States of Conflict: Gender, Violence and Resistance

Edited by Susie Jacobs, Ruth Jacobson and
Jen Marchbank

Zed Books
LONDON • NEW YORK

States of Conflict: Gender, Violence and Resistance was first published by Zed Books Ltd, 7 Cynthia Street, London N1 9JF, UK, and Room 400, 175 Fifth Avenue, New York, NY 10010, USA, in 2000.

Distributed in the USA exclusively by St Martin's Press, Inc., 175 Fifth Avenue, New York, NY 10010, USA

Cover designed by Andrew Corbett
Set in Monotype Ehrhardt and Franklin Gothic by Ewan Smith
Printed and bound in the United Kingdom by Biddles Ltd, Guildford and King's Lynn

A catalogue record for this book is available from the British Library.

Library of Congress Cataloging-in-Publication Data

States of conflict: gender, violence, and resistance/[edited by] Susie Jacobs, Ruth Jacobson, and Jennifer Marchbank.
      p. cm
  Includes bibliographical references and index.
  ISBN 1-85649-655-4 (hb) — ISBN 1-85649-656-2 (pb)
  1. Women—Crimes against. 2. Women—Crimes against—Prevention. 3. Violence—Prevention. 4. Women and war.
5. Women and the military. I. Jacobs, Susie M. II. Jacobson, Ruth. III. Marchbank, Jennifer, 1964– .

HV6250.4.W65 S77 2000
305.43'355-dc21

99-052432

ISBN 1 85649 655 4 cased
ISBN 1 85649 656 2 limp

Contents

About the Contributors

Lee-Anne Broadhead is Assistant Professor in the Department of Politics, Government and Public Policy at the University College of Cape Breton in Canada. She is currently working on a book, *Rhetoric and Regimes in International Environmental Relations*.

Heaven Crawley holds a doctorate from Nuffield College, University of Oxford. She works for the British organisation Justice and is the author of *Women as Asylum Seekers*.

Francine D'Amico teaches political science at the State University of New York College at Cortland and at Le Moyne College in Syracuse, NY, USA. She is co-editor with Laurie Weinstein of *Gender Camouflage: Women and the US Military*.

Judy El-Bushra is Research and Policy Officer for ACORD, an operational development agency working in seventeen countries in Africa. She is currently working on a book on Somalia and Somaliland as seen through the eyes of Somali women.

Jude Howell was formerly at the School of Development, University of East Anglia and is now a Fellow in Governance and Civil Society at the Institute of Development Studies, University of Sussex. She is working on gender aspects of state enterprises and has co-authored a forthcoming book on civil society.

Susie Jacobs teaches Sociology and International Studies at Manchester Metropolitan University and has published a number of articles on gender, agrarian change, land reform and the state in Zimbabwe, South Africa and comparatively. She is currently researching a larger comparative work on gender and peasants; other research interests include pedagogical issues in the teaching of 'race' in higher education, and diasporic identities.

Ruth Jacobson is a Visiting Research Fellow at the Department of Peace Studies, University of Bradford. She works on aspects of gender, conflict, political settlement and longer-term peacebuilding.

Liz Kelly is a feminist researcher and activist. She is Director of the Child
and Women Abuse Studies Unit, University of North London, and has
published extensively on sexual violence.

Fiona Macaulay's research interests currently include human rights and
the criminal justice system in Brazil, women and the law in Latin America
and gender, local government and political parties in Chile and Brazil.
From late 2000, she will be a Research Fellow at the Centre for Brazilian
Studies, St. Anthony's College, Cambridge.

Teboho Maitse is a longstanding member of the African National Congress
and holds a doctorate from the University of Bradford. Since the democratic transition in South Africa, she has worked as Gender Empowerment
Advisor to women parliamentarians in South Africa.

Jen Marchbank lectures in Women's Studies and Politics at Coventry
University. Her recent research interests include policy making and women
and feminist pedagogy and research practice. She is the author of a
forthcoming book on women and public policy.

Parita Mukta is a lecturer at the University of Warwick. Her research is
centred around questions of remembering, restitution, and narratives within South Asian communities.

1

Introduction: States of Conflict

Ruth Jacobson, Susie Jacobs and Jen Marchbank

This book is about the gendered nature of conflict. It explores conflicts at different levels and across national and social spaces. It examines, in particular, the relation of conflict to state power and to state regimes; while having a focus on gender, it also considers other social cleavages. Thus, for example, the reader will find themes such as 'race'[1]/ethnicity, agency and action interwoven with the discussion of militarisation. In this Introduction, we pay particular attention to the role of states in creating and perpetuating conflict, as well as their potential for creating the conditions in which conflicts, especially engendered ones, might be curbed or ameliorated. Above all, we are seeking to make connections – in a non-facile manner, we hope – between some global processes, conflicts at the level of the (national) state and those taking place at the community, household or individual levels.

The majority of situations examined in this Introduction and in the following chapters are characterised by physical, violent manifestations. However, this does not in any way presume that situations without such overt characteristics are not conflictual. In this sense, we are following Galtung's well-known maxim that 'the absence of war does not mean peace' (Galtung 1969). Instead, we recognise conflict as endemic in human societies; some is sexualised (see below) and most has a gender dimension. The collection emphasises women's agency, alongside men's, in both creating and challenging conflict. In so doing, we aim for a feminist analysis which is at the same time more consistent in its treatment of *gender* than is often the case when conflict and/or violence is under examination.

Although *States of Conflict* addresses global themes, we recognise that the world is not a single place, particularly when historical patterns of colonialism and contemporary global inequities are taken into account. We acknowledge that analysis of women's experiences must always be appropriately contextualised, rather than being appropriated by universalising notions. Yet we agree with Brah that 'feminism cannot be framed without reference to the international context' (Brah 1996: 168). Therefore, this collection offers a layered investigation of conflict, ranging from the international through to the local and the personal. Before we provide an outline of contemporary conflicts, we attempt some clarification of terminology.

The Language of Conflict

All human relationships are fraught with tensions and disagreements. However, those concerning sexuality and gender relations can be a particular focus for *violence*, and here distinctions need to be drawn between different conceptualisations, which will appear in the varied usage of 'sexual' and 'sexualised' violence in this volume. The argument that sexuality and sexual acts, including violent ones, are not just a matter of individual preferences but are bound up with power structures in society is, of course, closely tied to feminist theory and constitutes one of its principal challenges to mainstream social science.

Within this broad perspective, various debates have occurred. One concerns the definition of 'violence': should it be construed broadly or more narrowly? Thus, one position is that violence entails acts of physical coercion or their threat. In this view, violence which is 'sexual' may be differentiated from more general assault/murder. Terms such as 'cruelty' or 'abuse' may be more appropriately used for non-physical coercion.

An alternative formulation is that violence is a gendered phenomenon within the context of patriarchal social relations (Kelly 1988) and that *all* such violence should be situated analytically within a 'sexual violence approach' (Radford et al. 1996: 3) even where no overtly sexual act is involved. In this sense, male sexual violence includes: 'violence which takes place in the home or workplace and on the street corner; violence involving racism, homophobia, xenophobia and other prejudices; violence on international and global levels including trafficking in women and women's experience of war violence' (Corrin 1996: 1). This quotation indicates two further, and connected, concerns: the behaviour of men as a group and the issue of who benefits from sexual violence. For those who take the broad definitional stance, the issues are usually seen as linked; it is men as a group who are seen to benefit from sexualised violence or its threat, even if they do not directly participate, and regardless of their social positioning. Thus, women's class or racial position does not act as protection against violence. Inasmuch as state regimes define what is violent and what is not, the right of all men to abuse women is upheld (Maynard and Winn 1997: 178).

For those who see 'violence' as appropriately naming physical acts, the question of 'who benefits?' remains distinct from definitional concerns. Thus it is possible to condemn rape as a war crime and to support the indictment of perpetrators but not to make assumptions about the behaviour of men as a group. Indeed, in terms of this example, some men do not benefit, and may indirectly suffer, from acts of sexual violence carried out against female family members. Writers employing this perspective have drawn attention to the way in which some women wield power as a result of their class or racial position, which can result in violence against men (Davis 1982).

This volume does not attempt to take one definite position. However, our multi-layered approach does, for example, enable us to look at connections between global economic institutions, notions of 'security' embedded in the practices of actors within these institutions (Lee-Anne Broadhead, this volume) and militarised settings where pornographic images of women are standard (Liz Kelly, this volume).

For the sake of completeness, a brief note on 'gender' and 'resistance' is also necessary. We see gender relations as 'a primary way of signifying relationships of power' (Scott 1988: 4). The relational aspect within 'gender' is of central importance, and a restriction to 'women' or 'women's issues' often obscures the relevance to *men* and to concepts of masculinity in any given context. Our concern is particularly with the way in which gender relations impact/are acted upon in situations of conflict, whether these are situations of large-scale violence (see Judy El-Bushra on Central Africa, this volume) or much more localised (Ruth Jacobson on Northern Ireland).

Resistance carries not just its common-sense implications of 'acting in opposition' but a reflection of the 'potential for subversion and contestation in the interstices of established orders' (Kandiyoti 1997: 141). However, the volume will establish that there are many forms of gendered resistance and that women's collective actions do not axiomatically take the form of opposition to the exercise of violence by men, whether against other men or against women (see Parita Mukta, this volume).

Having established some terminological parameters, we now need to look at those situations where conflict is all too overtly characterised by large-scale physical violence. Illustrations are not in short supply.

The State of the World

At the international level, the brief period of optimism generated by the end of the Cold War has given way to a widespread concern with 'the new world disorder' (for example, Fetherstone 1996: 98). This is characterised by new regional conflicts (such as those in Central Africa and the Balkans) and an escalation in armed conflicts *within* states which appears to be taking the place of the 'classic' form of war between organised state armies. The capacity of some states to control armed violence within their boundaries is associated with overall shifts in global sites of power (see below and Susie Jacobs, this volume). Moreover, the nature of warfare has undergone major changes, involving a widescale retreat from even a qualified observance of those historic rules of war which had offered protection to non-combatants. Instead, protagonists deliberately target civilians, including children, using the increasingly available technologies of rocket-propelled grenades, mortars, land mines and small arms. Where these kinds of conflicts are combined with a collapse or at least serious contestation of the state – for example, capacity to maintain any form of state administration or public services – the result is particularly disastrous in humanitarian terms.

Certain regions of the South today have come to be seen as bywords for conflict. Thus, even though substantial areas within Sub-Saharan Africa are handling tensions without large-scale violence, the continent is largely represented in the media in uni-dimensional terms.[2] Analysis of conflict situations in *any* region of the world needs to take into account broad structural and geo-political features; thus Central America has been characterised by 'peripheral status in the global economy; dominance of agriculture, external vulnerability, colonial history, deep social divisions and high levels of poverty' (Pearce 1998) while major zones within Central Asia are dominated by 'bandit economies' (Duffield 1994).

Conflict, gender and protection   What have these developments meant for women and for men? First, it is essential to record that the dichotomisation of 'clean' versus 'dirty' wars ignores the extent to which women's bodies have historically been included in the privilege of the conqueror (as explored by, among others, Brownmiller 1975; Nordstrom 1997; Heaven Crawley, this volume). Secondly, the mainstream Western view of the Allied forces of World War II as fighting a 'just war' neglects other crucial features. Such a view perpetuates those hierarchies of 'race' which endorsed nuclear attacks on Asians in Japan. It also allows for the continued ignoring of aspects of the Nazi Holocaust. The latter is illustrated, for example, by the refusal of the Allied Command to bomb railway lines leading to concentration camps.

Women's experiences of war have never been uni-dimensional. For example, the British women's suffrage movement split over its members' different positions on World War I; some members joined the war effort while Sylvia Pankhurst established a pacifist organisation. As well as being civilian victims, they have contributed significantly to national liberation movements in countries as diverse as Eritrea (Silkin 1983), Nicaragua (Chinchilla 1990) and Indonesia (Sunindyo 1998). Against the backdrop of this diversity, there are some distinctive contemporary trends to be discerned.

Women from Western countries are increasingly forming part of the 'security' arm of their states, whether the police, the military or the various surveillance and control agencies, such as those dealing with immigrants and refugees. (This is also, of course, the case in some countries of the South but in much less significant numbers.) In some contexts, women are actively seeking a role in front-line combat (Francine D'Amico, this volume; Elshtain 1998). The choice of a military career has brought women into the new sphere of military interventions to back up political settlements that open the way to peace, raising a whole raft of new questions around gender relations. What, for example, is the position of women as part of military 'peace-keeping' operations?

Another consequence of the global developments are those situations where very large numbers of women have found themselves and their families to be no longer protected by former codes of conduct, whether formalised or not (see, for example, El-Bushra on Somalia, this volume). This loss of personal security may be intensely gendered, involving the seizure of young girls (and sometimes boys) for forcible sexual relations with troops or the deliberate selection of 'expendable' young boys to carry arms. There is thus a (belated) recognition among humanitarian agencies of the realities of sexual violence and abuse. For example, it is now more common to find rape and its consequences included in the 'costs' of conflict. This is reflected in the documents prepared for the UN's Fourth World Conference on the Status of Women in Beijing: 'as the burden placed on women to provide for the basic needs of their families increases exponentially, there is [sic] considerable spillover effects for their daughters. Consequently, girls are moved even further away from the realization of their socio-political rights' (World Vision 1996: 7).

However, it has been left to feminist work on violence against women over many decades to dismantle the distinctions between so-called 'private/domestic' violence and the public world. This has ranged from Frances Power Cobbe writing in 1878 through to the modern campaigns against 'dowry deaths' in India. Such work on violence has enabled the dichotomous classification to be replaced by a continuum (Kelly 1988) ranging from the sanctum of the family home to public spaces (gang rapes) or police stations and military barracks. The fact that the latter is perpetrated by those very state personnel who are charged with 'security' has a particular resonance with our concern over the role of the state in power relations. It is to this area that we now turn.

Globalisation, states and conflicts In common with other analysts within the social sciences (see Jacobs, this volume), we recognise that there are major changes occurring in the world today, which are significantly affecting the powers of individual nation-states. Jacobs notes the current debates over the extent and implications of globalisation within a range of social science disciplines. For example, from within the discipline of International Relations, Peterson discusses 'the complex of trans- and supra-national economic dynamics, new technologies, weaponry, diseases and pollution which make up globalisation' (Peterson 1996:10). With the rise of transnational corporations and supra-national economic institutions, individual governments have less capacity to determine their own economic policies. Rapid flows of money, technology and information across the world make state boundaries of less relevance while the internationalisation of commodity/consumer culture impacts on individuals who can compare their own societies with those of others.

The degree to which these developments translate into 'the death of the state' remains contested but it is clear that processes of globalisation are inter-twined with notions of gendered security. For example, there is the growth of 'the maids industry', which exposes large numbers of women to a new range of transnational opportunities and risks (Phizacklea 1996: 168). These processes are best reflected by the human security approach, which involves replacing the state as primary reference and giving primacy to 'human beings and their complex economic and social relations' (Thomas 1999: 1). This is further illustrated by Broadhead (this volume) in relation to economic and environmental security. The changing nature of nation-states has also had significant effects on their military regimes. Instead of being charged with 'the defence of the realm', national forces are assigned to regional military alliances and may find themselves carrying out military interventions which cause intense disquiet in their home countries.[3]

Feminists have been increasingly turning their attention to these issues (see, for example, Runyan 1996; Kofman 1996). Peterson and Runyan draw our attention to 'the challenge of both documenting how the world has radically changed' since the early 1990s (Peterson and Runyan 1999: xi). For some writers, these changes have created a central tension because 'however problematic women's relation with states and liberal citizenship, they are preferable to an internationalised market citizenship and the further erosion of state sovereignty by powerful transnational capitalist interests' (Pettman 1996: 23).

Diverse States

The above points notwithstanding, we take the position that state power and state policy remain significant in women's lives. This does not, however, mean that we conceive of states as monolithic and omnipresent. On the contrary, in some ways 'the' state is itself an abstraction, consisting of relations, practices and institutions (Pettman 1996: 9). As this collection illustrates, state formations differ across the globe in many respects, including the amount of control they actually wield over their populations. Rather, as Connell (1991) has noted, the state is implicated in the construction of 'gender regimes' that have specific outcomes in the lives of women and men. The process by which this takes place is too complex to be examined in detail in this Introduction (but see Jacobs and Howard 1987; Yuval-Davis 1997). Our principal concern here is to establish some primary features which are relevant to the gendered experience of conflict, without privileging the historically specific form of the Western liberal-democratic state.

In the late 1990s, the Western political configuration[4] has spread well beyond its place of origin but the world still shows a multiplicity of state forms. Large proportions of the world's population either remain within other state regimes or are in a state of very recent transition. This is demonstrated by Jude Howell's chapter (this volume) which points to the implications of the one-party regime in China for women's organisations and by Teboho Maitse's on South Africa. We realise, however, that we have not included any material on the former communist states; some of these are covered in Einhorn 1993.

Western liberal democracy: soldiers, citizens and welfare Despite the huge mainstream literature on the history and characteristics of liberal democracy in Western Europe, it has once again been the task of feminist analysis to critique both its theory and practice in terms of gender (see, for example, Phillips 1995; Bock and James 1992). Among other themes, these writers examine the way in which citizenship, originally resting on the capacity to provide military service, was eventually extended to *most* men[5] while women's relationship to their states remained defined through men (husbands or fathers). Women were ascribed the status of 'the protected' and located within the private/domestic sphere, even when lived realities were starkly different. This dichotomisation continues to resonate in current debates about women's entry into the military (see Francine D'Amico, this volume) and in the formation of international legal regimes as Crawley demonstrates in the case of refugee and asylum law (this volume).

In its more modern configuration, the Western state has also been characterised by its 'welfare' function, which provides at least a minimal economic safety-net to support women and their families but at the cost of constructing them more as 'mothers' than as citizens or workers in their own right (Karl 1995). Feminist analysis, along with feminist campaigns, has variously led to a view of the Western state as inherently oppressive or potentially empowering (see, for example, Franzway et al. 1991; Marchbank 1996 and 1998).

Given the classic liberal formulation of the state as 'a human community that successfully claims *the monopoly of the legitimate use of physical force* within a given territory' (Weber [1919, emphasis in original][6] in Weber et al. 1948), it is perhaps curious that, with a few noticeable exceptions such as Enloe (1990), there has been so little *specific* feminist examination of the state's machineries for the exercise of violence. This could contribute to a better understanding of contemporary situations where female members of the state's security institutions are given the power to police the conduct of other women. In contrast, there has been a growing body of work on women's representation in national legislatures (Phillips 1995). This suggests that as numbers of women increase, they can effect changes in state policies, such as improvements in maternity benefits. We need more examination of women's membership of those political institutions which at least formally have the ultimate control of national militaries and their budgets.[7]

Historically, it was the military might of the Western European states that enabled their imperial and colonial expansion from the sixteenth century onwards. In this regard, Rai reminds us of the non-universal nature of the Western model of the state and argues that 'Western feminist state theory has largely ignored the experience of Third World women under the post-colonial state' (Rai 1996: 5). Similarly, Afshar points to the marginalisation of women's political activities by not only the male-dominated discipline of political theory but also because of the earlier stage of Western feminism which 'had serious misconceptions about femininity, motherhood and the family' (Afshar 1996: 1). Even within the limitations of this Introduction, it will still emerge that there are some different questions to be asked about gender and conflict when the focus shifts from the modalities of Western liberal-democratic states.

Statehood, gender and conflict in the Third World When looking at the historical background of statehood, it emerges that nationalist opposition to colonialism was 'mounted largely within the modernizing parameters that were privileged by the colonists' (Rai 1996: 10). As a result, the indigenous elites who took over the reins of government at independence often professed a commitment to improving the lot of women through changes in the law and in public provision. This is demonstrated, for example, in accounts of the early independence period in Mozambique (Urdang 1988) and Algeria (Mehdid 1996). Subsequently, however, the narratives of gender and statehood have diverged.

Rai notes three main feminist approaches in the writings of Third World women analysts of the state. To the extent that post-colonial governments such as those of India have made interventions on behalf of women, it is possible to posit 'a binary *opposition* between the state and the patriarchal forces in society' (Rai 1996: 12, emphasis added). Conversely, other writers have concentrated on the *symbiotic* relationship between the state and patriarchy, seeing it as particularly pertinent to developments within some Islamic states (Kandiyoti 1991). Thirdly, Third World feminist writers and activists have examined the impact of global capitalism, although not necessarily from the same viewpoint (Rai 1996: 12). These diverse approaches, Rai argues, all demonstrate 'the importance of bringing the state back into any discussion of women's lives in the Third World' (Rai, 1996: 5) but not in terms of universalizing conceptual frameworks (p. 12). An illustration would be Lievesley's study which takes the experience of Peruvian women under the military regime to demonstrate the inappropriateness of both liberal-democratic and (Marxist-derived) structuralist approaches (Lievesley 1996: 47).

Waylen employs a four-fold typology of political formations in the Third World: colonialism, revolution, authoritarianism, democratisation (Waylen 1996: 4). Themes of gender, conflict and violence run through all four. Women's active participation in anti-colonial, revolutionary and national liberation campaigns has already been noted; newer elements, however, are accounts of betrayal of promises and expectations (see, for example, Baylies and Bujra 1993 on Sub-Saharan Africa). 'Authoritarian states' may cover bureaucratised military regimes, most typified in the Latin American experience and the neo-patrimonial form, where state authority is maintained through personal patronage. This latter has been more common in Africa (Waylen 1996: 93). Both forms of course have gender implications, whether for women serving in repressive state bureaucracies *or* for resistance movements, although there are still relatively few detailed examinations available (but see Mba 1996). As Macaulay (this volume) illustrates, women have been central in democratising processes. However, Pankhurst and Pearce point to the dangers of privileging gender as against other sites of exclusion, emphasising how 'poor peasants, indigenous peoples, some ethnic groups and poor urban dwellers' also remain marginal to political processes, even where the formal right to vote has been achieved (Pankhurst and Pearce 1996: 44).

Rai's analysis of the ways in which women negotiate their post-colonial states has a direct bearing on our topic. Given the absence in the majority of instances of a welfare network, all but a minority are reliant on non-state resources and this produces a situation where there is a 'startling difference' between their experiences of state regulatory powers and those

of women in the West (Rai 1996:16). They are further removed from the
status of full citizenship by factors such as illiteracy and lack of infra-
structural capacity which prevents enforcement of constitutional rights,
such as those of inheritance, divorce and maintenance (p. 17). Most
crucially for our theme, there is the question of the high incidence of state
violence against women which Rai sees as resulting from the weakness of
systems for internal regulation in many Third World states She cites the
instances of police brutality which profoundly affected the Indian women's
movement (p. 17).[8]

It is clear, therefore, that women's (and many men's) decisions about
whether or not to engage with the state cannot be posed in the same terms
as in Western discourses. However, this has not resulted in 'giving up on
the state' (Stewart 1996), as evidence from women's movements worldwide
attest. There is, however, one category of Third World states that have
reached a point of conflict where the state is itself a battleground or where
it has reached a point of collapse; these 'complex political emergencies'
also have specifically gendered outcomes (see El-Bushra on Central Africa,
this volume; and Jacobson 1999, on Mozambique).

Examination of the detailed causality of these conflicts lies outside the
scope of this collection, but it is necessary to engage with the assertion
that there is a rising tide of 'ethnic conflict' in the 1990s world. As
Sadowski (1998) establishes, several Third World internal wars have been
quite recently 're-classified' as arising from 'timeless tribal rivalry'; this
has been the case for Angola, where the roots lie in Cold War superpower
rivalry. Whatever the scale and origins of these conflicts, there can be no
doubt that the phenomenon of ethno-nationalism is intrinsically gendered.

Ethno-nationalism and violence against women   In recent years, principles of inclusive citizenship, however imperfectly realised, have given
way to exclusive forms of 'belonging' and 'not-belonging'. Some have
been resolved without violence[9] but, inevitably, these tend to be overlooked.
The conflict in former Yugoslavia[10] has attracted particular attention
because of the use of rape as a war strategy (see, for example, Kelly, this
volume; Benderley 1997; and for rape against men, Hague 1997).

Anthias and Yuval-Davis' (1989) exploration of women as guardians of
'the race' helps to explain heightened gendered vulnerability during armed
conflicts. However, unless the attention given to such episodes of violence
against women is placed within a wider framework, it can obscure the
ongoing realities of women's daily experiences. We stress again that it has
been feminist work on violence against women in their homes, on the
streets and in their fields that has provided essential conceptual tools in a
way borne out, for example, by El-Bushra's contribution to this volume.

Some of the earliest work on making violence visible was that of feminist activists and academics (Millett 1990; Griffen 1979; Hanmer 1978). By naming this violence, a feminist paradigm used initially to expose the abuse of women by men has been able to make public other forms of 'private' violence, such as that against children and elderly people (Campbell 1997). This book is not an ethnography of violence, so contains no extended investigation of the realities within the so-called 'sanctum' of the home (but see Maitse, this volume). While acknowledging that women are capable of perpetrating abuse against male and female partners as well as upon children (Hester et al. 1996), theorists of sexualised violence (see above) see male violence as a main factor in the construction of femininity and a principal or even crucial feature of women's subordination across different settings and societies, seeing it as shoring up patriarchy (Corrin 1996). Other analyses would emphasise the formation of specific modalities of male domination on the basis of class, age and state power.

There is now a growing awareness among policy-makers in humanitarian agencies of the continuities of war and 'non-war' for all women. This has been recognised at the global level by the UN's Beijing Platform and in the legislatures of countries emerging from military rule (Macaulay, this volume). There are myriad campaigns, such as Zero Tolerance in Britain (Hart 1994) or *Musasa*, working with the Zimbabwean police (Stewart and Taylor 1997).

We have sought to establish the relevance of an approach to gender and conflict that looks at the international, national and individual levels. The analysis has pointed to tensions and contradictions, particularly in the context of global change. We now, however, take up another initial theme, that of examining women's agency, alongside men's, in both creating and challenging conflict, bearing in mind that we are attempting to examine the totality of gender relations. This involves looking critically at the association between masculinity and violence and asking some difficult questions about what lies behind the visible layer of women's actions.

On Asking Difficult Questions (and Not Answering Them)

We first look briefly at the link between men, masculinity and aggression in the context of war.[11]

Men, masculinity and suffering It is the case that, in a wide range of societies and cultures, being 'a proper man' is inseparable from the capacity to use weapons. Works such as Bourke's (1999) stress the pleasure many men derived from killing during World War I and II, but it is not the case that this analysis applies to all groups of men. There remain many states around the world where young men face conscription and the result is gendered patterns of dissent, whether as conscientious objectors, 'deserters' or 'draft-dodgers'.[12] We suggest that this phenomenon deserves closer examination from feminist scholarship than it has received.

Male experiences of the military are fundamentally shaped by 'race'/ethnicity and sexuality (see D'Amico, this volume). Moreover, these intersecting hierarchies can have life or death implications; African-Americans were disproportionately represented in the front-line 'grunts' fighting the Vietnam War (Pettman 1996: 143). The analysis of men, masculinity and war becomes even more complex in the context of the 'new' conflicts outlined above. Young boys are subjected to forcible recruitment and complete severance from what otherwise might have been normal childhoods (see El-Bushra, this volume). At the least, therefore, when examining conflict we must question the notion of a 'one size fits all' model of masculine aggression and female victimhood. This makes an examination of women's actions in relation to violence all the more imperative.

Women and violent conflict: changing the parameters The relationship between women and violent acts has not, of course, gone unexplored in the past. Beyond women's membership of national liberation movements, there is also populist literature fascinated by their role as particularly dangerous 'terrorists'. The broader theme of women and war has received attention from, among others, Pettman (1996), Vickers (1993) and Elshtain (1987 and 1998). However, social groups do not readily investigate their own more negative record, and women are no exception. Such reluctance as exists among *feminists* to discuss women and violence must be seen in the light of well-founded fears that such investigations could be used to mask male violence.

Nevertheless, information does exist on, for example, women's involvement with fascist movements in Europe and this indicates that women joined the Nazi Party in large numbers and served in the extermination camps (Koonz 1987). Likewise, during the 1930s, many white women from the southern states of the USA enthusiastically associated themselves with the Ku Klux Klan (Blee 1991, quoted in Fangen 1997: 125). In the 1970s, Pinochet's regime in Chile received support from middle-class women (Bunster 1988) and in contemporary Norway, young working-class women are to be found in the ranks of neo-Nazi movements (Fangen 1997); Protestant and Catholic working-class women have also been present in intimidatory mobs in Northern Ireland (Jacobson, this volume). As well as serving in essential positions in the US military, women have rallied behind the use of force by successive US military initiatives (Pettman 1996: 115). There are even instances where women have condoned the use of rape against 'enemies' and those constructed as 'not proper women' (Sarkar and Butalia 1995).

How can such evidence be integrated into a feminist project? As Mukta points out (this volume), feminists have found it difficult to confront the violence of women at both the theoretical and programmatic levels. This is particularly the case with assertions around an *essential* link between women, motherhood and non-violence, often referred to as the maternalist position (Ruddick 1992). This position argues that those engaged in 'mothering work' have distinct motives for rejecting war which run in tandem with their ability to resolve conflicts non-violently. It is difficult, if not impossible, to accept the premises of maternalism in the light of evidence such as Mukta and Jacobson (this present volume). As Pettman reminds us: 'Some mothers understand their attachments and responsibilities as requiring either the sacrifice of their sons for the state or nation, or the use of violence against other women's sons – and daughters' (Pettman 1996: 12).

Turning from maternalism to some recent material on the theme of gender and conflict (Turshen and Twagiramariya 1998; Lentin 1997; West 1997), we find that there is an acknowledgement of these complexities. For example, Lentin and West both note the availability of evidence on women's involvement with violence. Lentin recognises that 'Viewing women as homogeneously powerless and as implicit victims does not allow us to theorize women as the benefactors of oppression, or the perpetrators' (Lentin 1997: 12); however, the point is not further developed. Similarly, West notes that 'Academia has not caught up with women in current political struggles' (West 1997: xiv) but does not expand on this point.

In raising this issue, we are acutely aware that where women are living under such coercive conditions that any form of protest would be at the least risky and quite probably life-threatening, questions of guilt may be, at a minimum, occluded. For just one example, see the statements of Rwandan women about how any attempt to refrain from participation in the killings of Tutsis (and moderate Hutus) would have meant their own deaths (African Rights 1995). Yet what are the consequences of continuing to shy away from these topics? One could be to open the door to allegations that, with social constraints removed, women are really 'just as violent as men'. This tendency appears to be already the case in some treatments of the increasing incidence of violent crime among young women (Pearson 1998).

The problem of understanding women's agency in relation to violence has been of particular relevance to some feminist researchers and activists. Jeffreys and Basu contrast the highly limited impact of feminist protests against dowry deaths in India with the numbers of women mobilised to support the destruction of the Ayodhya mosque, which sparked massive outbreaks of communal violence (Jefferys and Basu 1998: x). Goldblatt and Meintjes undertake the same painful task in relation to the actions of white (and some black) women in South Africa. Having listed the factors which are readily understandable, such as economic vulnerability and socialisation under apartheid, they are left with areas of sheer incomprehension in relation to the conduct of (women) informers, warders and even torturers, stating that 'Some of these reasons *do not adequately explain the degree of cruelty that certain women perpetrated, particularly against other women*' (Goldblatt and Meintjes 1998: 45, emphasis added).

Struggling with language and with numbers Along with the epistemological and ethical problems raised by this topic, we have a struggle with terminology. We have argued above that the act of naming violence has been of great significance. What then are the terms available? Talking of women's 'involvement' with violence is very imprecise and 'co-responsibility' can indicate that women and men stand in a precisely equal relationship.[13] 'Complicity' carries overtones of guilt, but is in use (Jefferys and Basu 1998; Mukta, this volume). These linguistic dilemmas raise profound questions of analysis and practice which require serious attention.

Another set of issues concerns the numbers, or percentages, of women engaging in violent actions. Given current media fascination with female violence, this is a fraught issue. As things stand, evidence is fragmentary; for instance, Husbands' research estimates that between one-quarter and one-third of the estimated 40,000 right-wing extremists in Germany are women but that they have made up only 4 per cent of actual convictions for punishable offences with neo-fascist features such as attacks on immigrant hostels (Husbands 1991: 192). Such evidence as exists is scanty but what there is suggests that acts of violence resulting in injury or death are rarer among women than men. However, it is still important to note the contrast between the attention given to the relatively few women antinuclear campaigners in Britain as against those who supported the (then) government's policy on nuclear weapons (Campbell 1987).

Ways forward? As Peterson has pointed out in relation to gender(ed) identities and nationalism, only by situating actors, identifications, discourses, institutions and dynamics *in context* ... are we able to render nonessentialist critiques (Peterson, 1996: emphasis in original). Such critiques would involve asking questions about actual range of choices available when attempting to evaluate particular strategies in relation to violence (p. 13). Yet this still only takes us so far. It remains 'a puzzle of extraordinary theoretical, ethical and political import' to explain how women who might reject any association with violence in their personal worlds can be persuaded to accept or advocate violence in the name of the state, or nation' (Pettman 1999: 3).

A possible key to unlocking the puzzle in terms of women's agency has been Kandiyoti's evolving notion of 'the patriarchal bargain'. (It should be noted that Kandiyoti's concern is with issues affecting the household, rather than conflict per se.) Her initial conceptualisation (Kandiyoti 1988) posed questions such as why were mothers-in-law in areas of 'classic' patriarchy such as North India so apparently unmotivated to change abusive patterns of behaviour towards daughters-in-law? Rejecting simplistic notions of 'false consciousness', Kandiyoti traced the link between the promises of protection contained in the bargain's terms. This bargaining can take place only within rules and she summarised her earlier conclusion that these rules informed 'both women's rational choices and the less conscious aspects of their gendered subjectivities predisposing them to favour differing strategies of resistance and/or collusion in different contexts' (Kandiyoti 1998: 136).

Taking up the notion in a later version (1998), Kandiyoti finds this approach to have been productive in looking at numerous instances of women's resistance, such as contestation of male power through song (Kandiyoti 1988: 141). However, she sees the approach as not having been entirely adequate to encompass women's positioning in social divisions *other* than those of gender. In this respect, she finds that: 'women's attachment to and stake in certain forms of patriarchal arrangements may derive neither from false consciousness, nor from collusion but from an actual stake in certain positions of power available to them' (p. 143). This approach leads us back to our original undertaking to contextualise gender and conflict in the context of other social cleavages in order to gain at least some conceptual hold over women's agency in violence.

We now take up the final theme of this Introduction: resistance.

Resistance, Risk and Protection

Throughout the contributions in this collection, there are examples of how women have refused to assent to violence carried out within their communities, sometimes in the name of their protection. This has even been manifested under life-threatening conditions. For example, Mukta points to how women offered refuge in their homes at the height of communal violence. At the institutional level, Macaulay and Crawley both illustrate how international regimes can be moved to recognise the fluid inter-relationship between public and private spheres that impacts on women's experiences of violence.

The role of 'women in movement' (Rowbotham 1992) has been crucial in processes of change. The agenda for the UN's 1993 World Conference on Human Rights in Vienna contained little mention of women or of gender-specific abuses; however, strategic organising by an alliance of women's organisations ensured that delegates listened to testimonies from Korea, Palestine, Peru, Somalia, Yugoslavia and Russia about violations of women's human rights in war (Bunch and Reilly 1994: 34). The ensuing Vienna Declaration affirms that 'the human rights of women and the girl child are an inalienable and indivisible part of universal human rights' and there are passages in the text on state accountability for violence against women. The historic decision of the International War Crimes Tribunal for the Former Yugoslavia on 10 December 1998 to pass a sentence which included guilt on the grounds of rape is also part of this process of resistance and activism.

Since there is a considerable literature in this area,[14] we do not feel it necessary to expand at this point about women's capacity for resistance that takes the form of mobilising against injustice and oppression. It remains important, however, to be open to some more complex manifestations. For instance, Howell (this volume) presents some challenging questions about 'resistance' in the context of China. The state women's organisation has not shown simple compliance with the government; it has taken on issues such as female infanticide. However, when faced with challenges from newer forms of organisation, Howell points to the complex trade-offs which took place. Jacobson (this volume) also problematises the notion of women's 'resistance' in the Northern Irish peace process.

Localities of power There is a complex dynamic between women's collective action at the local, national, regional and global levels. As argued above, women in Third World states may be highly distanced in spatial, social and political terms from their states. Although women in the West are not in a directly comparable situation, they can still be more affected by state actions at the local rather than central level. In some instances, the local–centre is a two-way process; as Macaulay illustrates (this volume), the female-led social movements which emerged in opposition to military rule in Brazil then took advantage of the country's federal structure to enter into regional politics. The development of municipal feminism in some Latin American and many Western states has changed the shape of local government, although this has often been against entrenched resistance from the local state (Marchbank 1994). This process can be described as 'penetrating and changing the structures which determine how we live' (Kane 1990: 24).

New Spaces, Old Problems?

This introduction has ranged widely in order to carry out its intentions of making connections between 'the front-line' and 'the home-front'. We have been able only to sketch out the multiple forms which gendered violence can take, as a frame for the contributions in this volume. We have also broached some questions about masculinity and about women's agency which we feel need more attention, to avoid essentialist constructions that will not ultimately contribute to a less violent world.

In relation to the central issue of the state, we have taken the view that the analysis of state power remains of importance to feminists, even where we have felt ourselves excluded from or threatened by state processes. Power may inhere at once in most relationships, including those of the family and of sexual relations *and* in particular institutions, especially those backed up by state institutions. It is necessary for gendered analyses to view these power relationships in their various guises.

Writing of power in mid-1999 has brought us face to face with a war in Europe[15] which also has wider, even global, implications. The events of March–June 1999 brought about massive civilian flight, great suffering and risk – but not, paradoxically, to the military personnel of either protagonist. During the period of NATO bombing, the West's political leadership (especially US President Clinton and British Prime Minister Blair) claimed its action as 'humanitarian', i.e. one where invervention into a sovereign state had been undertaken in response to humanitarian outrages and to ethnic cleansing (see, for example, Blair quoted on BBC News Online Network World, 20 April 1999). To counter this, opponents of the war pointed to the highly selective record of NATO's (and the West's) humanitarian priorities.[16] In this situation, choices have had to be made between trusting in the rationale behind NATO's claims for its bombing campaign or risking 'complicity through silence' in ethnic cleansing.

These dilemmas may be new, but images of the war were, as always, gendered. NATO's military personnel were variously portrayed as kindly protectors of refugees, skilled executors of 'precision-bombing' or primed fighting machines. However, it was noticeable that some other gender features were in evidence, which had not been the case in earlier periods of the Yugoslavian conflict. In addition to calls for special attention to the health and emotional needs of women refugees (see Mary Robinson, UN High Commissioner for Human Rights, cited in the *Guardian*, 19 May 1999), the use of rape as a strategy of terror and humiliation came to be specifically claimed as one of the justifications for interventions (British Defence Minister's statement quoted in the *Guardian*, 25 May 1999). This is an advance in feminist terms. Yet, like many human actions, it may be double-edged; recognising large-scale rape may also be part of constructing the entire population of Serbia as a collective Other.

Moroever, the way in which the military settlement reached in June 1999 was equated with 'peace' brings us back to the complex character of gender and conflict. The content of the settlement involved, effectively, the creation of a militarised protectorate within the province of Kosovo. At one level, this will provide a safe space for returning refugee women, but what other forms of violence will they face? More broadly, it seems certain that challenges to the state's security forces will continue to be loaded with risk.

In raising the themes of this Introduction, we have at times felt that we have been opening a 'Pandora's Box'. The myth recounts that Pandora opened her box against the advice of her elders and unleashed a flood of sorrows on to the world. Yet the underlying force of the myth lies in the fact that, once the sorrows had been released, right at the bottom she uncovered the slight form of 'Hope'.

Notes

1. In common with recent practice, the term '*race*' will appear in this form throughout this Introduction to indicate that it is a social construct with no inherent biological meaning.

2. This can result in the phenomenon which the organisation 'African Rights' calls 'disaster pornography' (quoted in Prendergast 1996: 4).

3. See below on the example of Kosovo.

4. Liberal nation-states are characterised by a formal adherence to democracy through multi-party representative legislatures and by the power of elected governments over the military. It is recognised that the content of 'democracy' and the nature of state violence are contested (see Jacobs, this volume).

5. There have always been exclusionary limitations for men, whether in terms of class, 'race' or religion.

6. Speech at Munich University published in 1919.

7. Such as the conduct of European women parliamentarians and US senators in relation to the deployment of troops against Saddam Husein's regime in Iraq.

8. It is not suggested that such incidents never occur in similar contexts in the countries of the West.

9. Such as the discriminatory citizenship rules initially imposed on Russian 'settlers' in the new Baltic states after the break-up of the Soviet Union, which have now been considerably modified.

10. Here we refer to the wars of the earlier 1990s between the successor states of communist Yugoslavia, not the events of 1999 (see below).

11. We acknowledge that there is a great deal of debate over this area; see, for example, the contrasts between Jabri's treatment (1996) and Bourke's (1999).

12. Armenia, for example, has *no* provision for conscientious objection to military service.

13. We are grateful to Francine D'Amico for pointing this out.

14. To cite just a selection: Radcliffe and Westwood 1993; Tetrault 1994; Basu 1995.

15. By 'war', we refer to the actions of the Milosevic regime in the nominal Federal Republic of Yugoslavia against ethnic Albanians in the Republic's province of Kosovo, the armed actions of the Kosovo Liberation Front and the response of the North Atlantic Treaty Organisation (NATO).

16. This was the case, for example, at a public meeting organised by the Department of Peace Studies at Bradford University on 14 May 1999 to discuss the rights and wrongs of the NATO bombings.

Bibliography

African Rights (1995) *Rwanda – Not So Innocent: When Women Become Killers*, London: African Rights.

Afshar, H. (ed.) (1996) *Women and Politics in the Third World*, London: Routledge.

Alvarez, S. (1990) *Engendering Democracy in Brazil. Women's Movements in Transition Politics*, Princeton, NJ: Princeton University Press.

Anthias, F. and N. Yuval-Davis (eds) (1989) *Women–Nation–State*, New York: St Martin's Press.

Baden, S. and A. M. Goetz (1998) 'Who Needs [Sex] When You Can Have [Gender]?', in C. Jackson, and R. Pearson (eds), *Feminist Visions of Development: Gender Analysis and Policy*, London: Routledge.

Basu, A. (ed.) (1995) *The Challenge of Local Feminisms: Women's Movements in Global Perspective*, Boulder, CO: Westview Press.

Baylies, C. and J. Bujra (1993) 'Challenging Gender Inequalities', *Review of African Political Economy*, no. 56, pp. 3–10.

Benderley, J. (1997) 'Rape, Feminism, and Nationalism in the War in Yugoslav Successor States', in West (ed.), *Feminist Nationalism*.

Blee, K. (1991) *Women of the Klan. Racism and Gender in the 1920s*, Berkeley: University of California Press.

Bock, G. and S. James (1992) *Equality and Difference*, London: Routledge.

Bourke, J. (1999) *An Intimate History of Killing: Face to Face Killing in Twentieth Century Warfare*, London: Granta.

Brah, A. (1996) *Cartographies of Diaspora: Contested Identities*, London: Routledge.

Brock-Utne, B. (1985) *Education for Peace: A Feminist Perspective*, New York: Pergamon Press.

Brownmiller, S. (1975) *Against Our Will: Men, Women and Rape*, New York: Simon and Schuster.

Bunch, C. and N. Reilly (1994) *Demanding Accountability: The Global Campaign and Vienna Tribunal for Women's Human Rights*, Rutgers University, Center for Women's Global Leadership.

Bunster, X. (1988) 'The Mobilization and Demobilization of Women in Militarized Chile', in E. Isaksson (ed.), *Women and the Military System*, Hemel Hempstead: Harvester.

Campbell, B. (1987) *The Iron Ladies: Why Do Women Vote Tory?*, London: Virago.

— (1997) *Unofficial Secrets*, 2nd edn, London: Virago.

Chinchilla, N. (1990) 'Revolutionary Popular Feminism in Nicaragua: Articulating Class, Gender and National Sovereignty', *Gender and Society*, vol. 4, no. 3, pp. 370–97.

Cockburn, C. (1998) *The Space Between Us: Negotiating Gender and National Identities in Conflict*, London: Zed Books.

Connell, R. (1991) 'The State in Sexual Politics', in Franzway et al. (eds), *Staking a Claim*.

Corrin, C. (1996) 'Introduction', in E. Corrin (ed.), *Women in a Violent World: Feminist Analyses and Resistance Across 'Europe'*, Edinburgh: Edinburgh University Press.

Davis, A. (1982) *Women, Race and Class*, London: Women's Press.

Duffield, M. (1994) 'The Political Economy of Internal War', in J. Macrae and A. Zwi (eds), *War and Hunger*, London: Zed Books.

Einhorn, B. (1993) *Cinderella Goes to Market: Citizenship, Gender and Women's Movements in Central Europe*, London: Verso.

Elshtain, J. B. (1987) *Women and War*, New York: Basic Books.

— (1998) '*Women and War*: Ten Years On', *Review of International Studies*, vol. 24, no. 4, October, pp. 447–60.

Enloe, C. (1983) *Does Khaki Become You? The Militarization of Women's Lives*, Boston: South End Press.

— (1990) *Bananas, Beaches and Bases: Making Feminist Sense of International Politics*, Berkeley: University of California Press.

Fangen, K. (1997) 'Separate or Equal? The Emergence of an All-Female Group in Norway's Rightist Underground', *Terrorism and Political Violence*, vol. 9, no. 3, Autumn, pp. 122–64.

Featherstone, B. (1996) 'Peacekeeping as Peacebuilding: Towards a Transformative Agenda', in L. A. Broadhead (ed.), *Issues in Peace Research, 1995–96*, Bradford: Department of Peace Studies, University of Bradford.

Franzway, S., D. Court and R. Connell (eds) (1991) *Staking a Claim: Feminism, Bureaucracy and the State*, Cambridge: Polity Press.

Galtung, J. (1969) 'Violence, Peace and Peace Research', *Journal of Peace Research*, vol. 6.

Goldblatt, B. and Meintjes, S. (1998) 'South African Women Demand the Truth', in Turshen and Twagiramariya (eds), *What Women Do in Wartime*.

Griffen, S. (1979) *Rape: The Power of Consciousness*, New York: Harper and Row.

Hague, E. (1997) 'Rape, Power and Masculinity: The Construction of Gender and National Identity in the War in Bosnia-Herzegovina', in Lentin (ed.), *Gender and Catastrophe*.

Hanmer, J. (1978) 'Violence and the Social Control of Women', in G. Littlejohn (ed.), *Power and the State*, London: Croom Helm.

Hart, S. (1994) 'Zero Tolerance', in M. Ang-Lygate, C. Corrin and H. Millsom (eds), *Desperately Seeking Sisterhood: Still Challenging and Building*, London: Taylor and Francis.

Hester, M., L. Kelly and J. Radford (eds) (1996) *Women, Violence and Male Power*, Milton Keynes: Open University Press.

Husbands, C. (1991) 'Militant Neo-Nazism in the Federal Republic of Germany in the 1980s', in L. Cheles et al., *Neo-Fascism in Europe*, London: Longman.

Jabri, V. (ed.) (1996) *Discourses on Violence: Conflict Analysus Reconsidered*, Manchester: Manchester University Press.

Jacobs, S. and T. Howard (1987) 'State Policy and State Action', in H. Afshar (ed.), *Women, State and Ideology in Africa and Asia*, London: Macmillan.

Jacobson, R. (1999) 'Complicating "Complexity": Integrating Gender into the Analysis of the Mozambican Conflict', *Third World Quarterly*, Special Issue on Complex Political Emergencies, vol. 20, no. 1, pp. 175–87.

Jefferys, P. and A. Basu (1998) *Appropriating Gender: Women's Activism and Politicized Religion in South Asia*, New York and London: Routledge.

Kandiyoti, D. (1988) 'Bargaining with Patriarchy', *Gender and Society*, vol. 2, no. 3, pp. 274–90.

— (1991) *Women, Islam and the State*, London: Macmillan.

— (1998) 'Gender, Power and Contestation: Rethinking Bargaining with Patriarchy', in C. Jackson and R. Pearson (eds), *Feminist Visions of Development*, London: Routledge.

Kane, M. (1990) 'From Inside the Council', in S. Henderson and A. Mackay (eds), *Grit and Diamonds: Women in Scotland Making History*, Edinburgh: Stanmullion.

Karl, M. (1995) *Women and Empowerment: Participation and Decision-making*, London: Zed Books.

Kelly, L. (1988) *Surviving Sexual Violence*, Cambridge: Polity Press.

— (1996) 'When Does the Speaking Profit Us: Reflections on the Challenges of Developing Feminist Perspectives on Abuse and Violence by Women', in Hester et al. (eds), *Women, Violence and Male Power*.

Kofman, E. (1996) 'Feminism, Gender Relations and Geopolitics: Problematic Closures and Opening Strategies', in E. Kofman and G. Youngs (eds), *Globalization Theory and Practice*, London: Pinter.

Koonz, C. (1987) *Mothers in the Fatherland: Women, the Family and Nazi Politics*, London: Jonathan Cape.

Lentin, R. (ed.) (1997) *Gender and Catastrophe*, London: Zed Books.

Lievesley, G. (1996) 'Stages of Growth? – Women Dealing with the State and Each Other in Peru', in S. M. Raiand and B. Lievesley (eds), *Women and the State: International Perspectives*, London: Taylor & Francis.

Lovenduski, J. and P. Norris (eds) (1996) *Women in Politics*, Oxford: Oxford University Press.

Macaulay, F. (1998) 'Localities of Power: Gender, Parties and Democracy in Chile and Brazil', in H. Afshar (ed.), *Women and Empowerment: Illustrations from the Third World*, Basingstoke: Macmillan.

Marchbank, J. (1994) 'Non-decision-making: A Management Guide to Keeping Women's Interest Issues off the Political Agenda', in G. Griffen et al. (eds), *Stirring It*, London: Taylor and Francis.

— (1996) *Going Dutch or Scotch Mist: Making Marginalised Voices Heard in Local Bureaucracies*, Research in Community Studies, Paper 11, Bradford and Ilkley Community College.

— (1998) 'Labour Pains', *Trouble and Strife*, no. 39.

Maynard, M. and J. Winn (1997) 'Women, Violence and Male Power', in V. Robinson and D. Richardson (eds), *Introducing Women's Studies*, London: Macmillan.

Mba, N. (1996) 'Kaba and Khaki: Women and the Militarized State', in J. Parpart and K. Staudt (eds), *Women and the State in Africa*, Boulder, CO: Lynne Rienner.

Mehdid, M. (1996) 'En-Gendering the Nation-State: Women, Patriarchy and Politics in Algeria', in S. Rai and G. Lievesley (eds), *Women and the State: International Perspectives*, London: Taylor and Francis.

Millett, K. (1990) *Sexual Politics*, London: Virago.

Molyneux, M. (1998) 'Analysing Women's Movements', in C. Jackson and R. Pearson (eds), *Feminist Visions of Development: Gender Analysis and Policy*, London: Routledge.

Nordstom, C. (1997) *A Different Kind of War Story*, Philadelphia: University of Pennsylvania Press.

Pankhurst, D. and J. Pearce (1996) 'Feminist perspectives on democratisation in the South: engendering or adding women in?' in H. Afshar (ed.), *Women and Politics in the Third World*, London: Routledge.

Pearce, J. (1998) 'Peace-Building in the Periphery: Lessons from Central America', commissioned paper for COPE (Consortium for Complex Emergencies) International Review Workshop, University of Leeds, February.

Pearson, P. (1998) *When She Was Bad*, London: Virago.

Peterson, V. S. (1996) 'The Politics of Identification in the Context of Globalization', *Women's Studies International Forum*, vol. 19, nos 1–2, January–April, pp. 5–15.

Peterson, V.S. and A. Sisson Runyan (1999) *Global Gender Issues*, 2nd edn, Boulder, CO: Westview Press.

Pettman, J. J. (1996) *Worlding Women: A Feminist International Politics*, North Sydney: Allen and Unwin.

— (1999) 'Theorizing Gendered Violence', paper presented at the International Studies Association Convention, 16–20 February, Washington, DC.

Phillips, A. (1995) *The Politics of Presence*, Oxford: Oxford University Press.

Phizacklea, A. (1996) 'Women, Migration and the State', in S. Rai and G. Lievesley (eds), *Women and the State: International Perspectives*, London: Taylor and Francis.

Prendergast, J. (1996) *Frontline Diplomacy: Humanitarian Aid and Conflict in Africa*, Boulder, CO: Lynne Rienner.

Radcliffe, S. and S. Westwood (eds), (1993) *Viva: Women and Popular Protest in Latin America*, London: Routledge.

Radford, J., L. Kelly and M. Hester (1996) 'Introduction', in Hester et al. (eds), *Women, Violence and Male Power*.

Rai, S. (1996) 'Women and the State in the Third World: Some Issues for Debate', in S. Rai and G. Lievesley (eds), *Women and the State: International Perspectives*, London: Taylor and Francis.

Randall, V. and G. Waylen (eds) (1998) *Gender, Politics and the State*, London: Routledge.

Rowbotham, S. (1992) *Women in Movement: Feminism and Social Action*, London: Routledge.

Ruddick, S. (1992) *Maternal Thinking: Towards a Politics of Peace*, Boston: Beacon Press.

Runyan, A. Sisson, (1996) 'The Places of Women in Trading Places: Gendered Global/Regional Regimes and Inter-nationalized Feminist Resistance', in E. Kofman and G. Youngs (eds), *Globalization: Theory and Practice*, London: Pinter.

Sadowski, Y. (1998), 'What Really Makes the World Go to War', *Foreign Policy*, Issue 111, Summer.

Sarkar, T. and U. Butalia (eds) (1995) *Women and the Hindu Right*, London: Zed Books, and New Delhi: Kali for Women.

Scott, J. (1988) *Gender and the Politics of History*, New York: Columbia University Press.

Silkin, T. (1983) 'Eritrea: Women in Struggle', *Third World Quarterly*, vol. 5, no. 4, pp. 909–15.

Stewart, A. (1996) 'Should Women Give Up on the State?', in S. Rai and G. Lievesley (eds), *Women and the State: International Perspectives*, London: Taylor and Francis.

Stewart, S. and J. Taylor (1997) 'Doing it Backwards and in High Heels', in A. M. Goetz (ed.), *Getting the Institutions Right for Women in Development*, London: Zed Books.

Sunindyo, S. (1998) 'When the Earth is Female and the Nation is Mother: Gender, the Armed Forces and Nationalism in Indonesia', *Feminist Review*, no. 58, Spring, pp. 1–21.

Tetrault, M. A. (ed.) (1994) *Women and Revolution in Africa, Asia and the New World*, Columbia: University of South Carolina Press.

Thomas, C. (1999) 'Introduction' in C. Thomas and P. Wilkin (eds) *Globalization, Human Security and the African Experience*, Boulder, CO: Lynne Reinner.

Turshen, M. and C. Twagiramariya (eds) (1998), *What Women Do in Wartime: Gender and Conflict in Africa*, London: Zed Books.

Urdang, S. (1988) *And Still They Dance: Women, War and the Struggle for Change in Mozambique*, London: Earthscan.

Vickers, J. (1993) *Women and War*, London and New York: Zed Books.

Waylen, G. (1996) *Gender in Third World Politics*, Milton Keynes: Open University Press.

Weber, M., H. Gerth and C. Wright Mills (eds), (1948) 'Politics as a Vocation', in *From Max Weber: Essays in Sociology*, London: Routledge and Kegan Paul.

West, L. (ed.) (1997) *Feminist Nationalism*, London: Routledge.

Wieringa, S. (1995) 'Introduction: Subversive Women and their Movements', in S. Wieringa (ed.), *Subversive Women: Women's Movements in Africa, Asia, Latin America and the Caribbean*, London: Zed Books.

World Vision (1996) *The Effects of Armed Conflict on Girls*, Geneva: World Vision International.

Yuval-Davis, N. (1997) *Gender and Nation*, London: Sage.

Part I

The Global Context

2

Re-packaging Notions of Security: A Sceptical Feminist Response to Recent Efforts

Lee-Anne Broadhead

> [T]he achievement of peace, economic justice, and ecological sustainability is inseparable from overcoming social relations of domination and sub-ordination; genuine security requires not only the absence of war but also the elimination of unjust social relations. (Tickner 1992: 128)

The Commission on Global Governance (CGG), an independent group of twenty-eight leaders, released its report, 'Our Global Neighbourhood', in 1995. Originally called together by Willy Brandt in response to the events of 1989–90, this group is the latest link in a long chain of such international commissions, the most notable of which are Brandt's review of development issues, Olaf Palme's on disarmament, Julius Nyerere's South Commission and Gro Harlem Brundtland's consideration of the environment. As with these previous commissions, the CGG has directed its report to a wide audience; it has been written in a straightforward manner and popularly marketed. The activities of the CGG did not, it must be noted, end with the publication of the report. Indeed, the committee has established a secretariat in London which seeks to promote awareness of the com-mission's report and recommendations. Teaching tools have been produced, a children's version of the book has been released, extensive internet sources were made available, and speaking engagements by members of the commission have been numerous. Others have now picked up on the CGG's work and have offered support for the commission's proposals.

There are two reasons why this report is of interest to those of us seeking to engender discussions of security and argue the centrality of social justice issues. First, the commission claims to be offering a radical people-centred way of thinking about security issues that, on the face of it, mirrors the feminist perspective; secondly, and of perhaps greater import, this group is offering up proposals for changes to the current ordering of the system that, given the status of its members, are guaranteed a hearing in the corridors of international power. Central to this effort is the attempt to frame the debate in a manner which establishes the boundaries of what seems possible in international economic and political relations. The establishment of such limits are in themselves of interest.

Despite their claim to present a 'radical' interpretation of the crisis facing the world, it is my contention that the similarities between the commission's suggestions and those of advocates of an engendered reconsideration of the nature of security/insecurity are of a superficial nature only. The purpose of this chapter is to consider the arguments and underlying assumptions of the CGG and to demonstrate the way in which it 're-packages' a traditional notion of security and world order. The way in which the commission's ideas have become the focus of reform discussions demonstrates the manner in which such debates are framed. The current positions of power held by members of the commission both within the United Nations and in individual states provide added incentive for us to understand the assumptions underlying the arguments presented.[1]

The Commission

Although endorsed by the then United Nations Secretary General, Boutros Boutros-Ghali, the commission on Global Governance was not directly sponsored by the UN. The commission, in fact, grew out of the Stockholm Initiative on Global Governance, a group brought together as the Cold War drew to a close. As a result of its 1991 report, the group was reconstituted as the CGG and met eleven times between 1992 and 1995 under the guidance of its co-chairs, former Swedish Prime Minister Ingvar Carlsson and former Commonwealth Secretary General Shridath Ramphal. Aside from the two high-profile co-chairs, the commission comprised twenty-six members, from twenty-four countries. These members are drawn from the senior ranks of government service and the private sector in their respective countries. In 1995, the 'findings' of the commission were presented to Boutros Boutros-Ghali and those world leaders gathered at the World Economic Forum in Switzerland. The forum claims to act as a bridge-builder between business and government; it brings together close to 2,000 business and political leaders, members of the media and academics every year and has as its motto, 'Entrepreneurship in the global public interest'. This choice of audience for the initial presentation of ideas was significant as we shall see.

A Radical View of Security?

The commission's stated aim was to develop a 'common vision' of the way forward for the world in making the transition from the Cold War to a more secure and stable world order. The task the commission set for itself was based on the belief that the existing co-operative arrangements at the international level are in need of updating and that the 'confluence of circumstances' would allow changes to be made which would result in arrangements better suited to the needs of the world's people.

The commission establishes six principles in international agreements to be used as norms for security policies:

> All people, no less than all states, have a right to a secure existence, and all states have an obligation to protect those rights.

> The primary goals of global security should be to prevent conflict and war, and maintain the integrity of the environment and life-support systems of the planet, by eliminating the economic, social, environmental, political, and military conditions that generate threats to the security of people and the planet, and by anticipating and managing crises before they escalate into armed conflicts.

> Military force is not a legitimate political instrument, except in self-defence or under UN auspices.

> The development of military capabilities beyond that required for national defence and support of UN action is a potential threat to the security of people.

> Weapons of mass destruction are not legitimate instruments of national defence

> The production and trade in arms should be controlled by the international community. (CGG 1995: 84–5)

The arguments put forth by the commission to eliminate nuclear and other weapons of mass destruction are comprehensive and convincing; they aim to get conventions entered into force which would allow for a nuclear-free world by the millennium. The section on arms control is impressive but the expansion of the definition of security goes well beyond the discussion of the arms trade, non-proliferation and arms control.

In attempting to articulate this new vision the commission appears at first glance to have taken on board the feminist challenge for a reconceptualisation of 'security'. The commission departs from the traditional discussion of inter-state military insecurity and insists on the need to view the insecurity felt by individuals as a result of a range of international problems:

> Despite the growing safety of most of the world's states, people in many areas now feel more insecure than ever. The source of this is rarely the threat of attack from the outside. Other equally important security challenges arise from threats to the earth's life-support systems, extreme economic

deprivation, the proliferation of conventional small arms, the terrorizing of civilian populations by domestic factions, and gross violations of human rights. These factors challenge the security of people far more than the threat of external aggression. (CGG 1995: 79)

The inter-linking of economic, social, environmental and political considerations with the notion of a broadly defined concept of security seems extraordinarily radical for an international commission of this ilk to be using as a foundation for proposed changes to the international system. Taken at face value, this critique of the widely accepted traditional view of security takes the crucial aspect of the way in which we *think* about the world as its starting point and challenges the centrality of states. By calling into question poverty, arms proliferation, human rights violations and the high cost – social and economic – of weapons of mass destruction and insisting on a discussion of the insecurity of *people* rather than the insecurity of *states*, the commission shifts the terrain of the discussion in a significant manner. Indeed, it presents the choice in stark terms:

[W]e can ... go forward to a new era of security that responds to law and collective will and common responsibility by placing the security of people and of the planet at the centre. Or we can go backwards to the spirit and methods of what one of our members described as the 'sheriff's posse' – dressed up to masquerade as global action. (CGG 1995: xix)

Along lines similar to those of the arguments offered by the feminist perspective on the security/insecurity of the planet and its inhabitants, the commission also makes the point that women's role in the global economy must be considered as a central part of this enlarged discussion of global problems. Indeed, by placing the concept of *empowerment* at the centre of its agenda, the commission gives the impression that existing political and economic structures which perpetuate inequalities are being called into question. The commission argues that the 'most pervasive denial of human potential is found in the discrimination that women suffer world-wide' (CGG 1995: 143). The report talks about the benefits reaped by society as a result of the unrecognised contribution of women and considers the catastrophic results of the traditional way of thinking: 'half the world continues to be systematically – though in varying degrees – denied their full rights as human beings, with stultifying consequences for them and at great cost to society, which is denied the many additional contributions they can make' (p. 143). This is an apparently powerful argument, especially when such observations are coupled with the tantalising claims that 'radical' proposals for a dramatically altered international order are contained within the pages of the commission's final report.

The commission is not alone in arguing for a broader definition of security than that which predominated throughout the post-World War II period. Numerous scholars of international relations have pointed to the inadequacy of a state-centred, military-based consideration of security/ insecurity in a time of ecological crisis, economic disparity and widespread human rights abuses. The critiques have been levelled at the traditional view by realist and critical theorists alike. Indeed, the United Nations Development Programme attempts to redefine the concept to give it a 'human dimension' as well (UNDP 1994). And from feminist studies comes a nuanced view of the nature of security/insecurity at all levels of inquiry (Grant and Newland 1991; Vickers 1993; Sylvester 1994; Tickner 1992; Peterson and Runyan 1993).

On the face of it, the consideration of individual insecurity offered by the commission mirrors that of J. Ann Tickner's critique of traditional views of security from a feminist perspective in which the *sources* of insecurity come under scrutiny and arguments are made regarding the way in which policy decisions taken to gain 'national security' can have the opposite effect for those individuals living within the state.

> [T]raditional notions of national security are becoming dysfunctional. The heavy emphasis on militarily defined security, common to the foreign policy practices of contemporary states and to the historical traditions from which these practices draw their inspiration, does not ensure, and sometimes may even decrease, the security of individuals, as well as that of their natural environments. (Tickner 1992: 127)

As Tickner's argument makes clear, the central point of any feminist analysis is not merely about 'adding' women to the list of important subjects to be considered and still less about merely offering platitudes about the importance of women to society; it is instead about looking at the hierarchical social relations (including gender relations) which lead to the injustices so prevalent in our world and the institutions and organisations that, either inadvertently or by design, perpetuate them. The feminist perspective on security insists on closer scrutiny being given to the impact on women of traditional state-security decisions but it does not address women's insecurities alone. As Tickner points out, its goal 'is to point out how unequal social relations can make all individuals more insecure' (Tickner 1995: 193).

Power – The Missing Concept

If we turn our attention to the commission's blueprint for a new international order with this consideration of unequal social relations in mind, a serious problem with the report presents itself. Power – the central concept in any fundamental rethink of the directions of international structures – is absent from the commission's work. In fact, its members have absolved themselves of responsibility for the truly difficult questions, which would indeed lead to an engendered analysis and more complex suggestions for the action we should be taking, when they argue that it is not their task 'to try to advance thinking of the underlying causes of poverty and its remedy.' (CGG 1995: 189). Alarm bells ring at the appearance of such a fundamental contradiction in the commission's belief that the stated goal of a radically revised international system can be realised *without* taking into consideration issues of structures which lead to the poverty, inequality and gender divisions that it acknowledges are of central import to the individual's insecurity. So, while broadening the conception of security on one hand, it subsequently allows a number of assumptions to pull it back to the status quo agenda of security.

The reason for the refusal to consider the underlying causes of poverty and the resulting insecurity which is a direct by-product of it, stems from a set of liberal assumptions which blind the commission to any truly 'radical' thinking. Indeed it argues that these deeper questions need not be examined because there is a 'broad consensus' on the methods which should be employed – everywhere in the world – to deal with it:

> [A] strong, long-term commitment to high rates of saving and investment; maximization of the opportunities potentially available through an outward-looking trade regime; release of the private sector from bureaucratic controls; and understanding of the importance of environmental sustainability; financial sustainability; and a strong social dimension to policy, emphasizing education (especially of women), health and family planning. (CGG 1995: 189)

In short, all we need to do to get rid of poverty is collectively to embrace the Western liberal international economic model, add a bit of education and family planning and we will be on the road to this 'radical' vision of a global neighbourhood in which everyone, everywhere, feels secure. The optimism inspiring this 'vision' stems from the belief that the Cold War polarisation which prevented the world from moving 'towards democratization and economic transformation, raising the prospect of a strengthened commitment to the pursuit of common objectives through multilateralism' has ended (CGG 1995: 1). Thus, in the place of a much-needed examination of the relations of domination and subordination which lead to insecurity and injustice, we have the re-articulation of the liberal project and an implicit acceptance of the argument that the insecurity of individuals throughout the Cold War was the result of an unalterable security balance. Now that economic consensus can be reached, the commission argues, security of individuals will follow provided that the democratisation of the international realm continues apace. If we closely examine the commission's view of power as well as the suggested alterations of the existing institutions, we can gain a clearer picture of the commission's idea of an international system dedicated to security for the individual.

'People Power'

The commission firmly believes that people all over the world now have more power than ever before, power which is evidenced by their participation in non-governmental organisations and the increase in 'democratic processes'. The commission argues, 'the collective power of people to shape the future is greater now than ever before, and the need to exercise it more compelling' (CGG 1995: 1).

The commission's view of the notion of power is a curious one. Contrary to the usual view of seeing groups of people with different interests and goals, the commission believes the post-Cold War world harbours an international civil society which acts to reinforce human solidarity. It is worth noting that the commission cites the rise of women's groups alongside trade unions, chambers of commerce (!), farming and household co-operatives and so on as evidence of the 'vigorous global civil society'. The commission believes that such groups 'channel the interests and energies of many communities outside government' (CGG 1995: 32). People have, the commission argues, come together to *share* a 'vision' and the supposed commonality of thought is defined as 'one of the most positive features of our time'. The commission sees its task as assisting with the shaping of that vision.

With the transformation of the world into a new global village – a *neighbourhood* in CGG-speak – all is possible provided that a set of core values, shared interests and neighbourhood ethics can guide the process, the description of which the commission accepts as part of its task. Global governance, it argues, 'would be greatly helped by common commitment to a set of core values that can unite people of all cultural, political, religious, or philosophical backgrounds' (CGG 1995: 48). This commonality of thought will in turn allow for changes to international organizations which will guarantee the democratisation of the international system.

Changes to International Structures?

The commission builds on its notion of *people power* and on the existing UN structure to articulate its vision of the desired *neighbourhood*. It suggests new mechanisms to allow for the input of citizens' organisations into the UN system in addition to recommending changes to the existing institutions.

In order that the active power of people is properly mobilised into the system of global governance, the CGG recommends the establishment of an NGO Early Warning Service and an Annual Forum of Civil Society. The former would be made up of a group of 'eminent persons' to which people's organisations (i.e. NGOs) could make representation. This, the commission argues, would enable groups to have direct access to the UN so that it can be forewarned of dreadful events and then be responsive rather than proactive. The latter is suggested to offer a formal opportunity for NGOs to provide direct input into the system by meeting once a year in advance of the General Assembly. It is also worth noting that to help put 'women at the centre of global governance', the commission recommends that a post of Senior Adviser on Women's Issues be established in the Office of the UN Secretary General.

In addition to the commission's attempts to deal with the power of people, it also suggests a concrete programme of action dedicated to ensuring that the global economic market-place runs smoothly. The proposals here are based on the premise that it is through the market-place that true international security can be found.

The commission argues that the international institutions which were established in the aftermath of World War II are now outdated. Although the Bretton Woods institutions are praised for the amazing growth they inspired, the commission believes that they need to be renewed to make them more responsive to the demands the world now faces. In short, the CGG argues, we need to democratise the process which already exists.

To do this, the commission argues that the International Monetary Fund and the World Bank should be given more central roles in the management of the international monetary system. It praises the IMF for the way it has 'managed to transform itself from an intimidating ogre to a welcome source of concessional assistance' (CGG 1995: 187) and, while acknowledging that the World Bank has 'made mistakes in the past', the commission argues that 'its overall record in producing a good social return on its investment is impressive' (p. 193). Both of these agencies receive the support of the commission and are seen as essential players in a world of globalised capital markets.

The commission suggests an addition to existing institutions and proposes that an Economic Security Council should be established to act as an *apex body* to assess the overall state of the world's economy and provide a long-term framework. The commission points to the example of the G-7 as a model but makes the point that this body is not very representative of the world's economies or population. A more democratic version, it argues, would allow for the surveillance of all the economic programmes of the various economic institutions which would in turn ensure that coherent action is taken in the best interests of the world economy. The commission argues that bringing together the heads of government (once a year) and the finance ministers (once a year) would redress the currently undemocratic nature of the economic decision-making process at the international level.

The World Trade Organization (WTO), in this new plan, would become a 'truly global body' whose comprehensive rules would govern trade and 'ensure' a democratic ethos. In addition to their efforts to institutionalise and update trading rules, the WTO would be charged with the task of initiating competition rules to watch over the actions of transnational corporations which are themselves given credit for being the 'driving force' behind the post-World War II prosperity. The commission acknowledges the uneven distribution of gains in the system but these proposals would, if accepted, institutionalise rules and norms that would put an end to the less savoury side of the market-place. Indeed, the commission argues that there now exists a 'high degree of convergence of attitude and common interest in creating a regime that supports business but outlaws abuse' (CGG 1995: 174).

New Security?

I want to return for a moment to my arguments about the absence of consideration given to power relations in this document. The most important point to be made about the insecurity of peoples – a cause which the commission claims to champion – is that the structure of power relations in the international system must be thoroughly examined. The unquestioned acceptance of the liberal international economic model and the attendant faith in its ability to right all wrongs leads the commission into an unpleasant contradiction. Giving more power and influence to transnational corporations and international economic organisations will not – even when coupled with institutional reform to encourage a greater degree of NGO participation – lead to a 'people-centred' world. The commission's 'democratic vision' is little more than a strengthened and re-packaged version of the existing unjust structures and as such can do no more than perpetuate the insecurity which their so-called 'radical' agenda proclaims to attack.

While a comprehensive feminist critique of the status quo view of security would necessarily include a consideration of the programmes and dictates of major international economic institutions, the commission itself valorises the efforts of such institutions and seeks to strengthen them. Despite its claims of recognising the place of women in the international economy, the commission has failed to offer (or even consider?) any critique of the International Monetary Fund and the World Bank's efforts to restructure economies. Indeed, the CGG refers to the way in which 'most countries have faced up to the crisis by introducing difficult and often painful structural adjustment programmes. Some, but not all, have as a result reversed economic decline' (CGG 1995: 20). Recognising the instability that can be caused as a result of capital flows does not leave them questioning the workings of the international economic system as a whole but of trying to uncover the best ways to 'adjust' domestic economies. The commission does not want to join with critics who make the IMF what it calls a 'scapegoat for failures that lie elsewhere' (CGG 1995: 184). In this argument, the commission misses the basic point of many of the critiques offered of conditionality programmes when it concentrates solely on the techniques and strategies for ensuring that the international system runs more smoothly and domestic economies conform more efficiently.

A number of critics have pointed to the gender bias of the dictates of macro-economic policy by these international financial organisations which tend to ignore the micro-economic level, a tendency which is usually at the cost of women. As Pearson (1992: 309) reminds us, 'economies do not only work through market relations'. Even in its own terms, however, the commission should see the structural adjustment programmes as a failure: it argues that it is essential to deal with poverty in order to realise a new security and subsequently turns a blind eye to the evidence that such policies 'reveal a serious deterioration in living conditions of low income populations' (Moser 1991: 105).

The space does not exist here for a comprehensive critique of the stabilisation and structural adjustment programmes enforced by the IMF and World Bank and indeed a substantial literature on the effect of SAPs on women exists (Gladwin 1991; Pearson 1992; Sparr 1994; Afshar and Dennis 1992; Elson 1991, 1992; Cornia et al. 1987). It is, however, important to recognise the fallacy of the commission's argument that the new global ethic can guarantee security of individuals as well as realise the potential of women when it has failed to recognise the problems inherent in the same global economic policies which are responsible for some of the existing injustice and insecurity, policies which it applauds and seeks to strengthen. Even when discussing what it refers to as 'persistent poverty', the commission fails to question the foundations upon which the international economy is built; its idea of *transformation* is not *of* the system but rather 'into successful market economies' (CGG 1995: 23).

Once again we come face to face with the commission's curiously contradictory belief that it wants to ensure a new form of security but (i) does not see the need to deal with power relations and (ii) that the economic arrangements of a liberal international order would remove the insecurity felt by individuals if they could be managed properly. The commission believes that the existence of NGOs in the number currently witnessed provides testament to the fact that the system has already fundamentally changed in such a way as to deny exploitation and injustice and indeed argues that the phenomenon is leading to more 'participatory development' (CGG 1995: 199). The sad reality is that, in the final analysis, the commission can be seen to assume gender neutrality in its suggested restructuring of the institutions designed to oversee the global economy.

The commission's confidence in the market and NGO involvement is misplaced. There will be no alleviation of military, economic and ecological insecurities without a challenge to the hierarchical social relations – including gender relations – intrinsic to each of these domains. The commission has, in short, framed the debate in such a way that guarantees the continuation of a set of economic relations which are in the interests of the few and at the expense of the majority. It is, on the whole, business as usual.

While the CGG seeks to translate 'concepts of security into principles for the post war era that can be embedded in international agreements' (CGG 1995: 84), the feminist approach seeks to examine the unjust and dangerous power relations embedded in the international system itself and indeed in the agreements which the CGG wishes to create. Anticipating and managing crises 'before they escalate into armed conflicts' (p. 85) is not enough and does not even begin to deal with the causes of insecurity as experienced by people around the world.

Ecological Insecurity

In addition to leading to greater insecurity of individuals (especially women) as a result of harsh economic restructuring programmes being dictated from the 'centre', the commission has also avoided dealing with the new levels of insecurity which will result from the ecological damage which will be caused by further exploitation of the natural world. None of the solutions offered for the re-vamping of the international economic order will lead to major improvements in the environmental crises currently facing the world.

The natural world continues to be seen as something to be exploited for economic gain – nothing more than the source of the raw materials for industrial progress. The adherence to the essentially vacuous notion of *sustainable development* guarantees that the central part of such a plan is continued economic growth at tremendous cost (Broadhead 1996; Clow 1996; Visvanathan 1991). The commission argues that 'in the long run ... there should be no conflict between free trade and the ambitions of sustainable development and improved social standards, since as countries develop they will naturally wish to adopt higher standards' (CGG 1995: 169). The argument that economic growth will eradicate poverty which will in turn allow for higher environmental standards is a fallacious one: increased exploitation of resources leads to deepened ecological crisis and thereby greater levels of insecurity. The commission furthermore fails to see the contradiction in the criticism it levels at developing countries for cutting down forests when this is, in fact, often done in an effort to diversify export funding and thereby conform to the dictates of the international economic agencies which it praises. Subsequent threats to society are obvious when one considers the potential for land erosion, migration and future conflicts.

The accepted way of dealing with the environmental crisis from a liberal point of view is to further the policy of developing *regimes* which are defined as 'social institutions composed of agreed-upon principles, norms, rules, and decision-making procedures that govern the interaction of actors in specific issue areas' (Osherenko and Young 1993). By their very nature, regimes are prevented from undertaking any radical action to alter the status quo view of either the natural world or indeed power relations. While they can seek limited areas of co-operation when the actors' interests converge, it must be remembered that in today's setting, free market orthodoxy is the centrepiece of any negotiations. Even in the successful cases of such multilateral action, the limitations of the process are evident. Indeed, if we consider the regime created to limit the production of chlorofluorocarbons (CFCs) in an effort to deal with stratospheric ozone depletion – widely considered to be the best and most effective environmental regime – we can see the futility of this line of action. Despite the 'strong' terms of this regime – and assuming full compliance with its terms by every state – 'another ten billion tons of CFCs will be emitted into the atmosphere – an amount equal to half of all production historically' (Litfin 1993: 110). The destruction continues largely because of the accepted view about economic growth. The outcome of the recent discussions at the Kyoto Conference on Climate Change serves further to highlight this point. The farcical compromise agreement allows the international trading of carbon emissions so as to allow the largest polluter (the United States) to continue on its environmentally destructive path despite the cost to us all. Likewise, the recent forest fires in Indonesia (and elsewhere) point to the environmentally destructive practices of states seeking to advance economic interests. Eco-feminists take the debate much further than the regime theorists and rightly argue that not until exploitation in all its forms (i.e. of both nature and people) is brought to an end will we realise an ecologically secure future (Tickner 1993: 59–69).

Finally, it is important to recognise that economic deprivation is unlikely to be ended through a deepening of free-market principles and, as states rush to lower environmental and labour standards in order to attract capital investment, human rights abuses are likely to increase. Indeed, instability is quite likely to rise. In short, of those sources of instability on the commission's list, only the proposals to deal with arms proliferation have any chance of realising the promised increase in international security and it is by no means certain that these are achievable given the way in which the suggestions have been removed from any consideration of the wider economic and political structures within which the arms industry and states seeking to increase their military capability operate.

The commission, rather than face the true causes of insecurity head-on or indeed even to consider the existing gender inequalities which deepen its effects, offers us changes within the system and not *of* the system. This is a retrenchment of the status quo dressed up as radical reform. The report, in short, avoids putting forth suggestions which would deal with issues of social justice; and, as a feminist approach demonstrates, unequal social relations are one of the major sources of insecurity. This holds true for both the domestic as well as the international level. The notion held by the commission that the market can act as a neutral force to increase the sense of security of individuals is debatable.

Framing the Debate

One might be tempted to argue that the attention given to the commission's work here is unwarranted. After all, it could be argued that such reports are released at regular intervals by well-meaning – if naive and/ or misguided – groups with little influence. Would attention not be better directed at those with *real* power? Who ultimately will listen to the CGG? It seems to me, however, that we should be considering both where the commission gets its support as well as the role the commission plays in the establishment of the boundaries of the debate on global economic relations.

This is not to suggest a conspiracy; it is merely to acknowledge that ideology is *not* dead merely because the Cold War has ended and, indeed, that there has been an on-going struggle to frame the debate. The commission accepts a broadly defined liberal line which seeks to assert the view that it is only through market principles – albeit with some watchful controls – that individuals can best experience freedom and security of person. The globalisation of market forces is seen as inevitable and therefore needing controls; it is also seen as a useful phenomenon for ensuring the economic well-being of individuals around the world. The CGG further believes that if individuals around the world can be convinced of a common agenda, then a smooth operation of institutions and practices will surely follow.

To acknowledge, as the commission did at the outset of its work, that the nature of international politics has irrevocably changed and that the security of individuals deserves a central place of consideration is an essential starting point. To close off debate subsequently by doing little more than tinkering at the edges of existing structures is nothing short of shameful and demonstrates an attempt to pre-empt what Vikki Bell describes as 'the most fearful moment for the liberal machinery, the moment at which the general vision is doubted and alternative paths left and right are dreamt and drawn' (Bell 1996: 82). The arguments put forth in the commission's report attempt to eliminate questioning of the economic structures within which these decisions are being taken; if the global ethic about which they speak can be articulated in such a way as to gain wide-spread acceptance, the structures can be further secured.

Commissions such as this are part of the struggle to frame the debate; to provide the terms of reference by which we discuss alternative visions of society. The CGG gives the impression of opening up the debate by redefining the causes and cures of insecurity but it is no emancipatory project. As Scholte (1996: 44) acknowledges, the consequences of globalisation 'will be considerably influenced by the sorts of knowledge constructed about, and fed into, the process' and, in this case, the liberal discourse has the upper hand. The promise here is one of freedom and stability but the suggested proposals do not offer much hope of this.

Through the rhetoric of a democratic vision of a people-centred world order one can see the way in which the commission prevents questions being raised about a transformation of the institutions it seeks to enshrine in a system of management through multilateralism. With its argument that the G-7 process is not representative of the world's people should come a serious reconsideration of the basic structures of the economic order. Instead, the commission uses the concept of democratic principles to argue for an institutionalisation of an apex forum – a democratic version of the G-7 but one undertaking the same functions. The dictates of the market logic in turn serve as a limiting force on states, an essential part of a disciplinary structure designed to organise world production and trade in a specifically liberal way. Its effects are neither ecologically sound nor guaranteed to produce a new sense of security.

The commission's belief that a core set of values is needed displays a further narrowing of the debate. When looking more closely at the core values which the commission seeks to instil in the citizens of the world, its claims for a new sense of security fade further. This is not about respecting or accepting diversity but about sharing values based on a Western notion of democracy, about the rule of enforceable law and, of greatest import, about the acceptance of the liberal international economic vision. Indeed, these core values which it praises so highly begin to appear as a means of further limiting the scope of debate. 'Without the objectives and limits that a global ethic would provide', the commission argues, 'global civil society could become unfocused and even unruly. That could make effective global governance difficult' (CGG 1995: 55). What does this mean? First of all it is important to examine the commission's view of civil society. It is clearly not about a site of diverse and sometimes contradictory interests and power struggles but about limiting the range of views which can be expressed. Second, while the concept of *governance* is considered in a complex manner elsewhere (Prugl 1996), the commission is simply using the idea to denote the promotion of 'systemic approaches' which will allow input into the system from a range of actors and locations. The rules, norms and institutions so beloved by liberal international theorists and practitioners are presented as guarantees for the effective implementation of global policies which they acknowledge in some cases 'must rely on markets and market instruments, perhaps with some institutional oversight' (CGG 1995: 5).

The suggested institutional change which would allow a Forum on Civil Society to have input into the policy-making process then begins to look more like an effort to keep people in line. Likewise, the Right of Petition looks to be tightly constrained by 'arrangements' to ensure that the process would be 'strictly circumscribed in scope for the facility to be manageable and effective' (CGG 1995: 261). These points may seem like quibbles but it is important to recognise the centrality of the concept of education is to ensure that people conform to the same ideal and the liberal notion of citizenship which is based on representation ('enlightened leadership') rather than participation.

Conclusions

This is not a report which is gathering dust; it is a programme which, if anything, is gaining momentum. The commission has sought to mobilise NGO, academic and popular support through speaking engagements and sponsorship of conferences. A notable example was the women's NGO conference held in London in November 1996 to mobilise the support of women's NGOs for the commission's perspective.

Support for the commission's agenda is coming from a variety of places, including major newspapers such as the *New York Times*. Barber Conable, former President of the World Bank, and Jacques Delors, former President of the European Commission (and both members of the commission), have added their voices to the calls for the establishment of an Economic Security Council. United Nations Secretary General Kofi Annan also got on the bandwagon when he appointed Maurice Strong (another member of the commission) as the UN adviser on reform and then argued at the World Economic Forum in February 1997 that the 'United Nations has a vital role in supporting and preparing the ground for domestic and foreign private investment' in an effort to move what he called 'beyond dogma' (World Economic Forum 1997). It is worth mentioning that the World Economic Forum – the international membership organization which annually brings business, government and academic leaders together – was the chosen site for the release of the commission's report; its central discussion topic in 1997 was methods of convincing people around the world of the benefits of economic globalisation.

These are powerful arguments being used by powerful people to convince us that a better and more secure world is just around the corner, provided we follow the liberal market dictates. These arguments are inevitably about shaping the system in a particular image and are thus attempting to prevent others from thinking, indeed dreaming, of alternatives which might call into question market logic. In a sense, the commission attempts to claim that its vision *is* the dream of an alternative. When, in a speech to celebrate the fiftieth anniversary of the United Nations, Shridath Ramphal argued that 'in the end, it is the people of the world that must secure their global neighbourhood for themselves and future generations' (Ramphal 1994: 2), he implied that insecurity, inequality or failure of this peaceful order will be the fault of individuals. His version of global governance promises 'peace and progress for all people' as long as they share the dream and make it happen. If the people fail to demonstrate the will to support this plan, the world will not realise the peaceful order which the commission seeks; the fault will be theirs and not structural.

My challenge to the commission's plan and their tactics for selling it to us can be summed up simply: the international system, with its economic inequality, its lack of ecological concern and its militarised structures, is the cause of insecurity and this in turn is related to the power relations embedded in the system. Not until a fundamental reconceptualisation of these root causes is undertaken will any progress be made towards a more just and secure world. Promises that the global market will raise standards of concern for the environment, human rights and individual security are illusory and are to be resisted. We must have the will to dream alternatives based on issues of social justice and refuse to be limited by the proposals on offer.

Note

1. As well as its co-chairs, its membership included high-profile public figures from around the Amarworld such as Jacques Delors, former President of the European Union, Barber Conable, former head of the World Bank and Maurice Strong, Chair of two UN Environmental Conferences. For further information on members, see the CGG's website: http:www.cgg.ch.

Bibliography

Afshar H. and C. Dennis (eds) (1992) *Women and Adjustment Policies in the Third World*, London: Macmillan.

Bell, V. (1996) 'The Promise of Liberalism and the Performance of Freedom', in A. Barry, T. Osborne and N. Rose (eds), *Foucault and Political Reason: Liberalism, Neo-Liberalism and Rationalities of Government*, London: UCL Press, pp. 81–97.

Broadhead, L. A. (1996) 'Watching the Waves: Peace Research and the International Environmental Crisis', in L. A. Broadhead (ed.), *Issues in Peace Research 1995–96*, Bradford: Department of Peace Studies, University of Bradford.

CGG (Commission on Global Governance) (1995) *Our Global Neighbourhood*, Oxford: Oxford University Press.

Clow, M. (1996) 'Sustainable Development: Our Next Path of Development, or Wishful Thinking?', *British Journal of Canadian Studies*, vol. 11, no. 1, pp. 1–10.

Cornia, G. A., R. Jolly and F. Stewart (eds) (1987) *Adjustment With a Human Face*, Oxford: Oxford University Press.

Elson, D. (1991) 'Structural Adjustments: Its Effect on Women', in T. Wallace and C. March (eds), *Changing Perceptions: Writings on Gender and Development*, Oxfam.

— (1992) 'Male Bias in Structural Adjustment', in Afshar and Dennis (eds), *Women and Adjustment Policies in the Third World*, pp. 46–68.

Gladwin, C. (1991) *Structural Adjustment and African Women Farmers*, Gainsville: University of Florida Press.

Grant, R. and K. Newland (eds) (1991) *Gender and International Relations*, Milton Keynes: Open University Press.

Litfin, K. (1993) 'Eco-Regimes: Playing Tug of War with the Nation-State', in R. Lipschutz and K. Conca (eds), *The State and Social Power in Global Environmental Politics*, New York: Columbia University Press.

Moser, C. (1991) 'Gender Planning in the Third World: Meeting Practical and Strategic Needs', in Grant and Newland (eds), *Gender and International Relations*, pp. 82–121.

Osherenko, Gail and Oran R. Young (1993) 'The Formation of International Regimes: Hypotheses and Cases', in G. Osherenko and Oran R. Young (eds), *Polar Politics: Creating International Environmental Regimes*, Ithaca, NY: Cornell University Press, pp. 1–21.

Pearson, R. (1992) 'Gender Matters in Development', in T. Allen and A. Thomas (eds), *Poverty and Development in the 1990s*, Oxford: Oxford University Press, pp. 291–312.

Peterson, V. S. and A. S. Runyan, (1993) *Global Gender Issues*, Boulder, CO: Westview Press.

Prugl, E. (1996) 'Gender in International Organizations and Global Governance: A Critical Review of the Literature', *International Studies Notes*, vol. 21, no. 1, pp. 15–24.

Ramphal, S. (1994) 'Who owns the U.N? We the Peoples?' Remarks at a luncheon hosted by UN50 Committee on Global Governance, 24 June 1994.

Scholte, J. A. (1996) 'Beyond the Buzzword: Towards a Critical Theory of Globalization', in E. Kofman and G. Youngs (eds), *Globalization: Theory and Practice*, London: Pinter.

Sparr, P. (ed.) (1994) *Mortgaging Women's Lives: Feminist Critiques of Structural Adjustment*, London: Zed Books.

Sylvester, C. (1994) *Feminist Theory and International Relations in a Postmodern Era*, Cambridge: Cambridge University Press.

Tickner, J. A. (1992) *Gender and International Relations: Feminist Perspectives on Achieving Global Security*, New York: Columbia University Press.

— (1993) 'States and Markets: An Ecofeminist Perspective on International Political Economy', *International Political Studies Review*, vol. 14, no. 1, pp. 59–69.

— (1995) 'Re-Visioning Security', in K. Booth and S. Smith (eds), *International Relations Theory Today*, Cambridge: Polity Press, pp. 175–97.

UNDP (United Nations Development Programme) (1994) 'Redefining Security: The Human Dimension', *Current History*, no. 592, pp. 229–36.

Vickers, J. (1993) *Women and War*, London: Zed Books.

Visvanathan, S. (1991) 'Mrs. Brundtland's Disenchanted Cosmos', *Alternatives*, vol. 16, pp. 377–84.

World Economic Forum (1997) *Press Release 13*, 1 February.

3

Wars Against Women: Sexual Violence, Sexual Politics and the Militarised State

Liz Kelly

Stories on the news, disconnected messages from war zones. The standoff in Drumcree [Northern Ireland]; women supporting the marchers and women protesting. But at root this is macho posturing; men of power, men who presume power refusing to give up one iota of historical privilege. I think about the stories my friend Monica McWilliams has told me of men's behaviour in the so-called 'peace talks', where their misogyny and bigotry are palpable. For days the headlines which followed tell of the rape and murder of women and girls: Jade Mathews aged nine; Lyn and Megan Russell, a woman and her child murdered in woods; Nicola Parsons, an eighteen-year-old. A man has walked into a nursery school in Wolverhampton waving a machete. Chaos and the breakdown of the social order, or just business as usual? There is a common thread, which none of the reporting seems to notice – these are all stories of men engaged in the pursuit of entitlement, men who rage at being challenged or denied, men who have no respect for the lives of women and children. (Journal entry, 10 July 1996)

This short reflection encapsulates the core theme of this chapter: that sexual violence[1] as a deliberate strategy in war and political repression by the state is connected in a range of ways to sexual violence in all other contexts. Sexual violence is one of the most extreme and effective forms of patriarchal control, which simultaneously damages and constrains women's lives and prompts individual and collective resistance among women (Kelly 1988). In exploring these connections the conventional distinctions in political theory between 'public' and 'private', 'war' and 'peace' become problematic. Gladys Acosta from Bogota notes:

Every war causes us pain and the last few years we have been removing the veil of suffering of women in these times of war. These wars concentrate the greatest destructive capacity of humankind ... but there is another war. There is an invisible war, a war more difficult to name, which is the one that

women suffer in those closed spaces called our homes, and from which some
of us survive and others don't. (Reilly 1996: 26–7)

This 'invisible' war has been variously named a 'shadow war' or, in the
early days of second-wave feminism, simply 'the sex war'; one question
this chapter poses is whether the use by feminists of the word 'war' with
respect to gender relations should be understood as a powerful metaphor
or as an accurate naming of a historical reality.

Victim and/or Agent: Women's Use and Support of Violence

In focusing in this chapter on men's use of violence against women I
am acutely aware of the potential criticism that the analysis is predicated
on an exclusion of women as perpetrators and supporters of violence in
both inter-personal and inter-group relations. Elsewhere, I have addressed
the necessity of feminists developing both theoretical frameworks and
practical strategies for dealing with women as perpetrators of interpersonal
violence (Kelly 1991, 1996). Other chapters in this volume draw attention
to the fact that women, in a variety of contexts, 'take up arms' as members
of the military and insurgent groups, and support, collude with, or
acquiesce to, the use of violence in civil unrest and international conflicts.

This does not, in my view, alter the fact that the use of violence – inter-
personal, state-sanctioned and insurgent – remains a primarily masculine
preserve, and that women who enter these terrains do so within a set of
long-standing gendered meanings. Recent debates about how a focus on
women as victims of violence constitutes a denial of women's agency are
revealing in this context (see Kelly et al. 1996). In many versions of this
argument agency appears to reside solely in the actions of the violator;
thus, the position of agent for women is confined to perpetration of, or
support for, violence. The agency which women exhibit (and feminist
research has documented) not only in resisting and coping with personal
victimisation but also through collective opposition to inter-personal
violence and/or war, is disavowed. In this construction, women's agency
is recognised only when women act in ways which resemble traditional
male behaviour. This restriction of the meaning of agency does a profound
injustice to survivors of sexual violence, and to feminist research, practice
and activism which have consistently sought to make visible the actions
involved in surviving, coping with and resisting victimisation.

To integrate women's use of (and support for) violence alongside the
connections between contexts in which women are victimised is beyond
the scope of this chapter. The volume as a whole none the less represents
a movement towards developing the tools to do justice to this challenging

area of feminist thought, without either valorising the use of violence or ignoring women's agency within victimisation.

War and Peace

An important motivation behind an earlier paper (McCollum et al. 1994) on which this chapter builds was to point out, in the context of extensive media coverage of war rape in former Yugoslavia, that knowledge of sexual violence in armed conflicts was not new. Brownmiller (1975) compiled evidence of its pervasiveness in 1975, including rapes of Scottish women in 1800 during the English occupation, during the German occupation of Belgium and France in 1914, and in World War II. Mezey notes: 'Rapes of German women by Russian soldiers during the liberation were widely reported and charges of the raping of Chinese women in the "Rape of Nanking" were heard at the trials in Tokyo in 1946: 20000 reports in the city during the first month of occupation' (Mezey 1994: 589).

Revealingly, the Japanese reluctance to prosecute perpetrators was justified on the basis that: 'If the army men who participated in the war were investigated individually they would probably all be guilty of murder, robbery or rape' (quoted in Brownmiller 1975: 62). Enloe (1987, 1988, 1989, 1993) has, for over a decade, been documenting the connections between masculinity, militarism, war and coerced and organised prostitution.

What requires exploration, therefore, is not only how sexual violence is implicated in armed conflicts, but also why and how violence against women has been minimised, denied and hidden in the documentation of these events. The central questions this chapter addresses include: how does the violence which is an essential part of armed conflict articulate with gender relations? Does militarism construct a particular form of brutal (or brutalised) masculinity? When is a war a war, and what constitutes peace from the perspective of women?

A central concern of 'second-wave' feminism has been to develop language and meanings which reflect women's reality; this is as relevant to international as to inter-personal politics. Key questions for feminist theory are: what are the conditions of 'war' and 'peace' for women? What is a feminist definition of war? The term 'sex war' was commonplace in feminist rhetoric and analysis in the 1970s. Undoubtedly in some contexts this was intended as a powerful metaphor, but in some of its uses the intention was undoubtedly to challenge the limited definition of war; to extend its meaning to the continuing social and political conflict between men and women. The concept has been less evident in the 1980s and 1990s (see French 1992 for an exception), perhaps because of the frequent use of it, usually in trivialised contexts, by the mass media. Nevertheless, the locating of gender relations as ongoing sites of conflict suggests that we should understand sexual violence in situations of national/civil armed conflict, as expansions in location, forms and intensity, as the intersection of two conflicts informed by, and constructed through, gender.

The conventional (patriarchal) definition of war involves associations with activity, heroism and masculinity. Peace, by contrast, is often understood as the absence of war, but in more developed formulations it is also linked to the quiet, mundane, feminine. Even within this conventional definition, 'peacetime' in one location involves conditions and actions which foster 'wartime' elsewhere. Between 1900 and 1988 there were 207 conventionally defined wars, in which 78 million people were killed; two-thirds of all nation-states were involved in at least one, and ninety-three states were created – most violently – between 1945 and 1985 (Morgan 1989: 144). Yet in the West we are repeatedly told that this century has been a relatively 'peaceful' one. 'Peace' is clearly defined here as what happens 'at home'; but there is a lengthy feminist tradition of questioning the attribution of 'peace' to the home/household where male tyranny presides.

Enloe's feminist definition of peace is 'women's achievement of control over their lives' (Enloe 1987: 538); she adds that any such peace is fragile and tentative, without the conditions which enable it to be continually re-created. For Enloe, a feminist theorisation of peace requires detailed understanding of women's oppression and its connections to the ways in which gender, and especially the construction of masculinity, inflects with capitalism, colonialism and militarism. A peace meaningful to women would require not just the absence of armed and gender conflict at home, locally and abroad, but also the absence of poverty and the conditions which re-create it. Other vital questions include: what are the connections between constructions of 'national security' and women's safety? How do acts of individual male violence connect with institutionalised state violence?

Which violent conflicts are attributed the title 'war' is not just an issue in relation to women but also for indigenous peoples in colonised countries where various forms of genocidal violence have decimated populations. One of the many legacies of colonisation has been institutionalised violence, and more exploration is needed of how this is gendered; especially the ways in which these legacies connect sexual violence. For example, why are Aboriginal women thirty-three times more likely to be violently murdered than white Australian women? How are we to account for the massive levels of reported rapes – and more recently sexual assault of girls – in South Africa (Vogelman and Eagle 1991; Mabaso 1992)? Neither patriarchal violence nor genocidal colonialism are termed war in mainstream accounts; the power to name war (and peace) is the prerogative of dominant nations and groups. It is this entitlement which feminist perspectives have sought to challenge.

Militarised Masculinity

Most feminists who have addressed international politics have urged a focus not on war but militarisation, since it is militaristic culture which legitimises violence as a way of resolving conflicts, of establishing and maintaining power hierarchies within and between states. Until recently, the military – both in terms of troops and policy – has been a masculine preserve, and it remains an institution which re-creates and reworks gender relations locally and internationally (Enloe 1987). Glib distinctions between wartime and peacetime are challenged by this perspective, since the power of the military within the politics and economics of nations, and the processes of militarisation, exist whether 'war' is being fought or not. Time-limited armed conflicts must, therefore, be located within wider social processes, which have become increasingly the concern of women from various Third World countries where foreign military bases have been located, and/or where their national state is explicitly militarised. How gender is deployed in the development, and changing forms, of militarisation has become an important arena of feminist investigation.

Enloe (1987) argues that state institutions for organised violence have historically and cross-culturally been dependent on maleness; and that this is the outcome of explicit political choices. The commonality constructed through militarised masculinity has facilitated the overriding of class, status and ethnic differences between troops and officers. The content of recent debates about allowing women in combat roles and ending the ban on 'out' gay men and lesbians within the military merely serve to confirm the historical centrality of heterosexual masculinity in militarisation.

Explicit patriarchal, heterosexist and racist attitudes and behaviour have been found in research not just on the military, but also on the police – the other organisation which state societies invest with legitimate use of violence. In both institutions sexual harassment of female members is institutionalised within organisational culture, leading to serious questions about the responsibilities invested in sections of the military and the police to protect civilian populations. In civil conflicts, and some 'peacetime' contexts, the police have also been implicated as perpetrators of sexual violence, but in many countries it is the failure of the police to act as enforcers of the law with respect to violence against women which has attracted most feminist criticism (see, for example, Campbell 1997; Gregory and Lees 1999; Kelly 1999). It is more than a little ironic that, across contexts and continents, the justification police traditionally offer for non-intervention in domestic violence has been 'keeping the peace'.

How far the symbols and ideological assumptions which underpin the military are common across societies and cultures is a further area for more detailed research. Are there, for example, a multitude of versions of the songs/poems/rhymes which we are familiar with from US and UK sources?

> This is my rifle
> This is my gun
> One is for killing
> The other for fun.
>
> (quoted in Morgan 1989: 154)

Cohn analysed the language of US military strategists, which is replete with sexual imagery and metaphors. She concludes that military discourse contains: 'strong currents of homoerotic excitement, heterosexual domination, the drive towards competence and mastery, the pleasures of membership in an elite and privileged group' (Cohn 1988: 97). Her central theme – the link between sex and death in military discourse – is echoed in much (Western) male philosophy, where heroism and the ultimate courage in death are central preoccupations (Lloyd 1986). Such intellectual voices have offered forms of justification for the use of violence by states and organised religion through the association with both manhood and nationhood. The ideas are especially potent where religion and the state (and religion and insurgent/oppositional groups) are explicitly connected. Morgan notes: 'History is a story of violence – public legitimised violence (men's relationships to other men) and private eroticised violence (men's relationships with women)' (Morgan 1989: 113).

History is also a story of male dominant violent cultures successfully overtaking, not to mention overwhelming and eliminating, other forms. Women's bodies and women as a group have in the process been constructed as the locus or carriers of culture. It is this, coupled with misogyny, which marks them as targets in military conflicts. Women's bodies are constructed as both territory to be conquered and vehicles through which the nation/group can be reproduced. The call by Ian Paisley, in the context of the conflict in Northern Ireland, to loyalist women to 'breed babies for Ulster' is just one example of a recurring theme. This positioning of women as carriers of culture has wider implications. Within any conflict or struggle about cultural 'authenticity' or national identity, gender is always lurking beneath (or closer to) the surface. It is these connections which feminist resistance, in a range of contexts, to religious fundamentalism has sought to highlight.

The relationship between militarised masculinity, violence and gender relations is, however, not confined to state organisations. Morgan (1989) explores the way oppositional, radical/left insurgent movements also draw upon and rework the masculinist values which underpin the structures they are challenging. From her location of involvement in an American far-left group in the late 1960s and her subsequent radical commitment to global feminism, she notes that national liberation movements have consistently been male-led. While small numbers of women may be 'full' and active members, they are invariably expected/required to sexually service men of the group. She maintains that, to date, all national liberation movements have sold out women if they succeeded in overthrowing the incumbent state, and the more statist the 'revolutionary' government becomes the more the reconstituted military returns to its usual masculinist form. Enloe echoes this analysis using the specific example of the Sandanistas in Nicaragua: 'it is interesting to note that when the Sandinistas were the insurgents, there were many women in their ranks. But today, seven years after the new state's creation, while women account for a major proportion of militia members, they have been exempted by the Sandanista regime from military conscription' (Enloe 1987: 35).

Both of these commentaries pre-date the transformation in South Africa, and extensive debates within global feminism as to the benefits, limits and dangers of nationalism for women. It is an open question whether there are now different stories to be told. What is incontestable, however, is the urgency for feminists to observe and record the ways in which large-scale reconstruction within, or of, nation-states and regions involve a realignment, and/or re-creation of, patriarchal power and control, and the similarities and differences in the 'patriarchal bargains' (see Introduction, this volume) which emerge.

Morgan also notes the shift in many localised movements of women in the USA (from civil rights to the ecology movement) who transform their daily individual resistance into loose coalitions of action. Once men become involved the participatory grass-roots structures are transformed, often developing into hierarchical, male-led, self-righteous organisations which increasingly espouse an 'ends justify the means' philosophy. Increasingly, activism is redefined in terms of the investment of manhood – the heroism of 'dying for the struggle' is one element in the resort to, and justification of, violent tactics. These transformations, for Morgan, signal that: 'A politics of hope has become a politics of despair' (Morgan 1989: 169).

The vast majority of women do not take up arms but are desperately trying to survive. Internal movements for peace are frequently led by women, who are committed to finding alternatives to violence. Such movements are invariably responded to with contempt and derision by male (military) leaders from all sides, and where women's agenda contains an explicit feminism this disparagement rapidly adapts to include overt hostility and misogyny (see McWilliams 1997).

Wars on Women

Helwig, reporting on an international conference, Women Overcoming Violence, held in 1992 in Bangkok, notes:

> Women stand in a relationship to violence and power which is probably unique among oppressed groups. Our primary oppressors are, almost invariably, found among our immediate family or our lovers. Terror for women is quiet, pervasive, ordinary; terror happens at home. We know what war is about because war is part of any woman's daily experience. Daughters or sisters or wives, we know about 'loving your enemy' in a particularly direct and painful way. (Helwig 1993: 7)

The route to connections between women, across nationalist and other divisions, was agreement that the most basic, shared, threat was being killed by a member of one's own family. These routine, unremarked, daily encounters with violence and coercion were understood as powerful constraints on women's freedom, including their ability to participate in movements for economic and political rights. That women are most likely to be assaulted by a man known to them, and particularly sexual partners, has been one of the most compelling findings of three decades of feminist research on sexual violence. It starkly illustrates a profound difference in the structure of gender oppression compared to other structures of power; not only are women required to live alongside and respect their oppressors, they are expected to love and desire them. The social relations of the sex war, are – in significant ways – constructed very differently from those in other conflicts, involving trust rather than distrust, 'love' rather than hatred, partnership rather than opposition. The complexity of the issues and questions this reality creates for individual women and for feminist theory and practice has produced some of the most intractable and irascible debates and differences within local and international women's groups and movements.

The defences which men draw on to justify their abuse of female partners and family members range from the disingenuous resort to 'love' to, in militarised contexts, notions of 'defending the fatherland' or even being 'on the front-line'. The Bangkok conference explored many more connections between the 'shadow war' and conventionally defined wars, including the costs to women of national and international conflicts: 70–80 per cent of the world's refugees are women and children; in many developing countries the military budget exceeds that for health and education combined; the intensification of sexual exploitation to service the military; the lack of sexual safety for women, including the rape of refugees and 'enemy' women. The connections between soldiers who come home and brutalise those close to them and, at a deeper level, between constructions of masculinity, patriotism and violence, and parallel constructions of women as 'other' as linked to nature, land and territory were key themes. Rather than view sexual violence in war as different, this group of women and many feminists before and since chose to see and make connections:[2] that militarised sexual violence is perpetrated by men who are some women's lovers, sons, brothers and neighbours. That their behaviour towards women in one context is connected to their actions in others.

Rape was used in former Yugoslavia to terrorise populations and inflict maximum humiliation on communities; but it was women[3] who carried the shame, who were later shunned and excluded, because they embodied the failure of the militarised men to 'protect' their homeland. Staja Zajovic, from Women in Black Belgrade, notes: 'A patriarchal brotherhood demonstrates its "male strength" through war. However, the rape of their women is not lived as pain in her body but as a male defeat: he could not protect his own property' (Zajovic 1993: 5).

Not only are women required to cope with the damage of sexual assault, but the meaning it has at a symbolic level results in additional layers of material consequences and injustice. 'In Bosnia the women who are raped are feared, hated and despised ... This is all the more extraordinary given the close, fully integrated communities that existed before the conflict and the fact that the perpetrators are previous friends and neighbours, colleagues and teachers of the women they later rape and kill' (Mezey 1994: 589). But is this so extraordinary? It is known men who are most likely to be rapists in so-called 'peacetime', and when women make the difficult choice to name them as rapists they frequently face disbelief and blame from their friends, family and community, including some women. Women in a variety of contexts may chose to opt for immediate self-protection by allying themselves with more powerful men, rather than support (believe) less powerful women and girls; that this happens in the context of armed conflict should come as no surprise to feminists – it is yet another example of the 'patriarchal bargains' women make in circumstances not of their choosing.

In drawing attention to the scale of the atrocities in war, and the injustices which follow, the fact that *all* women who are raped experience levels of shame, risk being disbelieved, blamed or shunned by friends and family disappeared. While more extreme, the responses to women in former

Yugoslavia are not that different from the stories women on crisis lines hear the world over. The choice between silence and stigma is one every woman who has been raped has to negotiate, weighing the costs of each. Self-blame and the absence of justice are also themes which connect work on rape across locations and contexts.

One issue which war rape has highlighted is the cultural meanings which rape embodies. In cultures where honour is still a core value, the meaning of rape for each individual woman and her family is filtered through this discourse. In former Yugoslavia, many still believe that following rape, women's honour, and that of her family, is retrievable only through suicide. Thus countless women face an impossible choice between silence and stigma. For it to be known publicly that you have been 'dishonoured' narrows women's life choices considerably, and anecdotal accounts suggest that many of the women who spoke about their assaults have subsequently survived through prostitution. The alternate choice of silence was a central theme in feminist lawyer Sarah Maguire's (1998) contribution to a recent conference.[4] Through Lawyers' International Forum for Women's Human Rights she has been working in former Yugoslavia to enable women who have been raped access to justice through the UN war crimes tribunal. Apart from the fact that neither this tribunal nor the one on Rwanda has been adequately funded, there is minimal recognition of the consequences for women of naming as their rapists men who now live in the same or the next village. It is unrealistic, not to mention potentially dangerous, to expect women to testify without making any provision for their protection. Some of the strategies feminist activists are developing to enable women to testify draw on the best elements of legal reform from various jurisdictions; indeed, some of the provisions move far beyond the current legal framework in the UK and most other countries. These efforts have, however, not been reflected in the actions of officials charged with implementing international law. But this is not the only reason why more cases have not been prosecuted. Women in former Yugoslavia are exercising agency in choosing to remain silent. They, like women everywhere, understand that speaking out can have unintended consequences, and may not result in either natural or formal justice.

This 'no-win' situation is echoed in Rwanda, and it could be argued that it is 'worse' since not only has less public attention been paid to the situation, but also the scale of international (feminist) solidarity work has been far less evident. Layika (1996) argues that explicit orders were given not to make the mistake of the 1959 war: sparing women and children. She states: 'the rape of Rwandan women was of a scale that surpasses the imagination' (Layika 1996: 39); there are some areas of the country where every woman still alive has been raped – by gangs and individuals and in refugee camps (p. 40). The 'punishment' of women continues, since there is limited judicial redress and little sympathy from others: 'people reproach them for having preferred survival through rape ... A wall of silence has been built between them and their families' (p. 40).

Feminist analysis of gender violence during war refuses to name it as fundamentally different from gender violence in other contexts. In the case of former Yugoslavia this has meant foregrounding both 'ethnic cleansing' *and* sexual violence.[5] Staja Zajovic comments: 'Ethnic hate is yet another argument which men use to justify violence against women. The hate of women, the oldest hate of all, is the hate of the Other. Violence against women becomes completely justified, especially when hate of the other permeates all spheres of life, becoming even part of state ideology' (Zajovic 1993: 3). Sexual violence in the context of armed conflict intensifies already existing attitudes and behaviours.

More Connections

The violence women experience from men is not confined to conventionally defined conflict situations. Rape and sexual murder have been used as forms of political repression recently in Haiti and Peru,[6] and 'custodial rape' by police and the armed forces has been an important organising focus in India and Pakistan (Human Rights Watch 1995). Varying forms of permission and legitimation exist prior to emerging armed conflict situations, and persist after there has been some form of resolution. A number of factors have been proposed as distinguishing sexual violence in armed conflict, but few survive detailed scrutiny.

In the reporting of forced pregnancy in former Yugoslavia the connection was seldom made with slavery, where black women were repeatedly raped, forced to bear children by white male slave-owners. This permission which powerful white men afforded themselves (often with the complicity of white women) did not end with slavery, African-American women continue to be differentially targeted for rape. Opal Palmer Adisa, exploring the representation of rape in African-American women's literature, calls it an 'undeclared war'; a war that has spread in the twentieth century to the extent that there is no demarcation to distinguish between battlefields and safe zones (Adisa 1992: 367). Connecting these contexts and understanding the ways in which women negotiate the contradictions of forced pregnancy, and what factors are most salient in their decision-making processes about whether they can mother children conceived in conditions of force and violation, deserve more critical feminist attention.

What armed conflict situations do foster are actions by groups of men, where all participate or some watch and encourage. But even here, there are other contexts in which sexual violence occurs in planned, organised and relatively public contexts – all forms of gang rape involve the co-operation and participation (even if only as observer) of more than one man. Peggy Reeves Sanday's (1990) research revealed the centrality of gang rape to some US male college fraternities; and both clients and pimps have been known to organise group rapes of prostituted women (Hoigard and Finstad 1992). Recently in Sweden stories have begun to be told of young people's parties which conclude with a mass rape (personal communication, Lundgren 1996). It might seem obvious that in a such a situation of powerlessness women would not blame themselves for the violation, but they do; and their sense of shame is often multiplied by the knowledge that their degradation was witnessed; the damage to trust is compounded by the fact that there were people who could have intervened but did not.

A case which was widely reported in the USA at the time connects the military, organised sexual violence and 'peacetime'. It was referred to as 'Tailhook', and involved organised public sexual harassment and assault of women at a naval social function (see also D'Amico, this volume). Some of the women in attendance, including fellow officers, were forced to move through a double column of men in the hotel corridor who awarded each other the liberty of touching the women and saying whatever they wanted to them. Paula Coughlin, a lieutenant, blew the whistle after watching Anita Hill testifying about sexual harassment by a member of government. In the investigation the 'gauntlet' was described as a 'time-honoured tradition' (Enloe 1993: 196).

Another commonly cited distinction between rape in war and other contexts is that the former is often public, whereas the latter usually occurs in private. This draws too great a distinction between the two circumstances; reality is more complex and messy with some rapes during armed conflicts occurring in private, and some at other times in public or semipublic. Moreover, recent reports of 'honour killings' of young women in Turkey took place in public, as a deliberate statement and warning to all young women (Kelly 1997). There are also many forums in which sex is a public and shared experience between men; for example, elements of the sex industry are based on this wish to act in the company of others who may be strangers or colleagues/friends. Rape by gang and fraternity members are also examples where violence against women is used as a form of male bonding. Conflicts between gangs are often referred to as 'gang warfare' and tend to be understood as disputes about territory; it is seldom only control of public space or forms of illegal activity which are at issue, but also access to/control of women within the territorial boundaries. Strong parallels can be drawn here with the ways some paramilitary groupings control territory and populations.

A further distinction which has been suggested is that during military conflicts men's violence is more ritualised, but sexual violence can be ritualistic in everyday, domestic contexts involving patterns in the acts, words and symbols used. One fascinating connection here is between 'ritual abuse' and political torture. The existence of ritual abuse has been strongly contested in both the child abuse literature and the Western media (Kelly and Scott 1992; La Fontaine 1994). What is remarkable, however, are the similarities between the accounts of child and adult survivors of ritual abuse and the documentation of political torture in military regimes, and by the military in other contexts. For example, Ximena Bunster-Burotto (1994) recounts how the southern cone countries in Latin America explicitly refined (through dedicated sections in the military) gendered patterns of punishment and sexual torture. Many of the elements she outlines – being deprived of sleep, food and drink, being made to witness the abuse and humiliation of family members, gang rape, the use of animals and objects and being offered the 'choice' of damage to onself or someone else – echo accounts by women and children of ritual abuse (Cook 1995/6; Cook and Kelly 1997). Thus what is recognised and practised as military strategy in armed conflicts or by military regimes is deemed 'incredible' in non-military contexts.

Ritual, in any context, uses the symbolic as a form of power; where this involves sexual violence it is often also invoked to absolve perpetrators from individual responsibility (Lundgren 1995). References to a greater power than the abusive individual have echoes in the defence many soldiers use that 'they were just following orders'. What is being enacted in most of these settings are reinforcements of the primacy of relationships between men, and the accompanying subordination of women which underpins male supremacy. Men affirm one another as men through the exclusion, humiliation and objectification of women. What we need to explore in more depth is whether any hierarchical grouping of men, organised as men, creates conditions in which coercive heterosexuality is promoted and enacted. These groupings would include sports teams, private clubs, gangs, secret societies as well as the military. An important question, which deserves attention, is what room there is in such groupings for dissent, and how many men chose this option.

The Military and the Sex Industry

The connection between the military and the sex industry does not require war to be currently fought, as the last thirty years in South-East Asia attest (Strudevant and Stoltzfus 1992; Troung 1990). Sexual access to women has been explicitly organised by the military for centuries, demonstrating a fundamental connection between militarism and coercive heterosexuality.

A recent example reported in *International Children's Rights Monitor* involved the presence of UN 'peace-keeping' troops in Cambodia resulting in a 'breath-taking increase in prostitution, in part involving children' (Arnvig 1993: 4). One health official estimated the increase in women and girls involved in prostitution in Phnom Penh from 6,000 in 1991 to 20,000 in 1992. Kane (1998: 7–9) confirms this account and notes that at least a third were minors. She provides another example in which the Italian component of UN peace-keeping forces in Mozambique not only availed themselves of the local sex industry, but became active in organising it (pp. 48–9). As in Bosnia, some of those involved are poverty-stricken, others are women and girls who have been raped by men of their own community and are 'unmarriageable'. These are the most common routes into the sex industry for all women and girls; what armed conflicts do is make survival even more fragile. Arnvig comments: 'The tragedy of Cambodia becoming a part of this sex-market is that it comes just at a time when the country is supposedly on its way to "new" society after more than two decades of violence, destruction and repression ... Someone might argue: but this is not war; this is peace' (Arnvig 1993: 6).

Individual use of pornography within the Western military is not just accepted, but virtually compulsory. Pornographic songs pervade Western military culture, being sung during manoeuvres and before and during combat. French (1992) notes how many of these 'war' songs explicitly equate the mutilation of women with male prowess; the recreational song book of the 77th Tactical Squadron of the US Air Force based outside Oxford includes many lyrics about sadistic sexual violence. Military equipment is often 'decorated' with pornographic imagery. Parallels can be seen here with men's sports, especially rugby and American football. In the context of international debates about the influence of pornography on behaviour, with positions ranging from it having no influence at all to an argument that it is in itself a form of violence, it is surely relevant to ponder on the question why the military goes to such lengths to ensure troops have access to it, especially before they are due to see 'action'.

While the connection between the military and adult prostitution has been well documented, rather less attention has been given to the sexual exploitation of children. Kane (1998) highlights that armed conflicts and displacement of populations create contexts in which children are often separated from their families. This increases their vulnerability to exploitation, and she cites cases of children having to trade sex for food in refugee and resettlement camps. She summarises a recent UN review of the sexual exploitation of children in situations of conflict. In all twelve of the case studies examined, troops from all sides were implicated in the sexual exploitation of children, and in six cases – Angola, Bosnia, Cambodia, Croatia, Mozambique and Rwanda – the UN peace-keeping presence was associated with an increase in child prostitution (Kane 1998: 46). As with military involvement in adult prostitution in South-East Asia, the process is extended by the emergence of civilian 'sex tourism' to areas where sex with children can be bought easily and cheaply.

These repetitious patterns, which transform local, and sometimes national, economies through the use of women and children's bodies, raise serious questions about military bases, military behaviour, and the 'peace-keeping' and conflict resolution roles of the UN. In the latter case at the very least there ought to be explicit disciplinary rules against involvement of UN troops in prostitution, and consideration ought to be given to including civilian women skilled in supporting women and children in the aftermath of sexual violence as core components of any UN team.

Resistance to their exploitation is emerging throughout South-East Asia. Redress has been demanded by hundreds of Asian women kidnapped into sexual slavery by the Japanese military during World War II (Asian Women's Human Rights Council 1993; Shin 1996),[7] and by Filipina women, who had worked in the sex industry, following the withdrawal of US troops and bases which resulted in many women being left destitute with children of US servicemen. Finding ways to make the military accountable for the consequences of extensive sexual exploitation, and taking issue with the presumed necessity of prostitution and pornography to the (presumed) heterosexual male military, must be key elements in any feminist response to militarisation.

The Home Front

Men returning from action do not leave the front-line behind. Military men who have been trained as 'lean, mean killing machines' return to their supposedly peaceful homes. Evidence from women in Croatia echoes the experience of women in Northern Ireland, that during armed conflict domestic violence involves many more incidents with weapons; the battle-field and home are not separate as ideology suggests they are. Nor are these effects limited to those living in the 'combat zone': Canadian shelter (refuge) workers noted that during the Gulf War women told stories of their husbands dressing in army uniforms before beating them, frequently after watching the TV news. Serbian and Croatian women have coined the term the 'post TV news syndrome' to describe men who began being violent to their partners after watching news coverage of the war (see also Introduction to this volume).

At the same time, Boric and Desnica (1996) maintain that domestic violence is never more invisible than in wartime. The national agenda shifts to the public sphere, requiring a spurious unity in the face of an external threat. 'Domestic' issues are subordinated to the 'war effort'; and any form of protest is defined as unpatriotic at best and at worst as subversion or treason.

Armed conflict also affects the forms of remedy and protection to which women have access. McKiernan and McWilliams's (1993) research on domestic violence in Northern Ireland outlines the consequences for women where the police become parties to an armed conflict, and 80 per cent of their time is spent on 'security' issues. Other areas of crime are thus under-policed, including sexual violence. In this context there are many areas which are controlled by paramilitaries, and the police refuse to enter them without the back-up of the army. Thus the agency which many women and children seek protection from in a crisis becomes unavailable to significant sections of the community. While paramilitary groups do often create alternative forms of policing, sexual violence is seldom high on their agenda. Even where they do choose to act, the sanctions tend to be forms of violence, and their own members are seldom if ever held accountable for abusing women and children.

What Difference Does War Make?

Armed conflict does make a difference, albeit not the absolute one which has been at times suggested. The limited protections available to women and implicit toleration are replaced by condoning and even an outright policy of sexual violence. There is an increase in the frequency of opportunistic and planned assaults within or close to the conflict zone. More of the violence occurs in public, so that women's violation and humiliation is witnessed by others in their community. These levels of permission constitute something of an 'open season' on enemy women and children, a licence to men to extend their range of violation. Even where sexual violence is not used as an explicit military tactic, implicit permission exists; which is why rape and coerced prostitution have never been properly encoded, or prosecuted as war crimes. 'History has shown that rape, even aggravated rape, in the context of war has been little prosecuted or punished. This is particularly true when the main perpetrators are political leaders whose cooperation is necessary for reaching a peace accord' (Koenig 1994: 131).

The destabilising effects of armed conflict have implications far away from the combat zone, changing priorities for many of the combatant nations. This may in turn result in the minimal policing and protection afforded to women receding (McKiernan and McWilliams 1993). This may be compensated for, to some extent, where a significant percentage of the male population is 'called up', possibly enhancing women's safety temporarily if they do not reside close to the conflict zone/s. The example of Sri Lanka (Rajasingham 1998) illustrates such contradictory processes. Both displacement and early widowhood have created circumstances in which women have had to ensure their survival, and some have embraced the autonomy which this has afforded them and in the process refused the traditional Hindu placement of widows. At the same time the armed conflict in Sri Lanka (as in many other areas) has generated its own internal logic, with small local paramilitary groups controlling movement of people and goods into and out of particular areas. This has drastically limited women's freedom and mobility, since 'checkpoint rape' is all too common.

To conclude I want to return to the three central questions which were posed at the beginning of this chapter: how does the violence which is an essential part of armed conflict articulate with gender relations? Does militarism construct a particular form of brutal (or brutalised) masculinity? When is a war a war, and what constitutes peace from the perspective of women?

I have endeavoured to show that sexual violence connects 'war' and 'peace' as conventionally defined, and that these conventional definitions rely on a construction of 'war' which women's experiences belie. Nevertheless, armed conflict do accentuate both the construction of a brutalised masculinity, and a suspension – especially within and close to combat zones – of the limited protections from violation afforded to women at other times.

The vast majority of troops are men, and militarised masculinity is constructed through the requirement that, when necessary, troops will use violence against other human beings. While some attention has been given to men who refuse military service, and rather less to the traumatic impact of military action on some men, there is as yet hardly any attempt to discover whether, and how many, men in the military resist and reject the sexual use and abuse of women and children which appears to suffuse military culture. Interestingly, little research has been done on men in any context who choose to eschew violence in their relationships with women and children. Yet these men may have critical insights into how non-violent masculinities can be constructed.

'War' is not easy to define – when did it start? When did it end? Did anyone win? How can we tell? When asked from the perspective of women these questions become even more complex. Some Western historians have argued that periods of national and international conflict are times when women 'gain', sometimes temporary sometimes permanent rights: for example, the vote in Britain in 1918, access to a wider variety of paid employment, and the link between warfare and welfare. There are two connected problems with this version of history. First, the focus is on the woman of the 'victorious' nation with minimal reference made to the consequences of 'the war' and 'the peace' for women of the defeated nations/groups. Hossain (1998), reflecting on the history of armed conflicts between India, Pakistan and Bangladesh, notes that displacement is not only a matter of physical location, but of much of women's experience. Even defeated combatants are welcomed home as heroes, but raped women are at worst ejected from their families, at best hidden away. The notion that women 'gain' from war involves not only ignoring women who belonged to the defeated side, but also not questioning elements of ideology, which parallel the discourses created in 'war' to recruit women into supporting it. The ending of many armed conflicts, between or within nations, have frequently required women to relinquish certain freedoms and/or forcible removal of what had previously been 'rights' – for example, to employment, abortion, childcare.

Any 'peace' involves a reworking of power relations, not just between nations or parts of nations but between men and women. Attempts are made to conscript women into a 'rebuilding the nation' agenda in which their needs are subordinated to those of repairing the damage to men and 'the society'. One central, but universally neglected, element of this is that violations women experienced during the conflict are silenced, since the male combatants need to be constructed as heroes rather than rapists (Davies 1996).

The centrality of masculinity and nationhood to armed conflicts creates a potent combination which displaces (silences) women's experiences of violation, poignantly illustrated by a former Yugoslavian woman: 'When the rapists came into our room all of us were crying; when some of us came back, all of us were silent, without voice' (Helwig 1993). Any attempt to make sense of state-sanctioned violence, of armed conflict within and between nations, which fails to include and take account of sexual violence in 'war' and 'peacetime' does a profound injustice to women, further contributes to the silencing of their voices, experiences and insights and reinforces the stigma which accompanies being a victim of sexual violence.

Notes

1. The term 'sexual violence' is used as a collective noun to encompass all forms of male violence against women and girls (Kelly 1988).

2. See also Mezey's (1994) discussion, from the perspective of a clinical psychologist,

of being part of an EC investigative commission into 'war rape' in former Yugoslavia. She notes that women were raped by soldiers, paramilitaries and male civilians, and that these (often multiple) rapists were 'normal' men, 'who were later welcomed back into communities as heroes' (p. 584); this reality challenges virtually all of the forensic constructions of 'rapists'.

3. Some evidence is emerging about the rape of men and boys in national/international conflicts. Euan Hague (1997) argues that gender and misogyny are at work in these contexts, through positioning assaulted men and boys as 'feminised victims'.

4. Rape and the Criminal Justice System, London, 14 June 1997.

5. One of the Croatian feminist services uses the term 'genocidal rape' to name the war rapes (Katarina Vidovic, personal communication, 1998).

6. In Peru the Marxist insurgent group Shining Path has specifically targeted feminists and women community organisers; for some of these women, activism has cost them their lives (see Americas Watch 1992).

7. Shin (1996) estimates that 200,000 women from Korea, China, the Philippines, Indonesia, Malaysia, Taiwan and the Netherlands were involved as 'comfort women', of whom only 10 per cent are thought to have survived.

Bibliography

Adisa, Opal Palmer (1992) 'Undeclared war: African-American Women Writers Explicating Rape', *Women's Studies International Forum*, vol. 15, no. 3, pp. 363–74.

Americas Watch (1992) *Untold Terror: Violence Against Women in Peru's Armed Conflict*, Washington, DC: Human Rights Watch.

Arnvig, E. (1993) 'Child Prostitution in Cambodia: Did the UN Look Away?', *International Children's Rights Monitor*, vol. 10, no. 3, pp. 4–6.

Asian Women's Human Rights Council (1993) *War Crimes on Asian Women: Military Slavery by Japan During World War II*, Quezon City, Philippines: AWHRC.

Boric, R. and M. Desnica (1996) 'Croatia: Three Years After', in C. Corrin (ed.), *Women in a Violent World: Feminist Analyses and Resistance Across 'Europe'*, Edinburgh: Edinburgh University Press.

Brownmiller, S. (1975) *Against Our Will: Men, Women and Rape*, New York: Simon and Schuster.

Bunster-Burotto, X. (1994) 'Surviving Beyond Fear: Women and Torture in Latin America', in M. Davies (ed.), *Women and Violence: Realities and Responses Worldwide*, London: Zed Books.

Campbell, B. (1987) *Iron Ladies: Why Do Women Vote Tory?*, London: Virago.

— (1997) *Unoffocial Secrets*, 2nd edn, London: Virago.

Cohn, C. (1988) 'Sex and Death and the Rational World of Defense Intellectuals', in D. Gioseffi (ed.), *Women on War: Essential Voices for the Nuclear Age*, New York: Touchstone Books.

Cook, K. and the 'A' Team (1995/6) 'Survivors and Supporters: Working on Ritual Abuse', *Trouble and Strife*, no. 32, pp. 46–52.

Cook, K. and L. Kelly (1997) 'The Abduction of Credibility: A Reply to John Paley', *British Journal of Social Work*, no. 27, pp. 71–84.

Davies, S. (1996) 'Women, War and the Violence of History', *Violence Against Women*, vol. 2, no. 4, pp. 359–77.

Dworkin, A. (1983) *Right Wing Women*, New York: Pedigree.

Enloe, C. (1987) 'Feminist Thinking about War, Militarism and Peace', in B. Hess (ed.), *Analysing Gender: A Handbook of Social Science Research*, Newbury Park: Sage.

— (1988) *Does Khaki Become You? The Militarization of Women's Lives*, London: Pandora.

— (1989) *Bananas, Beaches and Bases: Making Feminist Sense of International Politics*, London: Pandora.

— (1993) *The Morning After: Sexual Politics at the End of the Cold War*, Berkeley: University of California Press.

French, M. (1992) *The War Against Women*, London: Hamish Hamilton.

Gregory, J. and S. Lees (1999) *Policing Sexual Assault,* London:Routledge.

Hague, E. (1997) 'Rape, Power and Masculinity: The Construction of Gender and National Identity in the War in Bosnia-Herzegovina', in R. Lentin (ed.), *Gender and Catastrophe*, London and New York: Zed Books.

Helwig, M. (1993) 'We Know What War Is', *Peace News*, February, p. 7.

Hoigard, C. and L. Finstad (1992) *Backstreets: Money, Prostitution and Love*, Cambridge: Polity Press.

Hossain, H. (1998) 'Displacement: a Bangladeshi Perspective', paper presented at Regional Workshop in Violence Against Women, Calcutta, 18–20 March.

Human Rights Watch (1995) *Violence Against Women In South Africa: State Responses to Domestic Violence and Rape*, New York: Human Rights Watch.

Human Rights Watch Women's Rights Project (1995) *The Human Rights Watch Global Report on Women's Human Rights*, New York: Human Rights Watch.

Jackson, S. (1997) 'Against Our Will – a Classic Review', *Trouble and Strife*, no. 35, pp. 61–7.

Kane, J. (1998) *Sold for Sex*, Aldershot: Arena.

Kelly, L. (1988) *Surviving Sexual Violence*, Cambridge: Polity Press.

— (1991) 'Unspeakable Acts: Women Who Abuse', *Trouble and Strife*, no. 21, pp. 13–20.

— (1996) 'When Does The Speaking Profit Us?: Reflections on the Challenges of Developing Feminist Perspectives on Abuse and Violence by Women', in M. Hester, L. Kelly and J. Radford (eds), *Women, Violence and Male Power*, Milton Keynes: Open University Press, pp. 34–49.

— (1997) *Final Report of the EG-V-SL, Including a Plan of Action*, Strasbourg: Council of Europe.

— (1999) *Domestic Violence Matters: An Evaluation of a Development Project*, London: Home Office.

Kelly, L. and S. Scott (1992) 'Devils, Demons and Denial', *Trouble and Strife*.

Kelly, L., S. Burton and L. Regan (1996) 'Beyond Victim and Survivor: Sexual Violence, Identity, Feminist Theory and Practice', in L. Adkins and V. Merchant (eds), *Sexualizing the Social:The Social Organization of Power*, London: Macmillan, pp. 77–101.

Koenig, D. (1994) 'Women and Rape in Ethnic Conflict and War', *Hastings Women's Law Journal*, vol. 5, no. 2, pp. 129–41.

La Fontaine, J. (1994) *The Extent and Nature of Organised and Ritual Abuse*, London: HMSO.

Layika, F. U. (1996) 'War Crimes Against Women in Rwanda', in Reilly (ed.), *Without Reservation*, pp 38–42.

Lloyd, G. (1986) 'Selfhood, War and Masculinity', in C. Pateman and E. Gross (eds), *Feminist Challenges: Social and Political Theory*, Sydney: Allen and Unwin.

Lundgren, E. (1995) 'Matters of Life and Death', *Trouble and Strife*, no. 31, pp. 33–9.

McCollum, H., L. Kelly and J. Radford (1994) 'Wars Against Women', *Trouble and Strife*, no. 28, pp. 12–19.

McKiernan, J. and M. McWilliams (1993) 'Studying Domestic Violence in a Violent Society', paper presented at Fifth Interdisciplinary Congress on Women, San Jose, Costa Rica, February.

McWilliams, M. (1997) 'Taking on the Dinosaurs', *Trouble and Strife*, no. 35, pp. 7–15.

Mabaso, M. (1992) 'Gang Rape in the Townships', *Trouble and Strife*, no. 24, pp. 30–4.

Maguire, S. (1998) 'Dispatches from the Front Line: Bringing Rapists to Justice in Former Yugoslavia', *Trouble and Strife*, no. 36, pp. 2–5.

Matovu, N. (1996) 'Wartime Abduction and Sexual Abuse in Uganda: The Story of Agnes', in Reilly (ed.), *Without Reservation*, pp. 34–7.

Mezey, G. (1994) 'Rape in War', *Journal of Forensic Psychiatry*, vol. 5, no.3, pp. 583–93.

Molina, F. (1996) 'Sex Trafficking from Columbia to Europe: Marta's Story', in Reilly (ed.), *Without Reservation*, pp. 69–75.

Morgan, R. (1989) *The Demon Lover: On the Sexuality of Terrorism*, London: Methuen.

Rajasingham, D. S. (1998) 'After Victimhood: Women's Agency in the Hidden Economies of Armed Conflict in Sri Lanka', paper presented at Regional Workshop in Violence Against Women, Calcutta, 18–20 March.

Reilly, N. (ed.) (1996) *Without Reservation: The Beijing Tribunal on Accountability for Women's Human Rights*, New Jersey: Center for Women's Global Leadership.

Sadou, Z. (1996) 'Algeria: the Martyrdom of Girls Raped by Islamic Armed Groups', in Reilly (ed.), *Without Reservation*, pp. 28–33.

Sanday, P. R. (1990) *Fraternity Gang Rape: Sex, Brotherhood and Privilege on Campus*, New York: New York University Press.

Shin, H. (1996) 'The Situation of the Comfort Women: An Update', in Reilly (ed.), *Without Reservation*, pp. 43–4.

Sturdevant, S. P. and B. Stoltzfus (1992) *Let the Good Times Roll: Prostitution and the US Military in Asia*, New York: New Press.

Truong, T. (1990) *Sex, Money and Morality: Prostitution and Tourism in South East Asia*, London: Zed Books.

Vogelman, L. and G. Eagle (1991) 'Overcoming Endemic Violence Against Women in South Africa', *Social Justice*, vol. 18, nos 1–2, pp. 209–29.

Zajovic, S. (1993) 'Cleansing', unpublished paper, Women in Black, Belgrade.

4

Transforming Conflict: Some Thoughts on a Gendered Understanding of Conflict Processes

Judy El-Bushra

Travelling[1] in a number of very isolated and resource-poor communities in Africa over the last few years, and talking to women and to development agency staff working with them, I have often been struck by the dissonance between the language of gender studies and the language of women and men in these communities. A visit to Rwanda in 1995 (to facilitate a workshop on conflict resolution for Rwandese NGOs)[2] was the stimulus for the thought that those involved with gender and development approaches must now begin questioning both the discourse and the concepts they have elaborated in the light of the turbulent conditions in which Africa and much of the rest of the world are now living. This chapter aims to contribute to this process of questioning. One of the themes to be followed here is the notion of 'respect', which emerges frequently in field discussions as a major desire expressed by women in contrast to the 'autonomy' which gender literature presumes as a need on their behalf.

The 'field' of gender and development and that of conflict analysis have often found it difficult to identify their mutual relevance. A critique of both is appropriate. Conflict analysis, for its part, has tended to ignore how a gender analysis could enrich understanding of the motivations of different actors, or how it could articulate linkages between the personal dimension on the one hand and institutions, trends and interests at local, national and international levels on the other. Gender and development have overly focused on women's economic roles (Razavi and Miller 1995) to the detriment of developing a holistic body of theory that addresses the human condition in all its aspects and responds to the voices and the experiences of men and women at the grass-roots.

The approach taken to defining gender in this paper is that of the social relations framework (Kabeer 1994). 'Gender' (socially constructed differences between men and women) differences are embedded in social relations and therefore differ between different cultures; they are constituted through – and also help to constitute – the exercise of other forms of social difference such as those of age, race or class. Uncovering gender differences in a given society will lead to an understanding of power relations in general in that society, and to the illumination of contradictions and injustices inherent in those relations.

The notion of conflict adopted in this paper is one which envisages it as emerging through a complex process rather than as being a discreet event which imposes itself on a pre-existing situation (El-Bushra and Piza-Lopez 1993). Any specific conflict should be understood in relation to its historical antecedents, and as moving towards a variety of potential outcomes. At different key junctures in the conflict, individuals and interest groups may be confronted with options, and how they select from these options may determine the future direction of the conflict. Such moments (critical thresholds) and such people or interest groups or their capabilities (stabilising points) enable individuals and institutions involved in conflicts to situate themselves *as agents* within the evolving conflict, and stress their potential for influencing outcomes either positively or negatively. A range of gendered opportunities and choices is open to individuals and groups.

In this conceptualisation, conflict appears as an unusually dramatic form of ever-present social change, and adaptation to an evolving global environment. It may be understood as the disintegration of social relations, while also heralding opportunities for reconstruction and the assertion of new values. It may facilitate the emergence of new sources of conflict, or perhaps prompt the re-ordering of social relations in better adapted forms. It may, or may not, provide a window of opportunity through which marginalised and powerless groups find ways to exert influence over the shape of the world they live in.

This chapter focuses on two concepts which are intrinsic to both gender and conflict analysis, namely those of 'identity' and 'agency', and aims to examine them from the standpoint of communities caught up in violent conflict. 'Identity' for these purposes concerns the social process whereby individuals come to identify themselves with a particular configuration of social roles and relationships. 'Agency' describes the strategies used by individuals to create a viable and satisfying life for themselves in the context of, or in spite of, these identities. Both identity and agency, as concepts, have relevance for understanding the nature of violent conflict and especially for probing the motivations of different actors in that conflict. Violence thus provides a conceptual space in which to elaborate and redefine these two concepts, with the hope of enriching both conflict analysis and gender and development in the process.

The first section of this chapter sketches three brief illustrative case studies. The second summarises existing literature on the impact of conflict on women, men and gender relations. The third section elaborates on identity, agency and violence as conceptual resources.

Case Studies

Northern Uganda[3] The Ugandan civil war came to an end in the country at large in 1986, although it continued sporadically in the North and is now reaching serious and widespread proportions there. Testimonies from women in Northern Uganda, gathered in 1993, reveal how during the civil war families were split up because of the different security strategies which men and women were obliged to follow. By day families continued to farm their fields when possible, while by night women and their children stayed in their homesteads or gathered in nearby towns in the homes of kin, with men hiding out in shelters dug underground or built in trees. When soldiers passed through the area, men were liable to be forcibly conscripted while women risked being abducted and forced into prostitution or forms of enforced 'marriage'.

During the more recent phase of the war, the activity of the Lord's Resistance Army (LRA), an anti-government force led by Joseph Kony, has often taken the form of kidnapping adults and children from within their homesteads, and often from within the centres of towns, and abducting them to bases inside the Sudan where they are given military training. Abducted girls have frequently been allocated as 'wives' to LRA officers. Abducted children of both sexes have been forced to commit acts of extreme violence as part of the training process. Many of the children who have returned home evidence signs of acute emotional disturbance, although most recover with adequate care over a period of around six months. According to care workers, abused teenage girls tend to take longer time to recover.

At the same time, government policy of grouping rural families into 'protected villages' (often by force), while at the same time failing to provide adequate military protection (Amnesty International 1999), has encouraged physical attacks and abductions, as well as having major implications for food security and reducing the majority of the rural population to dependency on food aid. The inability of both men and women to provide adequately for their families is leading to loss of identity for both and to accompanying social problems such as alcoholism, principally among men. An ACORD report on a visit to a displaced settlement called 'Coo pe kwene' (trans. 'is there no man anywhere') notes a development worker's comment on alcohol consumption that 'men drink to forget how helpless they have become with the loss of their homes, cattle and privacy'.

The experience of married women during the war, coping unaided by their husbands, had a significant impact on their self-confidence and assert-iveness. The gender division of labour was changing: by the late 1980s/early 1990s women's perceived 'proper' responsibilities included purchase of soap and kerosine, items which had previously been men's responsibility to supply, and it was not unusual for women to contribute the lion's share of the various tax requirements increasingly being demanded in the form of cash. In addition, the previously strict division of roles in agriculture was perceived as having become more fluid, with women and men often working together on tasks which had previously been exclusively the domain of one or the other. On the whole women's testimonies show that they were happy and proud to accept this increase in responsibilities.

One impact of the war, then, was to increase the range of responsibilities and tasks shouldered by women, without reassigning men's roles back to them. Women and their children had in fact become a relatively self-contained unit, which men found difficulty in re-entering. Women com-plained of the breakdown of socialisation processes (due to men's absences and women's overwork) resulting in children and young people appearing to be increasingly 'out of control'. They perceived the disintegration of the household as it had once been, both in terms of economic roles and inter-personal relations and the emotional sphere. Men complained of feeling excluded from the family circle, having ceded much economic responsibility to their wives, and of being unable to re-establish close relations with their children. Socialising in the bars with other similarly excluded men was, as they saw it, their only option, thus guaranteeing even greater resentment from their womenfolk. Women often came to see their husbands as an unnecessary and functionless encumbrance. Many marriages were held together only by the power of 'respectability' as an overriding force in determining women's behaviour.

The perceived breakdown of the family as a system of complementary and mutually supporting roles has paved the way for the growth of forms of organisation linking women with other women, and sometimes with men, in economic and other community-based endeavours. These take the form of traditional groupings carrying out communal agricultural labour or saving for burials and other key life-cycle events, often built on (and sometimes displaced by) NGO-sponsored rotational savings and credit groups and community-based organisations. For women the important goal of such groupings is self-help and self-reliance, a way of demonstrating to the world the contribution that women can and do make to the com-munity's survival and its development in good times and bad.

The continuation of the war in its present phase has taken place during a time of growth of local organisations of different types, including an increasing involvement of women in peace-building initiatives and in support for, for example, raped and disabled women who are often also repudiated and without support.

Somalia and Somaliland[4] Although the most serious excesses of the civil war appear to be over, pockets of localised conflict continue. De facto local authority structures are in place in Somalia and Somaliland, but their legitimacy is still in dispute and none has been recognised by any outside government.

Violence and potential violence have been features of life in Somalia on a continuing basis since before the formal outbreak of the war, making the routines of everyday existence a dangerous business for the average citizen. During the most violent periods, and particularly during the 'Operation Restore Hope' period of famine relief, armed gunmen would fight it out for control of relief supplies, risking the lives of the (mainly) women, children and elderly who tended to be the ones standing in food queues. Landmines still litter fields.

As in Uganda, during the most critical periods security often required men and women to go different ways, with children most often staying with their mothers or members of their mothers' clans. The war occasioned massive displacement of populations in bewildering patterns, as individuals tried to ensure their personal security by regrouping in their clan territories or by rejoining other family members. Codes of conduct in warfare protected women and children and by all accounts were nearly always followed in past conflicts; in the recent civil war, however, there have been numerous occasions in which these codes were disregarded. Incidents of violent attack and rape against women and girls were frequent, adding to the limitations on their mobility.

The survival of households and communities can be attributed at least in part to the efforts of women to provide food, shelter and protection to their children and other family members throughout the war. As the division of labour changed under pressure from male absences, women's roles in livestock production, agriculture and trade intensified and families became increasingly dependent on women's economic contribution. Women's experience of coping in spite of extreme difficulties has contributed to an awareness of their key role, and has underscored in their own minds their resilience and capacity for autonomous action. There is evidence that, in the immediate aftermath of the war at least, women took on more proactive roles in making decisions about marriage and divorce, refusing to accept marriage with men who did not 'pull their weight' and reluctant to return to 'the way things were before the war'.

The mushrooming of women's organisations since 1993 or so is a feature of the present situation. The functions of these organisations vary from service provision to mutual support and solidarity to promoting women's role in peace-building. Local peace agreements have in some cases been reached as a result of pressure from women, organising in spontaneous and informal ways to mobilise traditional peace promotion activities such as holding prayer meetings and singing anti-war songs and poems on battlefields. In other cases women have played major, though not necessarily prominent, roles in setting up formal peace-building and reconciliation mechanisms. In Somaliland, women's organisations and other local organisations with prominent female leadership have had international funds directed through them for reconstruction purposes such as administering of food for work programmes or credit support to small enterprises.

Historically, women have always exercised an influence over whether men go to war or not, mainly through their roles as poetesses and recounters of stories to their children. This influence has often had the effect of inciting violence, when the women believed that the interests of the clan were best served thus. For example, during the 1988–91 civil war in the north in which the Somali National Movement (SNM) attempted to bring down President Siyad Barre and put an end to his hegemonic control of the north, women gave strong support to the latter. However, following Siyad Barre's defeat, further violence occurred among his erstwhile opponents, a development which women widely abhorred. The degree of energy which women devoted to peace and development appears to represent an altruism born of their disgust with the vicious circle of reciprocal violence which prolonged the war beyond any useful function. However, it may also reflect alternative interpretations of the clan system and its influence, interpretations which emanate from women's structural position within it.

The segmentary nature of clan units is important at several levels. In addition, historical links and enmities between different clans also play an influential role in permitting or excluding relations between individuals at system level. However, it is mistaken to cite clan as an exclusive ruling factor in people's real-life behaviour. 'Class', which may be defined in several ways (such as economic/income categories, occupational categories, and also the existence of caste-like outcast groups within most of the major clans), plays a part. Neighbourhood plays a role as important as, or more important than, clan in determining social networks, the more so since clan territories may be scattered, with different sections of a particular clan never actually meeting each other.

Preferential exogamous marriage (i.e. a preference for marriage between people from different clans) is a key element in the capacity of the clan system to manage 'fission and fusion' tendencies, as it creates a myriad of cross-cutting affinal linkages (i.e. ties through marriage) at all levels of the system and provides a framework for interaction between otherwise un-connected individuals. Women and men relate to clan structures in different ways: both men and women retain membership of their fathers' lineage throughout their lives, but since women are the ones who are perceived as 'moving out' through marriage, the strength of their clan allegiance is believed to be weakened as a result. Women therefore have affinal links with their husbands' clans which are qualitatively different from men's links with their wives' clans.

This fact enriches life for women in that it generates a wide nexus of social relationships; it can also have a destructive effect on them. When the system breaks down women are pulled in two directions: their fathers and brothers on one side demand one set of allegiances while their husbands and children demand another. In a three-generation female-headed house-hold atomised by war (imagine, for example, a woman who has sought refuge abroad with her aged parents and her dependent children), the general stresses of the situation can be compounded by oppositions between the woman's parents and her children.

Nevertheless, the relationships generated through exogamy have the potential to become a force for reconstructing social relations. In fact, the relationships which apply are more numerous than those between a woman's lineage and her husband's. Through marriage, she is also connected in specific ways with the lineages of her mother, her sons-in-law and her daughters-in-law, and with others through extension of the same principle. This networking tendency is underpinned by perceptions of individuals' relationships with their mothers (and by extension their mothers' kin), relationships which have a different and more intimate or supportive quality from those with fathers (and by extension fathers' kin). Women's position in clan structures affords them a capacity to move between potentially opposing groups through marriage and to create inter-personal relations between them. It is this 'social mobility' which enables them to be more detached than men from clan-specific identity. This provides them with both the desire and the capacity to see social networks in inclusive terms and to mobilise for inclusive ends.

Rwanda[5] The conduct of the 1994 civil war in Rwanda is fairly well known.[6] The most relevant aspect of the Rwanda context for this argument is the spontaneous emergence of women's groups in the post-war period.

Throughout most of Central Africa, the predominant kinship pattern is that based on patrilineal descent and moderated by bridewealth arrange-ments which transfer control over the bride's productive and reproductive capacities from her own lineage to that of her husband. Interpretations of this system, and in particular whether or not it implies that women are themselves property, transferable through marriage like any other item, vary. Whatever the case, the reality of life for women in pre-war Rwanda was that, as individuals, their decision-making remit was highly circumscribed.

Population pressure on land had reduced women's already limited land entitlements to virtually nil in favour of male kin. According to customary law, anything women produced (including crops, cash income and children) was under the control of the male family head, even when agricultural labour was carried out by women. In the mid-1980s new legislation was brought in which gave women the right to open bank accounts in their own names (though even after that, banks routinely limited the practice). The establishment of women's groups had been promoted for some years by government, and indeed they were seen as the major strategy for women's development, since it was only through the groups' agricultural or income-generating activities that women could retain any degree of control over what they produced. Thus the identification of niches, however small, for women's autonomy was a major development priority.

During the war of 1994, and particularly as a result of the genocidal massacres which precipitated it, it was principally the men of the targeted populations who lost their lives or fled to other countries in fear. In present-day Rwanda an estimated 70 per cent of the population are women. This targeting of men for slaughter was not confined to adults: boys were similarly decimated, raising the possibility that the demographic imbalance will continue for generations. Large numbers of women also lost their lives; however, mutilation and rape were the principal strategies used against women, and these did not necessarily result in death. In the areas most affected by the massacres – for example in Bugasera in eastern Rwanda – the proportion of women who have been widowed, raped or physically handicapped is very high. It is to a large extent these women on whom the responsibility for producing food is now falling. Their psychological as well as their physical status is therefore a major issue for the community's survival in the current stage.

Women's groups are now beginning to reappear, this time spontaneously and on the initiative of women themselves. The focus of activity is often to ensure that members succeed in overcoming whatever problems they have in getting their fields cultivated. Yet women often discuss these problems in terms of psychological needs as well as the need for physical labour power. The task of the women's groups is not simply to provide joint labour but also to enable women to 'watch out for' each other, to provide an environment of mutual emotional support.

Women's groups enable their members to recount traumatic experiences of attack, bereavement and rape. Such experiences are common to so many women that they are no longer peculiar or shameful. The issue is not simply that the women have witnessed traumatic events from which they need time and support to recover. It is also that the events they have witnessed call into question the very basis of their identity and self-esteem. If they have lost parents, children, husband and their own physical strength, where will they get the emotional strength from to carry on with life? If they have been attacked and betrayed by neighbours with whom they have shared a lifetime, who else can they have confidence in? The impact of these events on the mutual trust which forms the basis of all social interaction cannot be underestimated. The significance of women's groups lies in their potential for rebuilding relationships as much as their ability to offer emotional support and share productive tasks.

A further problem is that of women who have themselves been perpetrators or instigators of violence. Such women may also be traumatised by their experience, often showing various forms of denial, and may be as much in need of support as others. Yet their inability to speak up cuts them off from sources of this support and prevents them from re-establishing networks of social relations which could promote their psychological rehabilitation. The problem has wider community repercussions, since as long as such actions continue to be known but unacknowledged, mistrust between neighbours – and even between family members – will be unassuaged.

A major issue of concern to women in Rwanda is the impact of the demographic imbalance on marriages. Polygamy, which is not legally permitted in Rwanda, is often suggested as a means of solving the problem of the large number of widows and younger women whose prospects of marriage have become drastically reduced. Rivalry between women over potential husbands has become common, and an issue which sparks off heated debate. This is in some cases reflected in the composition of women's groups: some groups consist only of widows, for example, since their interests are seen as being separate from those of married women. The disadvantage of this for widows, however, is that they do not benefit from the dynamism of women whose physical and psychological health has been less affected. The importance of this issue in the discourse of women in present-day Rwanda highlights the significance of relational factors in women's personal world-view. Autonomy per se or by default is the least desired of all options.

The war has not yet resulted in radical or strategic change for women in Rwanda. The authority structures (the male commune leadership formed around the 'bourgemaistres') which make the principal decisions about resource management in rural areas are the same patriarchal ones as before. Women still have access to and control over land only in so far as they hold it in trust for their children or for male kin who may one day return. Yet changes in men's and women's economic roles are being seen as women take on, of necessity, previously male tasks. Women are asserting greater autonomy in decision-making about marriage, children and sexual relations. Organisations promoting women's legal rights are contributing to the preparation of new legislation on land and property rights. The Rwanda government is attempting to incorporate gender perspectives on peace-building into its highest policy levels (Government of Rwanda 1997).

Trends in Conflict Analysis: Identifying Gendered Impacts

Literature on the gendered impact of conflict falls into two main categories: empirical research, observation and testimony, and gendered analysis of conflict in international relations. Brought together, these two strands may indicate a framework for mapping the gendered impact of conflict on women and men and on gender relations. The theoretical implication of this framework is that the capacity of 'gender theory' to address the wide spectrum of significant factors, and their inter-relationships, needs to be re-examined.

Empirical documentation In the twentieth-century Western world, the dominant assumption about war has been that it is essentially a male pursuit from which women are excluded for their protection. Recognising that women's involvement (passive and active) in war was largely unattested, a number of empirical studies and oral testimonies (see, for example, Ridd and Callaway 1987; Bennett et al. 1996; Sayigh 1997) have attempted to raise the profile of women's experiences in conflict. Women have generally been the focus of this material, in an attempt to explore a perspective rarely given attention. However, one of the perhaps unintended consequences of this work has been to raise interest in individual experiences of war, whether by men, women or children, and indeed to raise interest in personal testimony as a method both of research and of consciousness-raising. (See Human Rights Watch [1997] for an example of testimonies from abducted children in Northern Uganda, and Lentin [1998] for discussion of the problem of memory in the method of oral testimony.)

Impacts vary in different situations. Behaviour during the immediate heat of the conflict tends to be self-preservatory and short-term, but still demonstrates the gendered nature of people's responses to immediate crises, determined by their distinct social roles and responsibilities. Decisions about where and how to seek refuge, for example, including whether or not to split the family, who should stay with the children and old people, and where to run to, may be determined by a person's ethnicity or political allegiance, or equally by social factors such as prevalent attitudes towards women's and children's vulnerability and need for protection. In more settled post-war circumstances or in protracted emergencies, readjustment and reintegration pose a range of problems for both men and women. Windows of opportunity often present themselves, paradoxically, for making changes in the arrangement of social relationships which may benefit both men and women. Indeed there are times when women seem to gain while men lose, to the extent that women gain strength, self-confidence and solidarity from their experiences while men may be at a loss to re-establish their roles. The experience of exile as refugees or displaced people imposes other constraints on men and women and requires a range of gendered coping strategies (Bennett et al. 1996).

Research in international relations A second strand in the literature on gender and conflict comes from the field of political science and inter-national relations. Here, international trends such as multilateral trade and Western military expansionism have been shown to shape gender relations in Third World countries affected by the presence of, for example, US military bases (Peterson 1993; Enloe 1993). Recurring themes include women's participation in politics and political struggles (Ridd and Callaway 1987), the role of the state in promoting or curbing violence against women (Ashworth 1992), the gendered structures of international economic hegemonies (Enloe 1993), and the use of gender imagery to mobilise populations in support of state establishments (Macdonald 1987).

A theme of these works is that supposedly gender-free structures and institutions – the state, or transnational trade structures – are in fact gendered, inasmuch as their continuation depends on differences between men's and women's social and economic roles, as well as on the use of symbols of masculinity and femininity to mobilise solidarity behind the institution's goals. For example, the hegemony of multinationals in Central American countries, which American militarism has done so much to preserve, depends crucially on economic structures in which women's domestic labour permits the survival of families whose only other income is the starvation wages of male plantation hands. In this way the sub-ordinate position of all women helps to preserve inequalities between men. Yet, women have also found new economic niches, offsetting contractions in male labour opportunities, and thus have set their own challenges to the current global hierarchy (Enloe 1993).

A framework for mapping the gendered impact of conflict The relationship between gender and power, attested in all these studies, is observed both at local and international levels. Linkages between local and international seem critical to a full understanding of the underlying factors in the generation of conflict,[7] since this requires identifying the articulations between global and local actors and mechanisms.

Potential impacts of conflict on women are summarised in Table 4.1 (adapted from El-Bushra and Piza-Lopez 1993).

TABLE 4.1 Potential impact of conflict on women

International	Changes to gender roles at local level resulting from structural adjustment, militarisation and economic globalisation
	Application of international law (e.g. issue of rape as a war crime)
	Behaviour of international peace-keeping forces
National/state	Contraction of services and infrastructure
	National legislation and mechanisms for protection of women's rights
	Behaviour of police and army
	HIV/AIDS prevention policies
	Representation of women in political and authority structures
	Changing attitudes towards women's participation in public affairs and decision-making
	Community
	Changing attitudes towards women's behaviour
	Violence against opponents' womenfolk as war strategy
	Growth in women's organisations and other solidarity mechanisms to withstand problems
	Protection mechanisms, attitudes towards violence against women
Household	Women's production and social reproduction roles emphasised and extended
	Intra-household negotiation and decision-making about survival strategies
	Forced marriage and prostitution
	Quality of marital relationships may change
Personal	Personal violence: rape, injury, disability
	Sexual and reproductive health stresses, including children conceived in rape
	Trauma from witnessing and participating in violence
	Psycho-social impacts: loss of self-esteem flowing from loss of roles and relationships, loss of home and community

Further lessons may be drawn about the longer-term impact of war on gender relations. Demographic imbalance resulting from higher male deaths and family splits affects the personal and reproductive life expectations of both men and women (see, for example, Panchavichetr 1993). As the case studies above demonstrate, it also promotes changes in the division of labour as women compensate for the absence or incapacity of the male labour force by learning new skills and adapting new economic and reproductive roles (for example, in self-defence and protection). These changes may or may not be permanent, and may themselves lead to new relationships between men and women being negotiated. Greater sharing of gender roles, higher rates of divorce, a breakdown in mechanisms for the socialisation of children, may all figure among the results.

Wider changes in political relations include women taking on greater public roles and/or developing more and stronger forms of women's organisation, including organisations that take on dynamic roles in reconciliation, peace-building and development. The role of women in decision-making about peace and war is contested; in reality women may also have important roles in inciting men to violence and in perpetrating it themselves.

Conceptual Resources for Understanding Conflict

The material presented in the previous two sections suggests that any gendered attempt to explain behaviour in conflict-affected environments will have to encompass, as a minimum, three sets of closely inter-twined issues:

- economic survival and organisation
- the personal, affective (feelings and emotions) domain
- social and political relations

Examples from the case studies above include Ugandan women's changing roles in food production, mistrust between neighbours in Rwanda, and the emergence of women's organisations as a new social force in Somalia. Commonly used approaches have much to say about the first of the above sets of issues but little about the other two, and little about the important inter-linkages between all three. Enhancing women's economic role may be important, both for their survival and as a route into women's 'empowerment' or 'autonomy', since it helps to raise women's awareness of their capacities as well as putting money in their pockets which they can use as leverage to improve their position vis-à-vis men.

Important though it may be to facilitate women's economic survival strategies, an approach which privileges the material domain has limitations inasmuch as it ignores both the personal and the social elements in a given context that impact on economic capacity. Physical and psychological status clearly have an impact on an individual's capacity for economically productive activity, and economic pressures clearly affect the former in turn. The role of material and non-material claims based on reciprocal social relations as a contributory factor in economic potential is explored by economists such as Sen (1990).

As the first section has established, there is a wealth of literature now available on gender and conflict in Africa and elsewhere. The challenge remains, however, to explore how it could effectively contribute to a fuller and more people-centred approach to conflict analysis. To do this effectively it may have to reconsider some of its fundamental concepts and in particular be more responsive to the voices of women and men caught up in the reality of warfare, now coming to the fore. What these voices are telling us relate to sociological concepts which can throw light on the social mechanisms of violent conflict at a community level: the meanings of power, issues of identity and personhood, the institutionalisation of masculinity.

Power The meaning of 'power' itself has been subject to philosophical debate over many centuries. Elshtain (1992) distinguishes between '*potestas*' (official power or authority) and '*potentia*' (informal power or potency) and notes that this has historically corresponded to notions of male and female power respectively. Power can comprise both overt, 'naked' power as manifested in violent conflict, and more subtle manifestations such as coercion, influence, authority and manipulation (Bachrach and Baratz 1970). Power may be observed in the way decisions are taken, but equally when decisions are *not* taken, i.e. excluded from the decision-making agenda. Indeed, it has been suggested that the most effective form of power is that which does not require to be exercised.

To promote a simplistic divide between power/men on the one hand and powerlessness/women on the other would be misconceived; men's power is limited by a variety of historical and institutional factors (including women's and other men's challenges to it), whereas women, even while denied the outward, publicly acknowledged forms of power such as public political office, do exert forms of influence. Hadendowa women in the Sudan who are virtually invisible in the public arena nevertheless contribute critically to decision-making in the key political issue of demands for compensation for injury; women ultimately decide at which moment the men of the group should take up arms or lay them down, using poetry, songs and taunts as means of conveying their opinions and the withdrawal of sexual relations as the ultimate sanction (Ilham Osman, personal communication).

Everyday forms of resistance within existing gender relations frameworks provide scope for women to exercise political influence, often in ways that confound the outside observer.[8] Women may claim rights, based on the *absence* of self- or group-interest, to approach powerful leaders to seek reconciliation (El-Bushra forthcoming; Callaway 1987). Thus, in various ways, women exercise agency in the pursuit of self-identified goals, demonstrating that their lack of formal power does not deprive them of their capabilities or resilience. Yet this requirement to interpret the nuances inherent in the notion of power should not obscure the importance of gender as a major axis of power in its own right, and of gender relations as the site of both personal and institutional struggle by individuals to carve out niches of self-fulfilment.

Nuanced concepts of power help to explain the important social differentiations which determine the scope individuals have to pursue their own interests and set agendas for change. However, to understand why the pursuit of such agendas may degenerate into violent action requires other dimensions to be taken into account.

Identity and personhood Debates about the nature and production of gender identity form a crucial thread in the evolution of gendered understandings of power relations. Much of the work done in this area delves into the essence of what constitutes 'gender' and its supposed oppositional relationship with biological sex, and has deliberately sought to explore the relevance of psychoanalytic theory to anthropological discourse on culture (Moore 1994). By associating gender differences with the 'performance' of social roles, rather than having a fundamental or fixed nature, this work enables links to be made between gender and other sorts of difference which are 'constitutive of gender' (Moore 1994: 24–5) and without which gender differences have no contextual meaning. It also expands on the notion that differences *within* genders may be as important as differences *between* genders. A varied range of 'masculinities' or 'femininities', or different masculine and feminine identities, may be produced by the intersection of a variety of different historical factors (Connell 1995). Different notions of masculinity and femininity derive in part from communal perceptions of appropriate behaviour and are hence underpinned by the desire of both men and women for the respect of their neighbours and kinsfolk, from whom reciprocal services and support may be expected.

The importance of this work for conflict studies is the light it has thrown on violence as an outcome of conflicting or shifting identities, especially masculine identities. One of the main component ideas in this configuration is the notion of 'hegemonic masculinity' (Connell 1995) in which the differences of power and status *between* men merge with those between men and women, with the result that certain groups of men are allocated characteristics normally associated with women, or are, paradoxically, categorised in terms of 'animal-like' behaviour (see Mukta, this volume). The notion of violence as an expression of conflicting gender identities also permits the accommodation of male-on-male or female-on-female violence, with neither being the result of purely individual motivations, but generated by a particular configuration of gender roles and ideologies.

Another important element is the idea that violence results from an individual being 'thwarted' (Moore 1994: 66–7) by the intersection of conflicting self-images, such as the non-compatibility often besetting men between the image of the family protector and provider on the one hand, and the sociable, generous buddy figure on the other (Wade 1994). The notion of 'thwarting' illuminates the framework proposed above; it permits an understanding of how individual identities are influenced by pressures created at macro-levels of the national and international political economy (Wade 1994), and of how previously subordinated identities may acquire dominant social positions and hence reproduce the same hegemonic relationship over others.[9]

Most of the work on identities and violence has focused on masculinity, and the dynamics of female violence tend not to be so well elaborated as that of men. This, for the present, presents opportunities still to be exploited in 'probing the motivations of different actors' as suggested in the introduction to this chapter. The notion of female conflicts of identity, giving rise to the performance of or complicity in acts of violence, may perhaps contribute to an understanding of women's violence in conflict, such as has been described for Rwanda (African Rights 1995).

The association of women's 'nurturing' role with the promotion of peace and compassion does not stand up to close examination, since, although women may well be active in peace-work in many contexts, they are also often in the forefront of demands for aggression in defence of their and their group's interests. They may be instrumental in perpetuating inter-communal mistrust through their role as educators of new generations, have taken active parts in many armed nationalist movements (Vickers 1993), have often been seen as more vicious fighters than men (see Bennett et al. 1996 on Liberia) and, indeed, where they achieve political power at a global level may be as ardent as men in promoting the global hegemonies that underpin wars. Women's involvement in violence should be considered not as an aberration but rather as a component of 'agency', or ways in which individuals carve out an acceptable life for themselves within the constraints imposed by their various and possibly conflictual identities.

The institutionalisation of masculinity Work on gender identities is particularly important for the light it sheds on the institutional arrangements which contribute to the socialisation of men and to their mobilisation around male interests. Some, such as the family, are common across all societies, while others are particular to specific cultures, such as age-grades in Africa. Other institutions which are critically responsible for the production of masculine identities include political parties and nationalist movements, which may make similar appeals to gender identities despite ideological differences.[10] Such institutions may be capable of perpetuating patterns of enmity and abuse over generations (see Richards [1995], on the Sierra Leonean 'warboys').

Transforming gender relations requires an understanding of both men's and women's constraints and motivations (White 1997). An emerging approach is one in which wars are believed to be generated by distorted images of gender identity, which can be rebuilt through the adoption of careful and informed strategies:

> The socialisation of boys and young men is of vital importance in understanding the causes of conflict, allied to a recognition of the structural factors which are creating conflict in resource-poor situations. Reclaiming positive cultural traditions of manhood alongside those of womanhood is an area of research in social theory that needs to receive more attention from development theorists and practitioners. (Large 1997: 29)

It must be acknowledged that this kind of approach treads a thin line between, on the one hand, *identifying* male power as a crucial element in conflict, and, on the other hand, *accepting* it implicitly. Turning some 'bad' men into 'good' men may reduce incidences of violence, and so help cut into the vicious circle, but may not in the long run solve the problem of gender as an axis of hegemonic power. The strength of the approach is more its assertion that the same institutions which shape the formation of destructive identities can also be employed to shape constructive ones (Kandiyoti 1993). In any case, looking at masculinities (and femininities), one can begin to unpack the 'persons' behind conflict, addressing the question of why and how people become active participants in conflict, and equally why and how they desist from it. However, the connection between violence at an inter-personal level (at which most of this work has been done) and the wider disruption of international militarism, civil war and predatory violence, has not yet been made satisfactorily.

Concluding Thoughts

This chapter has attempted to argue that, despite a well-established body of empirical and theoretical work of relevance, a gendered understanding of conflict remains conspicuous by its absence. Among the many unanswered questions offering a challenge to future research are several to do with violence. How does political conflict degenerate into pervasive, mass violence, generating new crises and new forms of violent conflict in future? How does a community pull itself *out* from the cycle of violence and set up sustainable ways of living in which different categories of people may all be encouraged to contribute to the process?

Addressing such questions offers up a challenge to social science for which its habitual concepts and methods are not at present well adapted. Many of these concepts, including those employed in the service of social and gender transformation, such as 'empowerment', 'control', 'subordination', are difficult to define, open to misuse, and communicated only with difficulty across cultures. Hence the sense of 'dissonance' I have experienced between social science language and the discourse of women and men on the ground.

Concepts which are articulated more frequently at the field level concern respect, harmony, co-operation and the sharing of jointly held responsibilities. Of these, the goal most ardently sought by many women is respect. Respect is valued not only for its own sake and for the sake of confirming in personal terms the relationships sanctioned by society in marriage. It is also an important component in women's economic survival. In the long term, acceptance of the prevailing ideology is a condition of survival; by their willingness to follow, and indeed exceed, the norm, women may claim support and protection from misfortune from family and neighbours. By seeking autonomy, they may well forgo their sympathy, and hence their material and moral support.

In practice, when 'respect' is unpacked, it frequently involves women carrying out their existing, subordinate, roles even more efficiently, thus relieving men from family responsibility and freeing up their time and money for leisure. So why is it that women regard respect as being so important to their well-being and their status? Some might suggest that they have not yet 'seen' how they are being exploited. But in my observation it is more that their priorities and values are different from those of outside researchers. In fact, that exploitation is a price they are willing to pay for the public acknowledgement that they make important contributions to society, and for the removal of doubt about the security of their marital and other relationships. Perhaps they see clearly how long the road to women's development is, and that respect is one of the first stepping stones on it.

If gender analysis is to be more relevant to the issues thrown up by armed conflict situations, it must seek to extend itself into new directions. It must pay greater attention to the personal dimension of gender analysis, examining terms such as 'self-esteem', 'identity' and 'respect' empirically in the same way that it has done for gender roles and social institutions, and determine how these affect, and are affected by, changing social relations.

At the same time, if conflict analysis for its part is to develop meaningful interpretations, it should not be content with conceptualising 'conflict' as having a separate identity from that of the individuals and societies involved in it. The propensity for uncontrolled conflict is rooted within individuals, communities and societies, which are not gender-neutral. Our under-standing of war and peace would be deepened if conflict analysts were willing to take as a starting-point the men and women who make war, and also those who are complicit in it, support it, benefit from it, or suffer from it.

Notes

The original research for this paper was undertaken during a visiting fellowship at the University of East Anglia in 1997.

1. As Research and Policy Officer in ACORD, an operational development agency working in seventeen countries in Africa, where I have worked since 1982.

2. At the invitation of Cecile Mukarubuga, ACORD's regional representative in the Great Lakes, who inspired much of this paper.

3. Material for this section is drawn from oral histories collected for Bennett et al. (1996), and from ACORD Gulu programme staff and collaborators.

4. Material for this section is taken from a variety of sources including El-Bushra and Piza-Lopez (1993), ACORD programme documentation and material in collection for a forthcoming book on Somalia and Somaliland through the eyes of Somali women, to be published by International Co-operation in Development (ICD), the development co-operation arm of the London-based Catholic Institute for International Relations (El-Bushra [ed.] forthcoming).

5. Material for this section is taken from ACORD programme documents and from El-Bushra and Mukarubuga (1995).

6. For a general account of the civil war, the genocide and its antecedents, see Prunier (1998).

7. Little work has been done linking the international humanitarian response to conflict with local gender power relations, but, as an exception, see O'Kane (1997) on WHO complicity with Taliban prescriptions against women's health services.

8. Edgerton in Ridd and Callaway (1987) describes how Catholic women in Northern Ireland developed a warning system for army raids by rattling dustbin lids.

9. Boas (1997) suggests that explanations for the inhumanity of the conduct of the war in Liberia may be found in the experience of the ex-slave American settlers, who then reproduced master–slave identities in their own relationship with indigenous groups, identities which were subsequently perpetuated – and twisted – at each historical turn.

10. For example, Hale (1996), writing about the Sudan, draws parallels between the National Islamic Front and the Sudanese Communist Party in the way they conceptualise and promote women's social roles.

Bibliography

African Rights (1995) *Rwanda – Not So Innocent: When Women Become Killers*, London: African Rights.

Amnesty International (1999) *Uganda: Breaking the Circle – Protecting Human Rights in the Northern War Zones*, London: Amnesty International.

Ashworth, G. (1992) *Women and Human Rights*, background paper for the DAC expert group on Women in Development Organisations.

Bachrach, P. and M. Baratz (1970) *Power and Poverty: Theory and Practice*, Oxford: Oxford University Press.

Bennett, O. et al. (eds) (1996) *Arms to Fight, Arms to Protect*, London: PANOS Institute.

Boas, M. (1997) 'Liberia – the Hellbound Heart? Regime Breakdown and the Deconstruction of Society', *Alternatives*, vol. 22.

Callaway, H. (1987) 'Survival and Support: Women's Forms of Political Action', in Ridd and Callaway (eds) *Women and Political Conflict*.

Connell, R. W. (1995) *Masculinities*, Cambridge: Polity Press.

El-Bushra, J. and C. Mukarubuga (1995) 'Women, War and Transition', *Gender and Development*, vol. 3, no. 3, Oxfam.

El-Bushra, J. and E. Piza-Lopez (1993) *Development in Conflict: The Gender Dimension*, Oxfam/ACORD.

El-Bushra, J. (ed.) (forthcoming) *Somali Conflict and Peace: The Perspectives of Somali Women*, ICD/CIIR.

Elshtain, J. B. (1992) 'The Power And Powerlessness of Women', in G. Bock and S. James (eds), *Beyond Equality and Difference: Citizenship, Feminist Politics and Female Subjectivity*, London: Routledge.

Enloe, C. (1993) *The Morning After: Sexual Politics at the End of the Cold War*, Berkeley: University of California Press.

Government of Rwanda (1997) *Paix, genre et developpement: exam critique*, paper contributed by Rwanda to the Pan-African Conference on Peace, Gender and Development, Kigali, March.

Hale, S. (1996) *Gender Politics in the Sudan*, Boulder, CO: Westview Press.

Human Rights Watch (1997) *The Scars of Death: Children Abducted by the Lord's Resistance Army in Uganda*, London: Human Rights Watch.

Kabeer, N. (1994) *Reversed Realities: Gender Hierarchies in Development Thought*, London: Verso.

Kandiyoti, D. (1993), 'The Paradoxes of Masculinity: Some Thoughts on Segregated Societies', in A. Cornwall and N. Lindisfarne (eds) *Dislocating Masculinities: Comparative Ethnographies*, London: Routledge.

Large, J. (1997) 'Disintegrating Conflicts and the Restructuring of Masculinity', *Gender and Development*, vol. 5, no. 2, Oxfam.

Lentin, R. (ed.) (1998) *Gender and Catastrophe*, London: Zed Books.

Macdonald, S. (1987) 'Drawing the Lines – Gender, Peace and War: An Introduction', in S. Macdonald et al. (eds), *Images of Women in Peace and War*, London: Macmillan.

Moore, H. (1994) *A Passion for Difference*, Cambridge: Polity Press.

O'Kane, M. (1997) 'A Holy Betrayal', *Guardian Weekend*, 29 November 1997.

Panchavichetr, P. (1993) 'The Impact of Armed Conflict on Gender Relations: Cambodia', in El-Bushra and Piza-Lopez, *Development in Conflict*.

Peterson, V. S. (1993) *Global Gender Issues*, Boulder, CO: Westview Press.

Prunier, G. (1998) *The Rwanda Crisis 1959 – 1994: History of a Genocide* rev. edn, London: Hurst.

Razavi, S. and C. Miller (1995) *From WID to GAD: Conceptual Shifts in the Women and Development Discourse*, UNRISD.

Richards, P. (1995) 'Rebellion in Liberia and Sierra Leone: A Crisis of Youth?', in O. Furley (ed.), *Conflict in Africa*, London: I.B.Tauris.

Ridd, R. and H. Callaway (eds) (1987) *Women and Political Conflict: Portraits of Struggle in Times of Crisis*, New York: New York University Press.

Sayigh, R. (1997) 'Engendered Exile: Palestinian Camp Women Tell Their Stories', *Oral History*, Autumn.

Sen, A. (1990) 'Gender and Co-operative Conflicts', in I. Tinker (ed), *Persistent Inequalities*, Oxford: OUP.

Vickers, J. (1993) *Women and War*, London: Zed Books.

Wade, P. (1994) 'Man the Hunter: Gender and Violence in Music and Drinking Contexts in Colombia', in P. Gow and P. Harvey (eds), *Sex and Violence: Issues in Representation and Experience,* London: Routledge.

White, S. (1997) 'Men, Masculinities and the Politics of development', *Gender and Development*, vol. 5, no. 2, Oxfam.

5

Engendering the State in Refugee Women's Claims for Asylum

Heaven Crawley

All refugees inhabit a space of extreme marginalisation and vulnerability by having moved outside the established pattern of states and citizenship, and female refugees share certain aspects of being 'out of bounds' with male refugees: loss of state legitimisation by crossing physical boundaries, and losing a sense of belonging. In this situation there is a need for them to reconstruct their own boundaries and identities in a 'foreign' place, while other people are imposing *their* boundaries (and identities) on them ... However, there are also experiences which are specific to the gender of the refugee. (Laurie et al. 1997: 130, emphasis in original)

The Gendering of Protection

Feminist scholars have increasingly criticised the failure of international human rights law to respond appropriately to women's experiences of violence.[1] These concerns are mirrored in a growing body of theoretical and empirical research which argues that women who flee violence and seek asylum in other countries are unable to benefit equitably from protection under the 1951 Convention relating to the Status of Refugees ('the 1951 Convention'). This research suggests that although international instruments make no distinction between men and women, their interpretation by receiving states both reflects and reinforces gender biases within states themselves.[2] As a result many women are denied protection for reasons that have less to do with the content of refugee law than with gender.

Women suffer the same deprivation and harm that is common to all refugees. Many are targeted because they are political activists, community organisers, members of women's movements or persist in demanding that their rights or those of their relatives or community members are respected. They are often punished not only because they oppose the political structures of the state, but because they challenge dominant gender ideologies by being politically active at all (Spijkerboer 1994; Pettman 1996). Women's political protest, activism and resistance may also manifest itself in different ways. Women may hide people, pass messages or provide community services, food, clothing and medical care; many are persecuted because they resist state-sanctioned rules and regulations regarding their behaviour; those who challenge or are unable to conform to either the moral or ethical standards imposed on them may suffer cruel or inhuman treatment; women are abused by members of their family and/or community. In addition the authorities may exploit family relationships to intensify harm and undermine political opposition by men. The failure to recognise the gendered processes through which political identity is constructed undermines women's access to protection.

The decision on whether or not an individual seeking asylum can be recognised as a refugee and therefore granted protection in the UK is usually the culmination of a complex legal process. There are many inadequacies in the current system which have affected both women and men and which have been documented elsewhere (see Refugee Council 1996; Justice, ILPA and ARC 1997). Most fundamentally, however, and contrary to its portrayal in popular discourse as fair and neutral (and therefore open to systematic abuse by so-called 'bogus' asylum-seekers), the process of asylum determination is highly racialised and shaped by wider geo–political and economic interests. This is reflected both in overall recognition rates and in government measures to limit or 'fast-track' applications from particular countries. In focusing upon gender, therefore, it is not intended that this chapter should generalise or essentialise the experiences of refugee and asylum-seeking women. As Anthias and Yuval-Davis (1992) suggest, because women's relationship to the state is racialised and ethicised as well as gendered, it is critically important to connect race, gender and class processes and identities and not to assume that they exist separately from one another. Women's political identities and their experiences of persecution are shaped by their racial, ethnic, cultural and sexual identities as well as by factors such as class, age and marital status. Their experiences of the process of asylum determination, as well as the final outcome of their claim, similarly reflect the intersection of these multiple identities with the political agendas of receiving states. One of the most obvious ways in which this happens is through the issue of credibility which remains one of the most pervasive problems for almost all asylum applications made in the UK (Refugee Council 1996). For example, Razack suggests that where a survivor of sexual violence is a black woman 'racism and sexism intersect in particularly nasty ways to produce profound marginalisation' (Razack 1994: 897). The likelihood that she will be disbelieved is intensified because of the existence of pervasive racist myths about black sexuality.

Even outside these racialised aspects of asylum determination there remain striking similarities in the ways in which the experiences of women asylum-seekers, regardless of their country of origin, are assessed. The evidence which has been collected during the course of my research suggests that in countries such as the UK, which are not only trying to restrict the arrival of potential asylum-seekers (for example, through the imposition of visa regimes and the deployment of officers overseas to prevent inadequately documented passengers from boarding aeroplanes in the first place) but also to limit the extent of their obligations under international asylum law, asylum-seekers whose experiences of persecution do not fit rigidly defined categories will be the first to be refused protection.[3] While a lack of gender-differentiated statistics in the UK context makes quantitative assessment difficult, evidence collected during the course of my research suggests not only that women are less able to gain access to the decision-making process in the first place (because of the assumption that they are dependent upon spouses or other male relatives) but also that they are less likely to be granted refugee status than men (at least at the initial decision-making stage) and more likely to be allowed to remain on compassionate or humanitarian grounds. As a result women often have little or no control over the costs or conditions of protection which, rather than giving them rights, often entails them behaving as victims, weak, passive and grateful (Pettman 1996).

This chapter therefore exposes some of the underlying gendered assumptions upon which current interpretation of international refugee law is based and considers the implications of these for women seeking asylum in the United Kingdom. It will be argued that while the rules of international law purport to be abstract, objective and value free, this preoccupation with neutrality serves to disguise the importance of gender. A feminist perspective, with its concern for gender as a category of analysis, is able to illuminate many issues in the areas of international law including state responsibility and the concept of human rights itself to reveal that that law is an inherently gendered *system* which in reality serves to reinforce male domination (Charlesworth et al. 1991). Thus when gender, rather than 'women', becomes the centre of the analysis, 'international law ... dissolves into a normative struggle whose outcome is determined largely by power' (Strizhak and Harries 1993: 6). This chapter argues that the gendered construction of categories associated with asylum determination has significant implications for the ways in which women's experiences of violence are *represented and analytically characterised*. As both Peterson (1992) and Tickner (1992) suggest, it is important to expose the gender *politics* of categorising practices; we should be concerned with the ways in which women's exclusion from the public realm (political identity, public sphere activities and politics per se) reflects the power and politics of defining or 'bounding' public and private. It is this process of 'bounding' – as opposed to the absence of an explicit recognition of 'gender-related persecution – which depoliticises women's experiences of persecution and obscures their relationship with the state for definitional purposes. In the context of asylum, a gendered analysis of the state which reconceptualises human rights law and 'reveals the gender bias of those social relations upon which the state is constituted' (Romany 1994: 91) provides considerable explanatory potential in assessing why women fleeing violence are all too often unprotected. Unpacking categories and relationships intrinsic to the definition of a refugee, which typically have been seen as 'natural', self-evident and un-gendered, is therefore a critical first step towards gaining a deeper understanding of gendered relations of power and process in asylum determination.

Engendering the State

> [T]he human rights discourse of protection has not been available to women. Women are the paradigmatic alien subjects of international law. To be an alien is to *another*, to be an *outsider*. Women are *aliens* within their states, *aliens* within an international exclusive club that constitutes international society. (Romany 1994: 85, emphasis in original)

International law has evolved as a set of rules intended to regulate relations between states and remains centred on the state; the state continues to be the only actor in international law that really matters and plays a decisive role in making, interpreting and enforcing international law (Knop 1995). This is reflected in Article 1(a) of the 1951 Convention which defines a 'refugee' as a person who 'owing to a well-founded fear of persecution for reasons of race, religion, nationality, membership of a particular social group or political opinion, is outside the country of his nationality and *is unable, or owing to such fear, is unwilling to avail himself of the protection of that country*' (emphasis added). In addition, therefore, to identifying the human rights potentially at risk in the country of origin and an enumerated ground to which the fear can be attributed, a decision on whether or not an individual should be recognised as a refugee within the meaning of the Convention must also comprehend scrutiny of the state's ability and willingness to respond effectively to that risk (Goldberg 1993; Thomas and Beasley 1993). If meaningful state protection is available, protection under the 1951 Convention will not be granted. This concept of state sovereignty, which is based upon the social contract discourse of liberalism, is used to construct a particular (ungendered) understanding of the world (Romany 1994; Bhabha 1996; Pettman 1996).

Feminist critiques by contrast reveal the state, and citizenship, to be gendered and suggest that the impact of state action and inaction affects women and men differently (Peterson 1992; Pettman 1996). The state has no necessary relationship to gender but is dynamic, evolving and dialectic. Gender (and other) inequalities are buried within the state but, through part of the same dynamic process, gender relations are also partly constituted through the state. The state therefore partly reflects and partly helps to create particular forms of gender relations and gender inequality through the law and public discourses which emanate from it (Waylen 1996b). This conceptualisation of the state as a battleground arena in which different social forces articulate their interests is critical when considering women's relationship to the state and, in turn, their experiences of persecution during periods of political and social unrest and/or nation-building (Anthias and Yuval-Davis 1989). These critiques also suggest that regardless of differences *between* states – which are not monolithic, uniform or unitary – the liberal construction of the state enables the maintenance of a state system which legitimates direct and indirect violence against women; while there are many sources of power shaping social relations, the state is strategic in that it acts as the centralised 'main organiser' of gendered power through its legislation and policies, *and the ways in which it is implicated in the construction of the public/private distinction* (Peterson 1992; Pettman 1996). This demarcation between public and private life within society is an inherently political process and one which reflects and re-inforces power relations including the power relations of gender.

One of the most critical functions of the state in constructing the public/private dichotomy is through its role in defining terms and categories and in shaping cultural institutions and norms, including the definition of politics itself. In this sense, the state strengthens its patriarchal base by not only constructing but also maintaining the ideology describing public and private life; the state constitutes itself as the realm of political action and promotes a definition of politics that narrowly construes power relations (Peterson 1992: 44). This definition of politics as paradigmatically masculine and relevant only to the public sphere of state institutions is highly problematic for many women who participate in forms of resistance to state-sanctioned rules and regulations regarding their behaviour but who are not recognised as refugees fleeing *political* persecution when they seek asylum in the United Kingdom. As Waylen (1996a) suggests, because of the dominance of a narrow view of politics which includes only the institutional echelons of the public sphere and concentrates on the actions of political elites, those activities outside the conventional political arena in which women participate are excluded. Equally as critical, however, the idea of state sovereignty gives states their claim to a monopoly on the legitimate use of violence (see Peterson 1992; Tickner 1992; Pettman 1996). Peterson (1992) argues that the state is critical in maintaining gendered power relations through the exercise of so-called legitimate violence (through legislation, policing and wars) and through its role in defining what constitutes the 'illegitimate' forms. In this sense, it is the state which institutionalises and reproduces the legitimisation of social hierarchy; women become the objects of masculinist social control through direct and indirect violence.

The state therefore plays a critical role in instigating and perpetuating violence against women through both its own acts of political repression and through condoning and/or failing to prevent the patriarchal oppression of women in the home, family and community. The state can, however, be held responsible under international law for its inaction as well as its action. *International law imposes a standard of due diligence or reasonable care on the state to prevent, investigate and punish individuals, even non-state actors, who have committed acts that constitute human rights violations.* The failure of the state to do so is a breach of its duties, and as such implicates the state in the commission of these human rights violations (Goldberg 1993; Romany 1994). International refugee law similarly accepts that violence committed by non-state agents 'can be considered as persecution if they are knowingly tolerated by the authorities, or the authorities refuse, or prove unable, to offer effective protection' (UNHCR 1979: paragraph 65). The reality, however, is that states have typically been held accountable only for what they do directly or through an agent (for example, a member of the police or the military). In the context of the asylum determination process, '[t]he consequences for women of this dichotomous perspective are fundamental and profound' (Binion 1995: 519). Violence within the family and/or community – which is one of the most widespread and pervasive forms of abuse experienced by women – has typically been considered outside the realm of international refugee law. As Copelon suggests, such violence and abuse 'is considered different, less severe and less deserving of international condemnation and sanction than officially sanctioned violence' (Copelon 1995a: 116). Indeed, it often tends not be viewed as violence at all; it is seen as 'personal', 'private' or a 'family matter', its goals and consequences are obscured, and its use justified as chastisement or discipline. There is some evidence that states have not even been held accountable for direct violations of women's human rights, particularly where this involves sexual violence.

Sexual Violence and the State

Political violence is often sexualised, and women are sexually assaulted by agents of the state in a variety of circumstances. Susan (not her real name) had been closely involved in organising and running meetings for a political opposition organisation in Zaire (now the Democratic Republic of Congo). She described how members of the military had harassed, threatened and physically attacked her and members of her family. Then they arrested her and took her to the central prison:

> One night they took me to a central prison and I stayed there for months. It was really bad … Sometimes one of the guards would just come in and kick you. For women it was worse but I was quite lucky. Some women were raped and sometimes one woman would be raped by five or maybe six men. It happened to one woman all the time and sometimes I think about her even now. It was terrible. Really terrible.

Women detained for political reasons may be sexually abused or raped (along with other forms of torture) with specific sanction from, or the tacit approval of, the authorities. Civilian women may be raped or sexually abused by government or opposition militia as part of a campaign to terrorise the local populace by attacking core constructions of identity and security, punish politically active males by proxy or 'reward' victorious combatants. The experience of many women who were interviewed during the course of this research emphasises the importance of understanding how the social and political discipline of women is effected through their sexuality, and through the use of sexual violence as a weapon of political repression. This violence is aimed not just at those whose bodies are attacked, 'but through them at the body politic, so that both person and society are so disintegrated they are paralysed and negated' (Pettman 1996: 102). In this way rape and sexual torture become part of the political process, as strategies of power and domination.

Many women who have been sexually abused and seek protection as refugees are often unwilling to talk about their experiences because of trauma associated with violence, and because they fear that these experiences will become known to others. Where the preservation of virginity or marital dignity is the cultural norm within the family or community, fears of ostracism are exacerbated. Even where a woman has made her own claim for asylum upon arrival, there is often little or no recognition by decision-makers in the UK that women may find it difficult to disclose their experiences of sexual violence. For example, in one recent case, it was argued that the appellant, a Pathan woman, would have been frightened to explain her fears regarding sexual violence at the asylum interview because of the presence of male Muslims. In refusing her claim to asylum the court stated:

> We reject that contention as it appears to us that the appellant is an educated

and sophisticated woman. She was not a rural agricultural worker from a remote village and we do not believe that had she anything to say she would not have done so simply because there were male Muslims present. Accordingly, in our view, our finding must reflect adversely on the credibility of the appellant.[4]

Given the 'climate of disbelief' which currently pervades the asylum determination process in the UK, the reluctance to discuss sexual violence, coupled with cultural differences and trauma, means that it may be more difficult for women to demonstrate that their claims are credible. Even if women who have fled their countries because of rape, or other forms of sexual violence, are willing to reveal their experiences, they often have difficulties in substantiating their claims, partly because torturers are specialists in inflicting pain which leaves no visible injury, but also because sexual violence often leaves psychological as opposed to physical scars. In some cases rape (even with supporting medical evidence) has been dismissed. For example, in the case of an Ethiopian woman who was raped by officers from the EPRDF (the ruling party), the adjudicator concluded that 'the appellant's emotional response to the doctor was calculated and false ... [her] rape is a complete fabrication'.[5] Perhaps most significantly, however, there is also evidence that even where women do reveal their experiences of sexual violence, and these are accepted as credible, they may face problems in demonstrating that the state has failed to protect them. Such is the extent of the distinction between 'public' and 'private' during the process of asylum determination that even *acts by the authorities are not attributed to them*' (Spijkerboer 1994: 29, emphasis in original). Sexual violence is considered to be 'private' even when the perpetrator is an agent of the state. Noting that this line of reasoning seems to be specific to acts of sexual abuse, Spijkerboer (1994) criticises the implicit view of sexual violence in asylum-related situations 'as derailed sexuality and not as torture', and suggests that it presupposes a very particular conception of male sexuality; male sexuality is seen as an innate, independent and quasi-biological drive which seeks satisfaction and can suddenly overwhelm a man. As a result it is viewed as 'private' even when it is committed during an interrogation, and dismissed as the aberrant act of an individual which is to be expected, rather than as behaviour condoned or encouraged by the government (Kelly 1993).

Sexual violence by agents of the state is therefore *normalised and legitimated* during the asylum determination process. This can be seen in the case of a woman from Turkey who was a member of a political party and who had been arrested and detained. She was taken to a cell, blindfolded, and led to an interrogation room where she was verbally abused.

She was then given electric shock treatment on her breasts, and after that her trousers were pulled down and lewd remarks made about her body. She was touched on her genitals while she was physically restrained, and was finally taken back to her cell, still blindfolded. Her claim for asylum in the UK was refused. At the appeal hearing, the Home Office questioned whether the harm she had suffered amounted to persecution, arguing that 'although the Turkish authorities do have a tendency to *roughly handle people*, it is not directed at anyone in particular … *it is their style*'.[6]

This conceptualisation of sexual violence or its threat as private and thus not of public concern is perhaps at its most lethal during periods of armed conflict (see, for example, Elshtain 1987; Bennett et al 1995; Thompkins 1995). Rape during war has been filed away as an inevitable byproduct, a matter of poor discipline and/or the inevitable bad behaviour of needy soldiers who are 'out of control' (Copelon, 1995b: 197). Despite increasing evidence that rape is used as a strategy of war itself, it appears to be accepted as inevitable by political and military leaders (Copelon 1994; Bennett et al. 1995; Thompkins 1995). Moreover, international law has failed (until very recently) to integrate gender-specific abuses into human rights discourse (while at the same time constructing any sexual acts falling outside the heterosexual as outside the boundaries of normality). International humanitarian law therefore underplays the brutality of rape and sexual violence against women in favour of a consideration of the assault on male or national honour.

A feminist reconceptualisation of the role and legal understanding of rape and war involves recognising the use of rape and sexual violence by the state or by parties that the state is unable or unwilling to control during armed conflict. As Pettman (1996) suggests, during war, bodies, boundaries, violence and power come together in devastating combination. Women's bodies become the site for signifying the dominance of one group over another. While the sexual violence on any individual woman must never be forgotten, it is also important to (re)conceptualise rape as an attack on the body politic and not just the physical body. Reconceptualising the relationship between sexual violence and the state reveals war rapes to be exercises in political power. For refugee women, such challenges to the legitimacy of violence by the state or its representatives are critical. Sexual violence is a form of control which is itself political; if there is no state protection against it, sexual violence is therefore persecution on account of political opinion (Mulligan 1990).

The Politics of the Parallel State: Violence Against Women
in the 'Private' Sphere

> The abuse was so severe and so much of it ... at least one thousand incidents
> of abuse, on a daily basis practically since I was born ... sometimes just my
> father and then other men my father allowed in to abuse me, and abuse by
> my siblings and family friends ... my father went from abusing me to beating
> me and he set a precedent for the whole family on how to treat me ... like
> a piece of dirt, someone you could go to at night to relieve yourself,
> excrement on, urine on, dogs ... all of this.

As the previous section has indicated, there is no shortage of examples
where women are persecuted directly by the state or through its agents.
However, much of the violence against women on a global scale occurs in
the geographically and conceptually 'private' sphere; 'for most women,
indirect subjection to individual men or groups of men' (Wright 1992,
cited in Macklin 1995: 232). This can take the form of, for example,
'honour killings', dowry deaths and domestic or familial violence. In many
cases, the violence experienced by women in these situations constitutes a
fundamental violation of their human rights. This is evident in the
testimony cited above from a woman seeking protection from her abusive
family. Kelly (1993), Romany (1994) and Copelon (1995a and 1995b) all
argue that there is effectively nothing to differentiate the position of a man
locked in a torture cell and a woman who is repeatedly abused within the
confines of her own home, since the same processes used to break the will
of political prisoners are used by domestic aggressors to break the will of
battered women. Such women are subject to unpredictable violence, including constant scrutiny, enforced isolation and physical suffering mixed
with intermittent kindness. Indeed, Copelon argues that 'the shock of
being beaten by a partner as opposed to a jailor can be [even] more numbing
and world-destroying' (Copelon 1995a: 138).

Despite this, the tendency of international human rights law, *because it
is centred on the state*, to separate out violence that occurs in the public
sphere with normatively male forms of oppression and resistance from that
which occurs in the private sphere, means that decision-makers frequently
view such violence as 'personal' (Charlesworth et al. 1991; Goldberg 1993;
Macklin 1995). Violence against women has escaped sanction because the
public/private dichotomy has insulated its most common, private forms
(Copelon 1995a; Sullivan 1995; Romany 1994). As a result the state is not
held accountable even for those violations which are the result of its
systematic failure to institute the political and legal protection necessary to
ensure the basic rights of life, integrity and dignity of women. This problem

also reflects in part the fact that international norms concerning the family call upon the state to protect the institution of the family and enshrine the right of privacy within the family, although in reality the state can and does intrude into private family life when it serves its own political, social or economic goals.

Theoretical arguments around the public/private distinction in the interpretation of violence within the home and community are reinforced by evidence that women seeking protection on this basis are denied access to the determination process. One Ghanaian woman who had been detained on her arrival in the UK told me that her husband 'started chasing girls after my son was born. If I said something about it he beat me with his hands, his belt. I had a very swollen face. He beat me for three years. He said if I tried to stop him he would cut me with knives and kill me.' Her application for asylum met with the following response from the Home Office:

> The Secretary of State noted that you had not approached the Ghanaian authorities for assistance and he was informed that there was no evidence to suggest that the authorities would be unwilling or unable to offer you protection should you feel at risk from your husband ... In the light of all the evidence before him, he has concluded that your application is frivolous.

The adjudicator who heard her case concluded that, *as he understood the law*, 'being beaten up by your husband is not a reason for asylum however deplorable it might be'.[7] She was subsequently deported.

An analysis of the appeal decisions of women refused asylum in the UK reveals not only an assumption that women should be expected to appeal to a masculinist state for protection against the violence of individual men, but also an assumption that such protection will be available; neither states nor protection are acknowledged to be gendered. For example, in the case of an Iranian woman beaten by her father, the Immigration Appeal Tribunal upheld an appeal by the Home Office against the decision of an adjudicator to grant her asylum, stating:

> [T]here is no evidence that the Iranian authorities would not have offered protection to members of the family subject to extreme violence ... we do not read the Convention as extending to ill-treatment within a family unit by the head of the family, whose social and legal responsibilities towards his children neither we nor an adjudicator could, as a rule, fully or properly assess.[8]

A similar position was taken in the case of a Pakistani woman refugee accused of prostitution by her husband who subsequently requested the authorities to return her to Pakistan where she could be arrested and punished by stoning to death under the law 'before her feet touch the purity of the soil'. Despite the Pakistani state's direct involvement in her fear of persecution (and death) through its enforcement of gender-based discrimination under the Hudood Ordinance, protection was refused on the basis that her husband could not be regarded as an 'agent of persecution'; the determination stated that 'the Convention does not cover the particular circumstances of a domestic quarrel between a husband and wife that may fall to be decided in a society where there is clearly a bias in favour of the husband and the wife is regarded as in the home and subordinate to the husband.'[9]

As was suggested earlier in this chapter, states act as centralised main organisers of gendered power relations not only through their use of 'legitimate' violence but also, and just as importantly, by institutionalising and reproducing the *legitimisation of social hierarchy* through manipulation of a patriarchal base (Peterson 1992). Women become the objects of masculinist control through ideological constructs that justify structural violence. When seen in this context it is unsurprising that many women are reluctant to approach the state for protection. The woman whose experiences of familial violence were cited at the beginning of this section told me: 'For the first time in my life I've stood up to my father ... In [my country] he'd be laughing because the police don't get involved and there is nothing in the law to protect me. He would have the right to do anything he wished ... I'm his property, his daughter and he can do what he likes. The state endorses this.' In addition a woman cannot be expected to approach the state for protection if this would itself put her life in danger (Castel 1992; Spijkerboer 1994; Crawley 1997). Similarly, arguments that women can simply relocate within their country to avoid persecution conceptualise violence against women as individually rather than structurally based despite the fact that 'the gruelling consistency of this violence contravenes explanations couched in terms of "isolated incidents" or "individual deviance"' (Peterson 1992: 46). In the UK this is referred to as the 'Internal Flight Alternative' and is often used to justify the refusal to grant refugee status to many women fleeing violence within the home and community. As Peterson suggests, this approach is not to suggest simply that women can or should avoid the state and its potential support, 'rather it is to insist on asking structural questions about the processes by which male domination and violence are reproduced' (Peterson 1992: 46).

For women seeking protection from violence in the 'private' sphere of the home and community, the extent to which the state is viewed as genderless – as not implicated in the construction of gender subordination – clearly has significant consequences because it means that the systematic perpetuation of such subordination in the realm of civil society is not acknowledged. The experiences of these women forces us to challenge the gender stratification embedded in the concept of the liberal state within international human rights law including refugee law. In particular, norms of attribution that establish state responsibility must be expanded by filtering them through a contextual framework (Romany 1994). Breaking down the public/private dichotomy illuminates the role of the state in setting the scene in which familial violence occurs and in directing and limiting the roles of the actors (Stairs and Pope 1990). This violence does not occur in a vacuum; the positions and relative strengths of the parties are greatly influenced by laws, enforcement of those laws and social mores resulting in part from those laws or their lack. Understanding conceptually therefore how the state can be seen to condone or even promulgate activities within the home both justifies and lays the basis for the establishment of state connection to family and community violence. Violence within the 'private' sphere must be seen in the context of wider power relations; it occurs within a gendered society in which male power dominates at all levels (Tickner 1992).

It is increasingly being argued therefore that states can, and should, be held responsible for systematic 'private' male violence against women because by systematically failing to provide protection for women from 'private' actors the state becomes complicit; in effect, 'the state creates a parallel government in which women's rights are systematically denied' (Romany 1994: 99; see also Goldberg 1993; Copelon 1995a). Romany argues that acts of violence and domination in this parallel state 'allow the official public sphere to maintain its patriarchal underpinnings while keeping its hands relatively clean' (Romany 1994: 100). Peterson (1992) similarly suggests that the state is complicit through its selective sanctioning of non-state violence, particularly in its policy of 'non-intervention' in cases involving violence within the family or community. The state has an affirmative obligation to prevent, investigate, prosecute and punish violations of human rights. The failure or refusal to act – the omission – is equivalent to the commission of the act itself in assessing culpability because, in its failure to respond, the state gives the abuser freedom to act with impunity; 'these failures are acts of persecution, accomplished with the acquiescence, if not overt complicity, of the state' (Goldberg 1993: 588). State violence therefore includes violence not directly inflicted by the state but tolerated or encouraged by states in order to create, justify, excuse, explain or enforce hierarchies of difference and relations of inequality. In this context '[t]he widespread absence of state intervention in crimes against women is not merely the result of government's failure to criminalise a class of behaviour (since the violent acts themselves usually *are* crimes), but rather is the result of governments' failure to enforce laws equitably across gender lines'

(Thomas and Beasley 1993: 46). Non-prosecution of individual men then becomes a human rights issue because the reason for the state's failure to protect can be shown to be rooted in discrimination along prohibited lines.

Beyond the Public/Private Dichotomy?

> The challenge is not to shift the focus away from gross violations of civil and political rights by the state but, first, to broaden the normative framework to include the abuses suffered by women that do not fit this paradigm ... The distinction between public and private life in international law is one of the principal theoretical barriers to this effort. (Sullivan 1995: 127)

This chapter has challenged the current conceptualisation of the genderless liberal state within international human rights law and has argued that the paradigmatically masculine interpretation of international asylum law has specific and profound implications for women seeking protection from violence. In particular it has asked why some kinds of violence are legitimated or privatised while others are condemned and punished, and has suggested that, although theoretically gender-neutral, international human rights law, including asylum law, interacts with gender-based domestic laws and social structures that relegate women and men to separate spheres to exclude systematically many violations of women's human rights (Thomas and Beasley 1993). The construction of a public/private dichotomy not only by (masculine) states from which women flee but by (masculine) receiving states that make decisions about women's eligibility for protection, obscures the relationship between systematic structural violence against women – which is historically constituted and contingent rather than natural – and the state (Peterson 1992). As a result, not only are many refugee women denied protection but when the state *does* intervene it typically does so from within a patriarchal ideology that at best 'protects' women while simultaneously reproducing masculinist givens that ensure women's 'need for protection'. Moreover, it has been suggested that even where agents of the state are directly implicated, violence against women, and particularly sexual violence, is 'personalised' and 'depoliticised'. In this way men's association with violence has been legitimated through war and the instruments of the state (Tickner 1992).

In order to break down the distinction between public and private life that operates to exclude gender abuses from the human rights agenda, violence against women cannot be seen in isolation from structural gendered inequality; '[a]n analysis of women's structural inequality should be substituted for the "mainstream" preoccupation with the public/private distinction' (Sullivan 1995: 133). As Peterson (1992) suggests, however, the rules of the game have been so effectively authorised that it appears that they are now taken as 'givens'. In addition, demanding that international refugee law reconceptualise human rights abuse to include that which has largely been deemed 'private' faces opposition from states such as the UK and others in Europe which are currently trying to narrow their existing interpretation. Nevertheless, violence against women has often been the catalyst for women organising between and within states, and women's responses to gendered international politics has included gendered resistance to exploitation and victimisation and organising to change these politics. Some states, most notably Canada, the United States and Australia, have begun to give recognition to gender in the asylum determination process. In the UK, efforts to ensure that women asylum seekers are protected under the 1951 Convention are being led by the Refugee Women's Legal Group (RWLG) which has called upon the government to adopt *'Gender Guidelines for the Determination of Asylum Claims in the UK'* (RWLG 1998). These guidelines highlight the multiplicity of women's experiences and challenge the conceptualisation of women as passive victims lacking political identity and a relationship to the state and therefore ineligible for protection under the 1951 Convention. They have been produced by legal practitioners, academics and others working with refugee women and were circulated for consultation and discussion to refugee community organisations, women's groups, human rights groups and non-governmental organisations as well as refugee and asylum-seeking women themselves. However, at the time of writing, the Home Office has yet to be convinced that such guidelines are either necessary or desirable.

Although the issue of state responsibility is only one hurdle that women face in gaining recognition of their experiences of persecution under the 1951 Convention, it is perhaps the most critical. By incorporating a feminist understanding of social arrangements and legal argument as part of a critique of international refugee law, it becomes apparent that the categories intrinsic to asylum determination procedures do not reflect the law itself but the politics and priorities of gendered states. The definition of a refugee as someone in need of international protection must respond to all types of violence, including violence produced by gender relations of domination and subordination. As Tickner (1992) suggests, the achievement of comprehensive vision requires alternative modes of thinking to describe the behaviour of states in the international system. Only by revealing the hierarchical social relations based upon gender which are reproduced and reinforced by the states in response to refugees' experiences of violence, can we begin to construct a language, and a dialogic framework, that speaks out of the multiple experiences of refugee and asylum-seeking women in the UK (Romany 1994; Tickner 1992).

Notes

This chapter draws upon evidence collected through in-depth interviews with refugee and asylum-seeking women living in the UK, interviews with those working with refugee women and analysis of case law and Home Office determinations. The research was conducted as part of a PhD. I would like to acknowledge the contribution of all those who participated, especially those women who were willing to share their experiences both in their home countries and in the UK. I would also like to acknowledge the work of the Refugee Women's Legal Group (RWLG), formed in 1996 by legal practitioners and others working with refugee women, which is concerned about the gendered effects of changes in immigration and asylum law in the UK. The RWLG can be contacted c/o ILPA, 40–42 Charterhouse Street, London EC1.

1. This literature is extensive but particularly useful feminist critiques can be found in edited volumes such as Cook (1994) and Peters and Wolper (1995).

2. Johnsson (1989) notes, however, that to the extent that gender is revealed in these legal texts, the masculine language used suggests that the refugee as male was in the minds of the drafters.

3. The UK is explicit about its aim of restricting refugee in-flows and is keen to emphasise that the majority of asylum-seekers are 'bogus' or 'abusive' because they do not fit a very narrow interpretation of the Convention.

4. *Salma Jamil v. SSHD*, Immigration Appeal Tribunal, 25 June 1996 (13588) (unreported).

5. Appeal no. HX/73594/94 (1995) (unreported).

6. Appeal no. HX/75889/94 (1995) (unreported), emphasis added.

7. Extracted from a letter from the Home Office to the applicant obtained during the course of this research.

8. *SSHD V Ranjbar*, Immigration Appeal Tribunal, 28 June 1996 (11105) (unreported).

9. Appeal no. HX/75169/94 (1996) (unreported).

Bibliography

Anthias, F. and N. Yuval-Davis (eds) (1989) *Woman–Nation–State*, London: Macmillan.

— (1992) *Racialised Boundaries: Race, Nation, Gender, Colour and Class and the Anti-Racist Struggle*, London: Routledge.

Bennett, O. et al. (eds) (1995) *Arms to Fight, Arms to Protect*, London: Panos Publications.

Bhabha, J. (1996) 'Embodied Rights: Gender Persecution, State Sovereignty and Refugees', *Public Culture* 9, 3–32.

Binion, G. (1995) 'Human Rights: a Feminist Perspective', *Human Rights Quarterly*, vol. 17, pp. 509–26.

Bunch, C. (1990) 'Women's Rights as Human Rights; Towards a Re-vision of Human Rights', *Humanitarian Rights Quarterly*, vol. 12, no. 4, pp. 486–98.

Castel, J. R. (1992) 'Rape, Sexual Assault and the Meaning of Persecution', *International Journal of Refugee Law*, vol. 4, no. 1, pp. 39–56.

Charlesworth, H. et al. (1991) 'Feminist Approaches to International Law', *American Journal of International Law*, no. 85, pp. 613–64.

Cook, R. (ed.) (1994) *Human Rights of Women: National and International Perspectives*, Philadelphia: University of Pennsylvania Press.

Copelon, R. (1994) 'Surfacing Gender; Re-engraving Crimes Against Women in Humanitarian Law', *Hastings Women's Law Journal*, vol. 5, no. 2, pp. 243–66.

— (1995a) 'Intimate Terror: Understanding Domestic Violence as Torture', in Cook (ed.), *Human Rights of Women*, pp. 116–52.

— (1995b) 'Gendered War Crimes: Reconceptualising Rape in Times of War', in Peters and Wolper (eds), *Women's Rights, Human Rights*, pp. 197–214.

Crawley, H. (1997) *Women as Asylum Seekers; A Legal Handbook, Refugee Women's Legal Group*, London: ILPA and Refugee Action.

Duncan, S. (1995) 'Law's Sexual Discipline: Visibility, Violence and Consent', *Journal of Law and Society*, vol. 22, no. 3, pp. 326–52.

Elshtain, J. B. (1987) *Women and War*, Brighton: Harvester Press.

Goldberg, P. (1993) 'Anyplace but Home: Asylum in the United States for Women Fleeing Intimate Violence', *Cornell International Law Journal*, vol. 26, no. 3, pp. 565–604.

Greatbach, J. (1989) 'The Gender Difference; Feminist Critiques of Refugee Discourse', *International Journal of Refugee Law*, vol. 3, no. 3, pp. 585–605.

Johnsson, A. B. (1989) 'International Protection of Women Refugees: a Summary of Principal Problems and Issues', *International Journal of Refugee Law*, vol. 1, no. 2, pp. 221–32.

Justice, ILPA and ARC (1997) *Providing Protection: Towards Fair and Effective Asylum Procedures*, London.

Kelly, N. (1993) 'Gender-related Persecution: Assessing the Asylum Claims of Women', *Cornell International Law Journal*, vol. 26, no. 3, pp. 625–74.

Knop, K. (1995) 'Why Rethinking the Sovereign State is Important for Women's International Human Rights Law', in Cook (ed.), *Human Rights of Women*, pp. 153–64.

Laurie, N. et al. (1997) 'In and Out of Bounds and Resisting Boundaries: Feminist Geographies of Space and Place', in Women and Geography Study Group (eds), *Feminist Geographies: Explorations in Diversity and Difference*, London: Longman.

Macdonald, S. (1987) 'Drawing the Lines – Gender, Peace and War: An Introduction', in S. Macdonald et al. (eds), *Images of Women in War and Peace*, London: Macmillan, pp. 1–26.

Macklin, A. (1995) 'Refugee Women and the Imperative of Categories', *Human Rights Quarterly*, vol. 17, pp. 213–77.

Mulligan, M. (1990) 'Obtaining Political Asylum: Classifying Rape as a Well-founded Fear of Persecution on the Grounds of Political Opinion', *Boston College Third World Journal*, vol. 10, pp. 355–80.

Niarchos, C. N. (1995) 'Women, War and Rape: Challenges Facing the International Tribunal for the Former Yugoslavia', *Human Rights Quarterly*, vol. 17, pp. 649–90.

Peters, J. and A. Wolper (eds) (1995) *Women's Rights, Human Rights: International Feminist Perspectives*, London: Routledge.

Peterson, V. S. (ed.) (1992) *Gendered States: Feminist (Re)Visions of International Relations Theory*, London: Lynne Rienner.

Pettman, J. J. (1996) *Worlding Women: A Feminist International Politics*, London: Routledge.

Razack, S. (1994) 'What is to be Gained by Looking White People in the Eye? Culture, Race and Gender in Cases of Sexual Violence', *Signs*, vol. 19, no. 4, pp. 894–923.

Refugee Council (1996) *The State of Asylum: A Critique of Asylum Policy in the UK*, London: Refugee Council.

Romany, R. (1994) 'State Responsibility Goes Private: A Feminist Critique of the Public/Private Distinction in International Human Rights Law', in Cook (ed.), *Human Rights of Women*, pp. 85–116.

Roth, K. (1994) 'Domestic Violence as an International Human Rights Issue', in Cook (ed.), *Human Rights of Women*, pp. 326–39.

RWLG (Refugee Women's Legal Group) (1998) *Gender Guidelines for the Determination of Asylum Claims in the UK*, London: RWLG.

Seith, P.A. (1997) 'Escaping Domestic Violence: Asylum as a Means of Protection for Battered Women', *Colombia Law Review*, vol. 97, no. 6, pp. 1804–43.

Spijkerboer, T. (1994) *Women and Refugee Status: Beyond the Public/Private Distinction*, study commissioned by the Emancipation Council, The Hague.

Stairs, F. and L. Pope (1990) 'No Place Like Home: Assaulted Migrant Women's Claims to Refugee Status and Landings on Humanitarian and Compassionate Grounds', *Journal of Law and Social Policy*, vol. 6, pp. 148–225.

Strizhak, E. F. and C. Harries (1993) *Sex, Lies and International Law*, New York: Women's Commission for Refugee Women and Children.

Sullivan, D. (1995) 'The Public/Private Distinction in International Human Rights Law', in J. Peters and A. Wolper (eds) *Women's Rights, Human Rights: International Feminist Perspectives*, London: Routledge.

Thomas, D. Q. and M. E. Beasley (1993) 'Domestic Violence As A Human Rights Issue', *Human Rights Quarterly*, vol. 15, pp. 36–62.

Thompkins, T. L. (1995) 'Prosecuting Rape as a War Crime: Speaking the Unspeakable', *Notre Dame Law Review*, vol. 70, no. 4, pp. 845–90.

Tickner, J. A. (1992) *Gender and International Relations: Feminist Perspectives on Achieving Global Security*, New York: Columbia University Press.

UNHCR (1979) *Handbook on Procedures and Criteria for Determining Refugee Status*, Geneva: UNHCR.

Waylen, G. (1996a) *Gender in Third World Politics*, Milton Keynes: Open University Press.

— (1996b) 'Analysing Women in the Politics of the Third World', in H. Afshar (ed.), *Women and Politics in the Third World*, London: Routledge, pp. 7–24.

Yuval-Davis, N. (1993) 'Gender and Nation', *Ethnic and Racial Studies*, vol. 16, no. 4, pp. 621–32.

— (1997) *Gender and Nation*, London: Sage.

6

Citizen-Soldier? Class, Race, Gender, Sexuality and the US Military

Francine D'Amico

What does it mean to be a citizen? International (actually, inter-*state*) law and the domestic laws of particular states connect citizenship and military service. These laws are based on a conception of militarised or *martial citizenship* that suggests that *real* citizens are soldiers, and, conversely, that only soldiers are *real* citizens. This model of martial citizenship has prompted groups excluded from political power within a state to seek 'full citizenship' by entering the armed forces. In the United States, African-Americans, women, and sexual minorities – that is, people who identify as lesbian/gay/bisexual – have sought to prove themselves worthy of citizenship through military service. In this chapter, I examine their efforts at inclusion and assess the impact of their service on the structures of hierarchy within and beyond the US military institution. In doing so, I problematise the concept of martial citizenship and explore alternative ways of thinking about what it means to be a citizen.

If we seek to understand global politics, why should we be concerned about the relationship between citizenship and soldiering? Traditionalist scholars of international relations would respond that we need not address such a question. While traditionalists focus on the study of war, they do so on the abstract level of state interaction. For example, in a work considered a classic of the traditionalist international relations canon, entitled *Man, the State and War*, Kenneth Waltz writes: 'Individuals participate in war because they are members of states ... .One *state* makes war on another *state*' (Waltz 1959: 179). Waltz's so-called 'realist' perspective, which sees the world through what I call a *Statist lens*, sees war as the natural and unavoidable condition of an abstract and universalised 'Man' within the essentialised structure of 'the state system'. He contends that inter-state war 'occurs because there is nothing to prevent it' (p. 188), that is, because there is no world government or global authority to make states behave.

What happens, though, if we look at the world, war and humanity in a different way? Suppose we paraphrase Waltz's original title as *Wo/men, the State, and War*. The shifts of *gender* and *number* call attention to the exclusive vision of hegemonic masculinity underlying the traditionalist/statist study of international relations as well as to both the diversity of men's and women's lived experiences and the intersectionality of hierarchies of nationality/citizenship, class/rank, 'race'/colour/ethnicity, gender/sexuality, and other socially constructed markers of difference.

Seeing the world this way, through what has been called a *gender lens*, reveals that people, not states, make war, *and* that these people are men and women who are differently situated in an array of intersecting power relations. By bringing into focus the people who decide to make war and who organise and populate 'the state' and the 'state system', a gender lens restores human agency in and therefore responsibility for war. A gender lens framed from what I call a critical feminist perspective asks how the current structures in international relations came to be, questions who benefits from or is hurt by these structures, and encourages us to think about how the structures may be reconstructed more equitably. The military merits special scrutiny from this critical feminist perspective because it is one of the primary sites for the construction and negotiation of power relations both within a state and among states.

As Jan Jindy Pettman has pointed out: 'Citizenship debates ... take us within the state and de-link the easy nation-state association' of traditionalist/statist international relations (Pettman 1996: 23). The prevalence and deadliness of 'civil conflict' today, such as the secessionist struggles in the Kosovo province of Yugoslavia and the Kashmiri region of India/Pakistan, clearly indicate that a complete understanding of contemporary world politics requires the study of the relationship between citizen and state. Further, we must examine the construction of citizenship to comprehend the transitions under way in Eastern Europe, the processes of state-building in Cambodia and Mozambique (and its failure in Angola), the prospects for the institutionalisation of democracy in much of Latin America, and the consequences of economic globalisation.

Citizenship and Military Service

Contemporary Western inter-state law defines a *citizen* as a person who belongs to a state: a citizen is state property. Belonging to one state offers citizens protection from other states. One of these protections is a right *not* to be forced to serve in some other state's armed forces (impressment). Only our own state can require its citizens to put their lives at risk in its defence.

Who is a citizen? That is, how do we know who belongs to a particular state? Under inter-state law, *citizenship* is conferred by birth (*ius soli*), by blood (*ius sanguinis*), and by the internal laws of the state, which may provide for naturalisation, marriage, adoption and other situations (Von Glahn 1996: 147–58). In many states, citizenship is granted in exchange for military service (Elshtain and Tobias 1990: 87).

For most of us, the notion of *citizenship* suggests more than this idea of simply belonging to a state. The Western tradition of liberal democratic theory posits a reciprocal relationship between citizen and state: citizens may belong to the state, but the state also belongs to its citizens. We think of citizens as *participating* in the socio-political life of the community; they have certain *rights* and *responsibilities* vis-à-vis the state and other citizens (Pettman 1996: 15). Citizenship rights often include the right to vote, to hold public office, and to dissent, and citizenship responsibilities usually include paying taxes and performing some service to the state, such as serving on a jury or in the military.

The concept of the *citizen-soldier* suggests that a person has a responsibility to defend the state in order to enjoy the right to participate—that is, that 'equal rights' demand 'equal responsibilities' (Kerber 1990: 89–103). While most states do not call upon all their citizens to be soldiers, liability to service – and willingness to sacrifice all for one's country – are the hallmarks of *martial citizenship* (Hartsock 1984). The more militarised the state, the more closely knit are citizenship and military service.

Class, Rank and Military Service

Western liberal democratic theory posits *equality* of all citizens and *mobility* based on *merit* (as opposed to *nobility*) as the selection process for both civilian and military leaders. In theory, soldiers may rise through the ranks of the military's hierarchical structure to become officers; they are not born to an hereditary warrior class. But these twin promises of equality and mobility for citizen-soldiers mask the reality of the military system of *rank*, which serves as a surrogate for socio-economic class. With some exceptions, US enlistees from poor and working-class families may rise only through the non-commissioned ranks, while those with more resources, education or connections receive commissions as officers, the elite of the military rank structure.

When a state conscripts (drafts) soldiers, class protects some people and makes others more vulnerable to service. For example, in the United States, early conscripts could hire substitutes to serve for them, and, during World War II, draft boards comprised of prominent citizens determined which community members would serve. Exemptions for people in particular professions and for university students protected the privileged.

When soldiers volunteer for military service, as in the United States since 1973, economic incentives and lack of other employment opportunities push more people from poor and working-class families to enlist. And while military service is not strictly hereditary, many recruits come from US military families who see the institution, rather than a specific location, as their home (Wertsch 1991). So when we begin to examine martial citizenship in practice, we see that class differences may be camouflaged by the concept of the citizen-soldier but are reinforced by military rank, and that these differences help determine who serves.

'Race'/Colour/Ethnicity and Citizenship

Class differences may also be camouflaged by and are bound up with the social construction of 'race'/colour/ethnicity. The organising principle of 'race' in the United States is a dichotomy of white/black in which people with any amount of African descent are categorised as black. Members of other racial-ethnic groups, such as Asian, Hispanic or Native Americans, are either equated with blacks' position of racial subordination because of dark skin pigmentation, or they remain invisible in the dominant culture because they are seen as relatively less threatening than African-Americans. In *Ethnic Soldiers*, Cynthia Enloe (1980) describes these other racial-ethnic groups as 'preferred minorities', that is, preferred by state leaders over blacks as military personnel resources. Because of this either/or construction of the white/black 'race'/colour dichotomy and the connection between 'race'/colour and military service, many African-Americans embraced the model of martial citizenship with the belief that their efforts as soldiers would help blacks claim an equal place in American society. Yet the experiences of African-American members of the armed services ultimately prompted a more critical evaluation of the concept of the citizen-soldier.

In mobilising troops for the American Civil War as well as the Spanish American war and World War I, the message both from the US government and from leaders in the African-American community was clear: real citizens – that is, real men – fight wars. African-Americans believed the ultimate reward for equal risk would be equal rights (Mullen 1973: 15–35; Mershon and Schlossman 1998).

Despite this promise of equality, African-Americans remained unequal in the US armed forces. Until recently, the numbers of African-Americans in the ranks was restricted to a proportion of personnel not greater than their presence in the civilian population. During World War II, this figure was set at 10 per cent. Despite this ceiling, African-Americans were drafted in greater proportions than were whites, and more than one million

African-Americans served during the war. Further, African-American soldiers were frequently assigned to menial or manual labour in the quarter-master or transportation corps rather than to combat or to skilled positions. They were also more frequently disciplined, court-martialled and executed than were white soldiers accused of similar crimes, and they were less likely to be promoted (Clines 1993; Mershon and Schlossman 1998; Moore 1996; Mullen 1973).

African-American women who wanted 'to serve their country and their race' (Moore 1996) under the model of martial citizenship were constrained by the intersection of 'race'/colour/ethnicity and gender hierarchies. As black women, they were either excluded from service or restricted in number, proportion and duties in the nursing corps and women's auxiliary corps of World War II. Like their male counterparts, African-American women served in segregated units until President Truman ordered de-segregation of the armed forces in 1948 with Executive Orders 9980 and 9981 (Moore 1996; Earley 1989; Mershon and Schlossman 1998).

In the early 1970s, the mobilisation for the war in Vietnam and growing public opposition to US involvement there created a personnel crisis for the American military. State leaders finally responded to popular political pressure to end conscription (the draft) and moved to a volunteer force in 1973. The proportion of African-Americans in service rose rapidly as a result of this policy change, and although the formal 10 per cent ceiling had been abandoned, policy-makers began to express concern over the 'representativeness' of the force. Part of this concern stemmed from the high casualty rates suffered during the Vietnam War by African-American soldiers concentrated in infantry and artillery units. This issue resurfaced during the Gulf deployment, as African-Americans remained concentrated in these units (Armor 1996). Today African-Americans comprise 21 per cent of enlisted personnel but only 8 per cent of the officer corps, despite the prominence of a few high-ranking officers such as now-retired General Colin Powell; other racial-ethnic minorities are better represented in the rank hierarchy. Hispanic Americans are 7.7 per cent of enlisted personnel and 3.3 per cent of officers; Asian Americans are 3.4 per cent enlisted personnel and 2.6 per cent of officers (Defense Equal Opportunity Management Institute figures for 1 March 1998).

The human cost of military service and the racial dimensions of Vietnam and subsequent conflicts, together with continuing discrimination and racism in US society, have left many African-Americans critical of US military policy and disillusioned with martial citizenship. Increasingly, African-Americans have begun to call for 'social citizenship', articulated as 'freedom' from the socio-economic inequalities remaining after basic political rights were achieved (Foner 1999). This articulation parallels the post-colonial critique of the legacy of economic dependence remaining after political independence was achieved by the states of the global South. Further critiques of martial citizenship come from women who have struggled to play the role of citizen-soldier.

Gender and Citizenship

In the United States before 1900, women were excluded from public life: they could not vote, hold political office, serve on a jury, receive a university education, own property or enter most professions. Social conservatives argued that women did not deserve the right to vote because they did not share equally the burdens of citizenship, based on the citizen-soldier model. This led some early advocates of gender equality to promote an alternative, feminised version of citizenship: mothers, they argued, needed to be full citizens themselves in order to teach their children to be good citizens. That is, because of their gendered roles of wife and mother in the family and society, women needed an equal but opposite or 'complementary' voice in political decisions. This *maternal citizenship* was thus constructed in opposition to *martial citizenship*.

The notion of maternal citizenship supported rather than challenged the hierarchy of citizenship being constructed by the new state (Elshtain 1987: 87–8). Early feminists urged that American politicians 'Remember the Ladies' in constructing the new state, and so they did ... as *ladies*, women were protected (that is, excluded) from participation in public life (Kerber 1990). The model of *maternal citizenship* left unchallenged the masculinised version of *martial citizenship* and ignored that women were differently situated: many were not mothers, and many working-class women and women of colour needed rights and protections that the concept of maternal citizenship did not address (Pettman 1996: 17–18).

The strategy of pursuing maternal citizenship met with little success, and feminist activists after the turn of the century were confronted with a dilemma: should they continue to claim citizen rights based on the distinctness of their gender roles and experiences, or should they support US entry into the war in Europe and embrace the concept of martial citizenship, emulating the model of the citizen-soldier? Some believed that women had a moral responsibility as life-givers to oppose the war. Others saw militarised patriotism as the price of full citizenship and feared that those who opposed the war would jeopardise the legitimacy of women's claims to equal rights. This difference of opinion split the women's movement (Berkman 1987).

Feminists who embraced the citizen-soldier model soon found that women would serve not as soldiers but as helpers or 'auxiliaries'. The military institution sought to maintain itself as quintessentially masculine and to construct feminine-gendered spaces for women first as outsiders and then at its margins.

As the American military mobilised women for successive crises, gradually formalising their participation and expanding its control over their energies, skills and activities, it masked its increasing reliance on *woman*power with what Laurie Weinstein and I call *gender camouflage* (D'Amico and Weinstein 1999). During World War II, the military needed personnel with skills which the gendered division of labour in civilian society was gradually feminising, such as health-care providers, office clerks and telephone operators. To maintain gender lines, these women were kept not-quite military: they were assigned auxiliary status, 'relative rank', and lower pay than 'real' soldiers, and segregated in separate corps so that they were serving *with*, not *in*, the military (Sadler 1999).

The first American women to be militarised during war were elite and middle-class white women with the education and skills the military needed. They were deemed a trustworthy personnel resource because they were believed to share the state elite's vision of the appropriate division of power and resources in society across class and racial/ethnic boundaries. Next mobilised were lower middle- and working-class white women and women of colour from 'preferred minority' (non-African) racial-ethnic groups (Enloe 1980). The last to be mobilised were African-American women, and they were among the first to be demobilised post-crisis (D'Amico 1997a). For example, African-American women were not permitted to serve in the Army Nurse Corps from its establishment in 1901 until 1918, and were excluded from service again between 1919 and 1941 (Reeves 1999).

After World War II, US policy-makers kept the women's corps rather than re-train combat troops for clerical and other 'women's work', and to assist future mobilisation. The women's services would be permanent and regular rather than temporary and reserve or auxiliary. That is, women would now serve *in* rather than *with* the military but would still be in gender-segregated corps, limited to 2 per cent of enlisted personnel and 10 per cent of officers, and restricted to non-combat positions (Sadler 1999). These restrictions were designed to protect the masculine-gendered space of the core of military service – *combat* – from the incursion of women, to maintain gender hierarchy despite the greater degree of militar-isation of women.

The 2 per cent ceiling on enlisted women personnel and 10 per cent cap on women officers remained in effect from 1948 until 1967, and the actual proportions did not reach these levels until the end of the draft, when the number and proportion of women in service began to climb precipitously. This pattern continued through the military expansion of the 1980s under the Reagan administration, despite rhetoric about limiting women's participation until the impact of their growing numbers on 'military readiness' could be assessed. During the drawdown (personnel reduction) of the 1990s, the number of women in service decreased, but their proportion relative to the size of the shrinking force increased. At the end of March 1998, 197,322 women were in service, comprising 13.8 per cent of the total force of US military personnel (Defense Equal Opportunity Management Institute 1998).

The Militarised Woman Patriot

In *The Morning After*, Cynthia Enloe argues that American women's military participation from the 1970s to the 1990s underwent a process of 'professionalisation', creating the militarised woman patriot (Enloe 1993: 222). In this period, military women challenged restrictions on their service. Families of military women were accorded equal access to dependent benefits in 1973, and military academies, where officers are trained, were forced to admit women in 1976. A federal district court ruled that the navy had to allow women to serve aboard non-combat ships in 1978. However, in 1981, the Supreme Court upheld women's exemption from conscription because federal law exempted them from combat (D'Amico 1996a, 1997a).

The laws that barred women from sea and air combat duty were re-scinded on 30 November 1993. The policy is now under control of the military services rather than the Congress, and each service has enumerated 'exceptions' to the rule that women may serve in combat positions. These include submarine billets in the navy, ground combat in the army and the Marines, and all special forces, such as the navy SEALS and the army Green Berets. Under the new law, the Pentagon must notify Congress in advance before announcing any change in assigning women to these units (D'Amico 1997a). So the military has preserved a masculine core of combat from which women are excluded; or, as congressional representative Patricia Schroeder phrased it, protected one last tree house with a sign reading 'No girls allowed'.

In *Citizenship Rites: Feminist Soldiers and Feminist Antimilitarists*, Ilene Feinman explores 'the episodes of US political history' which have shaped the process of military women's professionalisation as 'the articulation of a proper role for women as martial citizens took center stage' (Feinman 1999: 253). This process has left the model of the citizen-soldier intact but gendered in a particular way. As a result, Feinman argues, women will continue to be held to the militarised and androcentric model of citizenship individual women have shown they can achieve. The cost of doing so and the alternatives to the model remain unexamined, except by 'outsiders' (feminist academics and activists) or those who have left the institution, such as navy veteran and psychologist Donna Dean. In her recent book, *Warriors Without Weapons*, Dean (1997) analyses the hostility and abuse American women experience in military service (see also, Herbert 1997).

Despite these problems, I believe women's continued military participation has a potentially positive (and subversive) effect on the military's gender hierarchy in the long run. In talking with women in the United States who have made the military a career, I am always struck by their articulation of their experiences in reference to the general pattern of social gender relations. Many of these women see themselves as engaged in a battle to redefine gender-appropriate behaviour; they do not accept the construction of gender relations as 'given' or natural. Women on the front-lines in the military's 'gender wars' (Francke 1997) are in a position to challenge the traditional gender hierarchy underlying the foundation of both the masculinised military and the state itself.

Thus, the potentially 'radical future' (Eisenstein 1981) of women's military participation is that when women are admitted to places from which they have previously been excluded, they may critique from within rather than only from the outside (Reppy and Fainsod Katzenstein 1999). For example, attention to what have been constructed as 'women's issues', such as the effect of military service on families, has come in response to demands from women professionals in the ranks who carry more authority in the institution than have wives and civilian employees (Fainsod Katzenstein 1998). But finding a voice within the institution remains difficult because of the intersecting hierarchies of class/rank, 'race'/colour/ethnicity, gender and sexuality. As the next section explores, military women's sexuality, as well as that of military men, has been policed to maintain the gender hierarchy of the institution (Zimmerman 1995; D'Amico 1997a, 1997b).

Sex/uality and Citizenship

Since its inception, the US military has attempted to police the sex/uality of those who serve. The first gay soldier was drummed out of the service in 1778; and during World War I, soldiers convicted of forcible sodomy were court-martialled, imprisoned and then dishonourably discharged. After the war, consensual same-sex relations were also criminalised, and the military routinely engaged in 'gay dragnets' to purge gay men from the ranks. During World War II, men suspected of being gay were deemed mentally unsuitable for service; those already in service whose sexuality became suspect were either dishonourably discharged or forcibly 'rehabilitated' and retained, as military authorities feared troops would claim to be gay to avoid service (Shilts 1993). Similarly, only unmarried women 'of good moral character' were recruited for the women's corps, and military women suspected of either heterosexual promiscuity or lesbianism were discharged (D'Amico 1999).

Since World War II, American military members who are gay/lesbian/ bisexual have been striving to end harassment by their peers and discharge by the institution. Because sexual minorities seek an end to expulsion from the military rather than access to the institution from the outside, their service is constructed more as a civil right than as a citizen responsibility. That is, their 'right to serve' (Humphrey 1990) is presented as a right to a particular job and to protection from discrimination. Because they are routinely denied this right to participate (rather than the right to vote or to hold public office) and because many have been able to serve undetected, their quest for inclusion may best be interpreted as one of a *recovery* of full citizenship rather than as a claim of a group completely excluded from political power in the state.

However, like African-American men and military women, gay/lesbian/ bisexual members of the armed forces appear to accept the equation of citizenship with military service. Yet not all in the civilian gay/lesbian/ bisexual community have done so, as many have also worked in the anti-militarist/anti-nuclear movement. Still, many have come to believe that ending military exclusion of people who identify as sexual minorities will help to overcome discrimination in civilian employment and housing, to decriminalise same-sex intimacy, and to reduce the incidence of harassment and physical assault, known in the United States as gay-bashing.

Between 1980 and 1993, 19,267 people were discharged from the US armed forces because of their sexuality. In the five years since the new 'Don't Ask, Don't Tell' policy came into force, another 4,429 servicemen and women have been discharged, bringing the total discharged since 1980 to 23,599 (D'Amico 1999).

For each year since 1980, the proportion of women discharged under the exclusion policy has exceeded the proportion of women in the armed forces overall, such that women have been from two to three times as likely to be discharged as have servicemen. In 1998, women accounted for 28 per cent of exclusion discharges yet were only 14 per cent of armed forces personnel. Military men pressure military women to prove they are not lesbian by engaging in heterosexual relations; failure to comply with this sexual extortion risks investigation and discharge. So the military closet affords little protection for military women; their sexuality is suspect because their presence in the military institution violates gender boundaries (D'Amico 1996b, 1999).

As Carol Cohn (1998) points out, the debate over allowing sexual minorities – and other previously excluded groups – to serve in the military has been constructed around the opposition of individual rights and national security. Cohn sees this dichotomous construction as a smokescreen to 'direct and divert our attention … from questions about the military's role in civil society and the cultural assumptions about that role' (Cohn 1998: 133–4). This diversion maintains the model of citizen-soldier and the concept of martial citizenship, and these are now held up to other communities as models to emulate, leaving little room for evaluation, critique or alternative definitions of citizenship.

Exporting Martial Citizenship

As Cynthia Enloe has pointed out, the US military plays multiple roles in the post-Cold War world; chief among these is that of *drill instructor*, in which United States military personnel teach other states' military personnel, recasting them in their own image through foreign aid defence dollars, joint training and exercises, and military socialisation at US academies and institutes (Enloe 1990, 1993). In so doing, the United States seeks to maintain its hegemonic position in the global political system.

For example, the admission of Eastern European states to the North Atlantic Treaty Organisation (NATO) requires their 'modernisation'– that is, their Americanisation – since US forces and strategies are the models to be emulated because of US military predominance. Beyond the lessons on battle techniques, foreign military officers learn about the construction of class/rank, 'race'/colour/ethnicity and gender/sexuality underlying the US military institution (Enloe 1990, 1993). One such lesson has been that modernisation requires the 'professionalisation' of military women's roles and the protection of the masculine-gendered core of the military from female incursion. The export of the citizen-soldier model means that excluded groups in these countries may be encouraged to seek access to the military institution. This will leave unchallenged the concept of martial citizenship.

At the School of the Americas in Bennington, Georgia, foreign military personnel are trained in the latest counter-insurgency methods. What other lessons are they learning from their American counterparts? What messages are conveyed from the instructors at Aberdeen Proving Ground, the US army's largest training facility, who forced women trainees into sexual relationships? What lessons are derived from the failure to convict *any* of the military personnel who participated in the infamous gauntlet at the naval aviators' Tailhook Convention in 1991, in which scores of women were sexually assaulted? (see D'Amico 1997b). The continued export of the US citizen-soldier model leaves the concept of martial citizenship and its foundations in hierarchical power relations unchallenged.

Yet these foundations can eventually be exposed as the military becomes more representative of the diverse society from which its members are drawn. For example, as more women enter, their presence challenges the gendered dichotomy of 'man as warrior'/'woman as pacifist' described by Jean Bethke Elshtain (1987). How will this change affect our ideas about gender? The formal militarisation of 'women' may allow a rethinking of the militarisation of 'men' (people gendered 'masculine') whose military service has been previously deemed 'natural'; more men may thus be enabled to cross these now exposed gender boundaries to embrace peace politics. The end result may be a calling into question of the nature and purpose of the military institution itself. There are no guarantees here, only possibilities; but the possibilities seem greater when these groups are present to critique the military from 'inside' as well as from 'outside'. Raising such critiques reveals class/rank, 'race'/colour/ethnicity and gender/sexuality boundaries as socially *constructed* and therefore capable of *re-construction* along more equitable lines.

Towards a New Form of Citizenship?

The idea of 'earning equality' or of proving one's excluded group worthy of 'full citizenship' appears problematic. Not all citizens are soldiers simultaneously, even in the most militarised societies. Many people's services are not needed; age and ability disqualify some, and others have commitments which appear incompatible with military service. Even those who are soldiers are not treated as full citizens, as African-Americans returning from the 'integrated' army in the Korean conflict to a segregated America learned.

Allowing previously excluded groups to serve contributes towards a *pluralisation* of the military institution, which is not weakened or made less capable because of this heterogeneity, as critics contend, but rather strengthened because it is both *democratised* in the sense of becoming more representative of the population at large and *humanised* by being made to pay attention to the basic human needs of *all* personnel: people with partners, parents with young children—in short, people with personal relationships with other people rather than atomistic individuals. Not long ago, the idea of the United States addressing dual deployment and quality of life questions would have appeared absurd. Being forced to confront these questions has the potential to turn the military from a tool for the maintenance of a particular set of power relations within and among states to a force for change in those structures.

The US experience suggests that the more broadly inclusive the military institution, the more possible is its control by citizens in a democratic system: political officials are now extremely reluctant to deploy US forces without broad public support. Leaving the military apparatus in the hands of a select few widens the gulf between the military institution and the civilian community and abdicates citizens' responsibility to hold the state accountable for military policies and actions undertaken in our names. When the state portrays itself in the mantle of democratic ideology as a product of its citizens, we must hold it to this promise in the peopling of the military institution.

Access to military service is important not just for the 'right to serve' but what that right represents in terms of the hope to change societal structures and practices, much as the right to vote was seen by suffragists as a means to a greater end. Just as suffragists found the vote inadequate to accomplish the transformation of gender hierarchy, so, too, are working-class families, African-Americans, women and sexual minorities finding access to the military institution inadequate to transform the intersecting power hierarchies underlying not only that institution but the rest of society. What is needed is a fundamental revision of the concept of citizenship.

Must one serve in the military to claim the rights of a citizen, as the model of *martial citizenship* asserts? Early advocates of women's rights staked women's claim to citizenship on the status of motherhood: *maternal citizenship* argued that women had different but comparable responsibilities to the community. Both martial and maternal citizenship are grounded in our ideas about gender, that is, our ideas about what behaviours are appropriate for people we call men (male people gendered masculine) and women (female people gendered feminine). Just as not all men are soldiers, not all women are mothers. So there must be another, broader basis for citizenship, one which is inclusive and demilitarised.

Some analysts have suggested that we construct a gender-neutral citizenship. For example, Jean Bethke Elshtain calls for a form of 'civic membership' which she labels the *chastened patriot* (Elshtain 1998: 447, 459). According to Elshtain, the chastened patriot or 'sceptical citizen' (p. 458) is critical both 'of the excesses of nationalism' and of 'feminist arguments that express contempt for forms of identity … embodied in loyalties to ways of life shared by men and women', yet acknowledges the 'dignity and rights of woman' (p. 447). Elshtain sees an opening for the renegotiation of the citizen-soldier concept here because she believes that although 'citizen and soldier were tightly tethered in Western history, this is no longer the case' (p. 455). She argues that contemporary citizens must 'be neither warriors nor victims' but 'seek, instead, an image of men, women, and civic life that links men and women alike to the social and political world, that narrows the gap between them, and that defuses the seductions of war' (p. 456). We must also consider how the increasing numbers of women serving in the military affect the dominant narrative of 'women's social location as noncombatants and men's as soldier-citizens' (p. 454) and analyse what 'justifiable grounds for war' might be from feminist perspectives (p. 457).

While Elshtain's conceptualisation of a more critical and engaged citizenry improves upon the citizen-soldier model, her revision seems to require participation in the traditional 'public sphere' of formal politics rather than to redefine the scope of civic life. Other theorists have attempted to conceptualise an explicitly *feminist citizenship* which does not just redraw the boundaries of citizenship but change its meaning. For example, Ruth Lister seeks to move citizenship from its traditional use as a tool of political exclusion grounded in inequality and xenophobia to a more inclusive and progressive practice of accommodating difference and diversity (Lister 1998). Jan Jindy Pettman observes:

> Citizenship is conventionally understood as the individual's relationship with the state, and as an association of equals in its political community ... Citizenship's construction of the individual citizen making up 'the people' can silence or marginalise minorities and those whose interests or beliefs are different ... This is especially so ... in international relations where the state speaks for 'the people'. (Pettman 1996: 17)

Both Lister's and Pettman's visions of citizenship require an uncoupling of the citizen-soldier model and an acknowledgement of different ways of belonging to and contributing to the life of one's community.

Because much feminist critique focuses primarily or exclusively on gender alone, I propose an alternative phrasing, *pluralist citizenship*, to describe a form of citizenship which attends to not only the legal equality of individuals but also the diversity of cultural groups within a particular state and the human rights of all in our larger global society. Pluralist citizenship requires an active rather than a passive citizen, one willing to participate, to take responsibility for actions the state does in her/his name, and to challenge the state when those actions contradict the values citizens cherish.

The martial citizenship of Western liberal democratic theory assumes a uniformity of condition among individuals in which treating people fairly means treating them *equally or the same*. Pluralist citizenship demands that where people are not the same, treating them fairly means treating them *differently*. Pluralist citizenship recognises not only the rights of the individual but also the rights of the group, not just individual interests but identity interests.

Citizen-Soldier?

Martial citizenship requires *sacrifice* – in the words of Abraham Lincoln, the 'last full measure of devotion'. Yet many besides soldiers sacrifice themselves in the performance of services to one another, to family, to community and to country. Those in the 'service professions'– teachers, counsellors, health-care providers, child/elder caretakers – sacrifice high pay, status, prestige (the markers of success in America's materialist society) to devote themselves to the care and education of young, old, ill and infirm. But sacrifice in these service professions is poorly rewarded and unrecognised as the work of citizens precisely because they are feminised. Unpaid volunteer work at all but the highest echelons of non-profit organisations (and some even here) is also accomplished largely by women. Similarly, community organisations, churches, synagogues and other places of worship rely on the energies and talents of women to meet the needs of the community. Why not broaden our conceptualisation of citizenship to include these activities which do so much for the life of the community?

Am I suggesting that we adopt the 'national service' model in which all youths are 'drafted' for some time of enforced service? No, because in that model, the hallmark of citizenship remains service to the state rather than to other people in our communities. Rather, civic or community service (not as a sentence for those convicted of crimes, which delegitimises service) or work in a service profession should be recognised as an act of citizenship, as should public dissent and civil disobedience, which clearly take seriously the responsibility of the citizen to hold the state accountable for its actions.

Conclusion: Citizens, States, and Communities

Waltz and others of the structural realist school of international relations theory have argued that we can understand world politics by focusing on the state system or 'third level' of analysis. But this focus at the structural level provides only a snapshot of a particular historical moment rather than an understanding of the complex processes which construct that moment and the consequences our decisions will have. In order to understand choices about war and peace, we need to examine the power hierarchies in which we are enmeshed and which compel and constrain us in our daily lives. As Jean Bethke Elshtain observes: 'Thinking about men, women and war implicates one necessarily in the politics of representation and identity, and such considerations, in turn, force one to cut through and across the "levels-of-analysis" framework that has so dominated international relations theory and that now unnecessarily hobbles it' (Elshtain 1998: 449). Elshtain argues that asking questions about the meaning of citizenship 'compels the scholar to move in and through all three levels of analysis' to consider the

complexities of history and experience that define the range of political
possibilities available to people in one community in their interactions with
peoples in other communities (p. 455). I concur with her assessment: we
must seek to understand the complex array of intersecting power relations
which shape militaries, states and the state system.

Bibliography

Armor, D. (1996) 'Race and Gender in the U.S. Military', *Armed Forces and Society*, vol. 23, no. 1, Fall, pp. 7–27.

Berkman, J. (1987) 'Feminism, War, and Peace Politics: The Case of World War I', in Elshtain and Tobias (eds), *Women, Militarism, and War*, pp. 141–60.

Chapkis, W. (ed.) (1981) *Loaded Questions: Women in the Military*, Amsterdam and Washington, DC: Transnational Institute.

Clines, F. X. (1993) 'When Black Soldiers were Hanged: A War's Footnote', *New York Times*, 7 February, p. 20.

Cohn, C. (1998) 'Gays in the Military: Texts and Subtexts', in Zalewski and Parpart (eds), *The 'Man' Question in International Relations*, Boulder, CO: Westview Press, pp. 129–49.

D'Amico, F. (1996a) 'Feminist Perspectives on Women Warriors', *Peace Review*, vol. 8, no. 3, September, pp. 379–84.

— (1996b) 'Race-ing and Gendering the Military Closet', in C. A. Rimmerman (ed.), *Gay Rights, Military Wrongs: Political Perspectives on Gays and Lesbians in the Military*, New York: Garland Press, pp. 3–46.

— (1997a) 'Policing the U.S. Military's Race and Gender Lines', in L. Weinstein and C. White (eds), *Wives and Warriors: Women and the Military in the United States and Canada*, Westport, CT: Greenwood Press, pp. 199–234.

— (1997b) 'Tailhook: Deinstitutionalizing the Military's "Woman Problem"', in L. Weinstein and C. White (eds), *Wives and Warriors: Women and the Military in the United States and Canada*, Westport, CT: Greenwood Press, pp. 235–43.

— (1999) 'Sex/uality and Military Service', in C. Rimmerman, K. Wald and C. Wilcox (eds), *The Politics of Gay Rights*, Chicago: University of Chicago Press.

D'Amico, F. and L. Weinstein (eds) (1999) *Gender Camouflage: Women and the U.S. Military*, New York: New York University Press.

Dean, D. M. (1997) *Warriors Without Weapons: The Victimization of Military Women*, Pasadena, MD: MINERVA Center.

Defense Equal Opportunity Management Institute (DEOMI) (1998) *Semiannual Race/Ethnic/Gender Profile of the Department of Defense*, Patrick AFB, FL: DEOMI.

Earley, C. A. (1989) *One Woman's Army: A Black Officer Remembers the WAC*, Texas: A & M University Press.

Eisenstein, Z. (1981) *The Radical Future of Liberal Feminism*, New York: Longman.

Elshtain, J. B. (1987) *Women and War*, New York: Basic Books.

— (1998) '*Women and War*: Ten Years On', *Review of International Studies*, vol. 24, no. 4, October, pp. 447–61.

Elshtain, J. B. and S. Tobias (eds), (1990) *Women, Militarism, and War: Essays in History, Politics, and Social Theory*, Savage, MD: Rowman and Littlefield.

Enloe, C. (1980) *Ethnic Soldiers: State Security in Divided Societies*, Athens: University of Georgia Press.

— (1983) *Does Khaki Become You? The Militarization of Women's Lives*, Boston: South End Press.

— (1990) *Bananas, Beaches, and Bases: Making Feminist Sense of International Politics*, Berkeley: University of California Press.

— (1993) *The Morning After: Sexual Politics at the End of the Cold War*, Berkeley: University of California Press.

Fainsod Katzenstein, M. (1998) *Faithful and Fearless: Moving Feminist Protest Inside the Church and Military*, Princeton, NJ: Princeton University Press.

Feinman, I. (1999) *Citizenship Rites: Feminist Soldiers and Feminist Antimilitarists*, New York: New York University Press.

Foner, E. (1999) 'African-Americans and the Story of American Freedom', *Souls*, Winter, pp. 16–22.

Francke, L. B. (1997) *Ground Zero: The Gender Wars in the Military*, New York: Simon and Schuster.

Hartsock, N. C. M. (1984) 'Masculinity, Citizenship, and the Making of War', *PS: Political Science and Politics*, no. 17, Spring, pp. 198–201.

Herbert, M. (1997) *Camouflage Isn't Only for Combat: The Management of Gender and Sexuality Among Women in the Military*, New York: New York University Press.

Humphrey, M. A. (1990) *My Country, My Right to Serve: Experiences of Gay Men and Women in the Military, World War II to the Present*, New York: HarperCollins.

Kelly, S. H. (1997) 'Seven WWII Vets to Receive Medals of Honor', www.defenselink.mil/armylink/news/medal, 13 January 1997.

Kerber, L. K. (1990) 'May All Our Citizens be Soldiers and All Our Soldiers Citizens: The Ambiguities of Female Citizenship in the New Nation', in Elshtain and Tobias (eds), *Women, Militarism, and War*, pp. 89–103.

Lister, R. (1998) *Citizenship: Feminist Perspectives*, New York: New York University Press.

Mershon, S. and S. Schlossman (1998) *Foxholes and Color Lines: Desegregating the U.S. Armed Forces*, Baltimore, MD: Johns Hopkins University Press.

Moore, B. L. (1996) *To Serve My Country, To Serve My Race: African-American WACs Stationed Overseas during World War II*, New York and London: New York University Press.

Mullen, R. W. (1973) *Blacks in America's Wars*, New York: Pathfinder Press.

Pettman, J. J. (1996) *Worlding Women: A Feminist International Politics*, London: Routledge.

Reeves, C. (1999) 'Invisible Soldiers: Military Nurses', in D'Amico and Weinstein (eds), *Gender Camouflage*.

Reppy, J. V. and M. Fainsod Katzenstein (eds) (1999) *Beyond Zero Tolerance: Discrimination in Military Culture*, Savage, MD: Rowman and Littlefield.

Sadler, G. C. (1999) 'From Women's Services to Servicewomen', in D'Amico and Weinstein (eds), *Gender Camouflage*.

Shilts, R. (1993) *Conduct Unbecoming: Gays and Lesbians in the U.S. Military*, New York: St Martin's Press.

Von Glahn, G. (1996) *Law Among Nations: An Introduction to International Law*, 7th edn, Boston: Allyn and Bacon.

Waltz, K. (1959) *Man, the State and War: A Theoretical Analysis*, New York: University of Columbia Press.

Wertsch, M. E. (1991) *Military Brats: The Legacy of Childhood Inside the Fortress*, New York: Crown.

Widnall, S. E., Secretary of the Air Force. (1997) 'Carrying the Flag of Equal Opportunity into the 21st Century', *Defense Issues*, vol. 12, no. 40, www.defenselink.mil.

Wynn, N. (1976) *The Afro-American and the Second World War*, New York: Holmes and Meier.

Zimmerman, J. (1995) *Tailspin: Women at War in the Wake of Tailhook*, New York: Doubleday.

Part II

Resistances and Responsibilities

7

Shifting Relationships and Competing Discourses in Post-Mao China: The All-China Women's Federation and the People's Republic

Jude Howell

For the past two decades gender policy theorists and planners have been concerned with the institutional articulation of gender interests (Stetson and Mazur 1995; Goetz 1992; Kabeer 1994; Moser 1993; Ostergaard 1992; Staudt 1990). Advocates of separate gender units within organisations, specialised ministries and departments for women's affairs and local women's centres would argue that it is essential that an institutional space is created where women's needs can find expression. Given the history of women's oppression and in particular the patriarchal nature of the state, its construction and reconstruction of oppressive gender relations, only a separate arena of organisation and policy-making can provide the autonomy for women to define their practical and strategic interests independent of male-dominated, statist agendas. Critics would maintain that institutional segregation leads not only to a marginalisation of gender issues but also a reproduction of a gendered division of labour where gender matters become typified as female concerns. The dangers of marginalisation have in turn prompted a debate among feminist theorists as well as policy-makers about the relative merits of mainstreaming gender issues or indeed a combination of mainstreaming and institutional specialisation.[1]

In former and contemporary socialist states where women's organisations have served as organic extensions of the party-state and gender issues have been subordinated to national and party interests, the debate has been less about choosing between alternative institutional arrangements and more about defining the degree of autonomy from the party-state. The failure to resolve this meant that once the various communist parties of the the Soviet Union and Eastern Europe began to fall from 1989 onwards, the official women's organisations likewise met a similar fate. Nevertheless, with their long histories of ideological and organisational support for gender equality and removing discriminatory practices, such states offer useful insights into the challenges of institutionalising gender issues.

The case of China is particularly interesting. In contrast to the former Soviet Union and Eastern Europe the Chinese Communist Party (CCP) has managed to institute a radical programme of market reform since 1978 and remain at the helm, while the All-China Women's Federation (ACWF) has retained its position as key organisational representative of women's interests. However, in the post-Mao era the close relationship between the ACWF and the CCP has increasingly been called into question and the struggle for greater autonomy for the ACWF has surfaced more prominently. The gendered consequences of rapid socio-economic change have likewise stimulated the ACWF to rethink its activities and purposes. Furthermore, the gradual emergence of more autonomous women's organisations from the mid-1980s onwards presents a potential challenge to the authority of the ACWF, thus drawing attention to the complex inter-relationships between official women's organisations and non-governmental women's groups. How the ACWF reconciles these different pressures will be of immense interest to both gender theorists and policy-makers concerned with identifying appropriate institutional forms for addressing gender inequalities.

This chapter thus explores the changing nature of the ACWF with a particular focus on its quest for greater autonomy from the CCP. We begin by tracing the historical relationship between the ACWF and the CCP, highlighting the different moments when a redefinition has been attempted and drawing out the constraints to more autonomous forms of organisation. We then go on to examine three factors which have contributed towards the ACWF's struggle for a more independent role from the CCP, namely, the socio-economic consequences of reform, competition from new women's organisations and the impact of the UN's Fourth World Conference on the Status of Women.

Struggling for Autonomy

Background The All-China Women's Federation (ACWF) is the official body representing women's interests in the People's Republic of China. Since its resurrection in 1978 the ACWF has developed extensive roots, with representation down to the village level. By 1994 it laid claim to 68,355 branches, 30 at provincial level, 370 at city level, 2,810 at county level and 65,145 at township level and between 80,000 and 90,000 cadres throughout China. It has full-time staff down to the city level, all paid for and appointed by the state. Compared with grass-roots women's groups in Western and many developing countries, the ACWF is very much a top-down organisation. However, at the lower levels the ACWF has historically tended to be in closer touch with the direct concerns of women and more ready to raise gender issues than the national-level organisation. During the land reform campaign in the early 1950s local branches of the ACWF often used the campaign to raise gender issues as well. Andors (1983: 32–3) gives the example of the Women's Association in Henan Province which, at a meeting in July 1949 to mobilise women for the land reform campaign, raised simultaneously vital issues such as attitudes to women, child brides, arranged marriages and female infanticide.

Like other mass organisations, such as the All-China Federation of Trades Unions (ACFTU) and the Communist Youth League, the ACWF serves as a transmission belt between the party and society, relaying party policy downwards and reflecting grass-roots opinion upwards, in democratic centralist fashion. The ACWF thus has the dual function of representing women's interests to the party and the party's interests to women. When these interests conflict, then the ACWF faces the crucial dilemma of whose interests it should prioritise.

Recent developments In the post-Mao era the clash of interests is starkly evidenced, for example, in the 'one child one family' policy. As ACWF cadres have been required to become involved in its implementation, they have had to preside over a policy which is not only unpopular but also anti-women as manifested in the incidence of late and forced abortions and female infanticide. As officials of the ACWF are frequently also party members, the dilemma becomes not only an organisational matter but also a personal one; for example, of the 196 Women's Federation heads in Suzhou City at county level, 78 per cent were party members (Wang Yi et al. 1991: 20–1). This tension between the competing pull from the party and the push from members has crucially informed the process of change within the ACWF in the reform era.

Although the ACWF has played an important role in keeping gender issues on the political agenda, in the last instance it has tended to subordinate these to the priorities of the party, as has occurred in all socialist states (see, for example, Johnson 1983; Davin 1976; Andors 1983). If the ACWF is to retain its legitimacy as a body representing, articulating and promoting women's interests, then the notion of organisational autonomy is clearly of importance. An organisation might be defined as autonomous if it meets the following conditions: first, it is able to set its own goals, determine its own priorities, and decide its own structures and principles of organisation; second, it is able to appoint its own personnel and recruit its own members; third, it relies primarily on its own sources of funding. In terms of this definition the ACWF leaves much to be desired.

While the ACWF has historically been subordinated to the CCP, some cadres have sought to resolve the dilemma of competing interests by seeking greater autonomy for the organisation. Such sentiments have been voiced with growing intensity at the various annual congresses. The Sixth Annual Congress of the ACWF in 1988 marked a turning-point in the attempts of the ACWF to adapt to changing circumstances and in particular to redefine its relationship with the party. One of the key themes at the meeting was how to convert the ACWF from an administrative organisation to a genuine mass organisation (Wang Qi 1988). Numerous women voiced the need for greater autonomy and self-direction. For example, the female vice-governor from Qinghai complained that the ACWF had become an implementing organ of the party and government. Similarly, Chen Xiaolu argued vociferously that mass organisations needed to reduce interference by the party in their affairs, manage their own affairs, enjoy autonomy, both according to the constitution and in law (Wu Ying Zeng et al. 1988: 22–4).

This spirit of openness and desire to prioritise members' interests met a setback after the dramatic events of 1989 and 4 June in particular. The subsequent clampdown on democracy dissidents, on organisers of auto-nomous trade unions and students' organisations and cadres in the mass organisations who had shown support for the movement served to dampen any expression for a more autonomous Women's Federation. Cadres in mass organisations retreated into their familiar party-speak. The 1989 democracy movement did not, however, stimulate any independent women's organisations to challenge the authority of the ACWF, as was the case with the autonomous trade unions in relation to the ACFTU.

The demonstrations of 1989 highlighted the growing gulf between the party, the mass organisations and society. Aware of the need to restore the legitimacy of the party, mass organisations were encouraged to strengthen their work at the grass-roots and address the issues raised by their members. As the political situation began to ease from 1991 onwards, we find the ACWF reiterating the need to act more autonomously, albeit in a more restrained fashion than in 1988. ACWF officials interviewed in 1992 claimed that the 'Double Compete, Double Study Campaign', which was organised to raise technical and cultural levels in the countryside, was the first activity where the ACWF enjoyed some independence (author's inter-view, ACWF, Beijing, 22 September 1992). Open discussion of a desire for greater autonomy did not surface at the seventh National Congress in September 1993. Although leading cadres underlined the importance of addressing crucial gender-specific issues such as the protection of women's rights and interests and female infanticide (see, for example, *Renmin Ribao*, 2 September 1993 and *Zhongguo Funu Bao*, 8 September 1993), constant references to party goals pointed to the continuing subordination of the ACWF to party objectives. Indeed the Congress highlighted the importance of the approaching Fourth World Conference on the Status of Women for displaying the achievements of reform and opening up (see, for example, *Women of China*, 8 September 1993).

The ACWF's historical alliance with the CCP has thus been a significant constraint upon any efforts to gain greater organisational autonomy. Its close ties have proved to be a doubled-edged sword. On the one hand these have given it a degree of influence with regard to gender issues that it might not otherwise have enjoyed; on the other hand they have also required a compromise where competing interests overlap. Where demands for autonomy have emerged, they have been confined mainly to the first two conditions. While in the last eight years the ACWF has become much more entrepreneurial in raising its own sources of funding, it has not simultaneously sought financial autonomy from the state. Having explored the quest for autonomy, we proceed in the next sections to discuss the factors which have stimulated this process. Thus we focus on the socio-economic consequences of reform, the competition from new women's organisations and the impact of the recent Fourth World Conference on the Status of Women.

Socio-economic Consequences of Reform

Almost two decades of fundamental economic reform have brought significant and contradictory changes in the economic opportunities and working conditions for women. In rural areas the introduction of the household responsibility system, domestic sideline production as well as the rapid growth of rural industry have increased the employment opportunities for women. Migration to the cities has not only provided a source of remittances to rural areas but also extended horizons, changed values and raised expectations. In the urban areas the gradual flourishing of the private and collective sectors, the expansion of the tertiary sector as well as the greenfield sites of industrialisation in the new Special Economic Zones (SEZs) have similarly opened up new avenues for women.[2]

However, the effects of the reform on women have been contradictory, sometimes bringing new, unexpected benefits, at other times reinforcing old patterns and creating new forms of oppression. The pressure on enterprises to become more profit-conscious has had a negative impact on women, evidenced in higher unemployment rates, reluctance to employ women (Honig and Hershatter 1988: 244–50; Jiang and Zhang 1997), numerous attempts to deprive women of their statutory rights such as maternity leave, dismissing women first and differential payment.

Some consequences The commoditisation of the economy has begun to permeate the realm of sexuality and redefine the nature of female subordination. While prostitution was initially seen as an undesirable consequence of setting up the SEZs, by the late 1980s it had become an issue of national concern, evident in most urban parts of China. Increasing numbers of reports of sexual harassment in the workplace, particularly in the SEZs and private enterprises, provided further evidence of the power imbalance in gender relations and the objectification of women (*China Women News*, 3 October 1993 and *China Daily*, 4 February 1988). Poverty, the draconian family-planning policy as well as agricultural reforms which initially rewarded households with larger labour forces have combined to turn women into commodities. The lesser value attached to female labour in a context where the size of family is subject to state scrutiny and control underpins the increasingly widespread practice of female infanticide in the rural areas. By 1994 demographers were already expressing concern at the noticeably unbalanced sex ratio.

The reforms have thus served to reinforce old patterns of gender subordination which had continued in post-liberation China as well as to create new avenues of opportunity which promise materially better life-styles for some women. This repositioning of women in the urban and rural economies has in turn presented the ACWF with new challenges. The expansion of the private and tertiary sectors has created new socio-economic groups such as private traders, entrepreneurs, specialised farmers and workers and managers in foreign factories, with particular needs, expectations and values. They encounter specific problems in operating in an economic environment where both market and state are constructed in gender terms. The difficulty for the ACWF lies in reaching these women, both institutionally and ideologically. While in the urban state and collective sectors the ACWF could link up with women through their work-units, those employed in the private and tertiary sectors fall outside the institutional scope of the ACWF.

The ACWF has encountered similar problems in the rural areas. The intensification of women's work due to male migrant labour and diversification of income-generating activities has left rural women with less time to engage in public affairs. To the extent that women have become more bounded within the household, particularly where they are engaged in sideline activities or are mainly responsible for agricultural work, they are more difficult for the ACWF to reach. As the household responsibility system has undermined the work of party and government rural cadres, the ACWF has also lost an important channel of communication and participation.

The ACWF response Despite the fact that the Women's Federation is still caught in the same contradictory position which has bedevilled it since its foundation in 1949, it has made significant attempts to respond to the changing needs of various types of women in the reform period. It has expanded its functions, experimented with new types of activity and created new departments. While in the pre-reform period the ACWF paid attention to the sub-categories of women along the urban/rural and class axes, in the post-Mao period it has begun to recognise the finer distinctions between women along class, occupational, rural/urban and regional lines. It has proved more dynamic than the ACFTU in its efforts to reach women in new socio-economic groups such as entrepreneurs, traders, managers, employees in foreign-invested enterprises and rural industry. To the extent that the process of commodification has led to a worsening of women's social status and security and economic reform has exacerbated discrimination in the workplace, the ACWF has come under increasing pressure to represent its members' interests and prioritise these over national and party policy. The ACWF has taken up the gauntlet, albeit warily and slowly, and tried to address some of the newly emerging needs such as the Social Fund for Child-bearing Women and the provision of free legal counselling in parks and on the street as well as the establishment of women's legal rights centres. This is reflected in the 1988 and 1992 legislation protecting the rights of women workers as well as the formation of special committees to protect women's rights at the local level and numerous legal consultation sessions in public places.[3]

The process of restructuring, devising new strategies for reaching women and seeking to address gender-specific issues inevitably has financial implications. Given the current pressure on state institutions to rein in their expenditures, the ACWF too has had to become more entrepreneurial. Unlike the ACFTU which by law receives 2 per cent of the total wage bill from enterprises, the financial position of the ACWF is far less rosy. While for most of its life the ACWF has relied on the state for financial sustenance, from the mid-1980s it has been permitted, along with other mass organisations, to fund-raise, using the profits to pay local cadres.

Following the go-ahead given by Deng Xiaoping in his much-cited Southern China speech in February 1992, the ACWF leadership embarked whole-heartedly upon a more entrepreneurial strategy for raising funds. In this spirit they decided to sell a building which was to be used for staff accommodation and use the proceeds to set up a joint venture hotel complex with foreign investors. Part of the profits would be used to provide housing for women cadres. The need to raise some of its own funds has thus given the ACWF greater room for manoeuvre and could potentially weaken its institutional obligation to comply with and prioritise party objectives.

In brief, the gendered impact of the reform process has complicated the category of woman, requiring a conceptual framework that goes beyond the limits of a reductionist, class content. Moreover, it has created new needs and demands which have highlighted the inadequacies of the ACWF and in particular the constraining effects of its dependent relationship on the party. In turn the ACWF's efforts to respond to new needs have led it to prioritise gender over party interests and, at particular junctures, to seek a more autonomous relationship with the party.

The Rise of Competitors

A second factor pushing the ACWF towards a redefinition of its relationship with the party has been the rise of new, more autonomous women's organisations in the reform period. These have emerged within the context of a more general expansion of the intermediary sphere. The new social organisations such as business organisations, professional bodies, cultural associations, friendly societies and chambers of commerce began to appear in the early 1980s. Their growth accelerated from the mid-1980s following the introduction of urban reform and reached a peak in the dramatic year of 1989. Following the tragic events of 4 June the CCP clamped down on these organisations. Since October 1989 all social organisations have been required to register with the Ministry of Civil Affairs. While politically oriented organisations perceived as a threat to the party-state were banned, those in the economic, cultural and welfare sphere were not only allowed to continue but positively encouraged by the state. By October 1993, there were over 1,460 registered national social organisations, 19,600 branch and local organisations registered at provincial level and over 160,000 social organisations registered with county authorities (interview, Ministry of Civil Affairs, Beijing, October 1993 and *China Daily*, 7 May 1993, p. 3).[4]

As part of this clampdown on social organisations, the Ministry of Civil Affairs issued a regulation prohibiting associations from organising along ethnic, religious or gender lines. Those women's organisations which had already formed before 1989 such as the Shanghai Journalists' Association were allowed to continue but all new organisations had to become second-level organisations to a more general organisation. So, for example, the Women's Mayors' Association is a second-level association under the Mayors' Association.

Women's organisations today Like other social organisations the new women's organisations enjoy a range of relationships to the state and few of these are genuine grass-roots associations, indicative of a vibrant civil society. We can identify three different types of women's organisations in contemporary China. First is the ACWF which is the least autonomous from the state. Then there are the semi-official women's organisations which are predominantly professional associations such as the Women's Journalists' Association, the China Women's Mayors' Association and the China Household Services Association.[5] These are hybrid organisations, drawing their leaders both from government and their membership. They receive some financial support from government in terms of an office, salaries of transferred government staff and support for activities. In the post-Tiananmen period they have increasingly been initiated from above rather than from below. Given their quasi-state character, they are more likely than the next category of popular women's organisations to come under pressure to put party or national policy interests over those of their members.

Compared to their semi-official counterparts, popular women's organisations enjoy greater autonomy from the party-state. They appoint their own leaders, determine their own priorities and goals and depend on their own efforts to raise funds. Their lack of financial support from the state is, however, a constraint on their ability to expand or organise more regular and grand activities.

To the extent, however, that the ACWF or government departments begin to encroach upon popular organisations, the latter are in danger of losing some of their spontaneity and grass-roots characteristics. The Intellectual Women's Associations provide a pertinent example of such a process. These began to mushroom at provincial and city levels from the mid-1980s. As the ACWF was keen to find an inroad among women intellectuals, it began to take an active interest in these organisations, wanting to shape their constitutions in its image and play a major role in their activities. From the point of view of some of the members, however, the ACWF's moves to incorporate the associations undermined their original impetus. As a result they are reluctant to set up a proper national organisation, fearing this would be taken over by the ACWF.

More autonomous than the semi-official organisations are those women's organisations which are in the process of registering or which have not sought to register but are not officially prohibited. An example of the former is the Xiaoshan City Women Writers' Small Group which, at the time of interview, was seeking registration. The local Women's Federation was concerned that it would not be approved and so was reluctant to act as its superior unit.[6]

Preparing for the UN Conference: the role of new organisations The Fourth World Conference on the Status of Women was an important

stimulus to the growth of more autonomous women's organisations, particularly those that lie in the limbo-land of non-registration and non-
prohibition. International organisations began to foster and support gender
initiatives. The Ford Foundation, for example, hosted regular group discussions on women's issues, which culminated in the production of a bilingual
book for the conference. Enterprising projects such as the Women's Hotline
and the Jinglun Family Centre received financial support from various
international agencies. The British Cultural Communication Centre ran a
training-course in the summer of 1994 to facilitate better communication
between Chinese and foreigners at the approaching conference.[7]

In hosting the conference it would have been ironic indeed if China
could not have presented its own contingent of women's NGOs. Hence the
CCP took a much more tolerant attitude to the new women's organisations,
particularly those that sought to discuss feminist theories that would be
perceived as divergent from orthodox Marxist interpretations of female
oppression. It would be safe to assume that if China had not hosted the
conference, there would have been far less of a relatively non-governmental
Chinese presence at the NGO venue.

Also related are the new Women's Studies Units which have sprung up
since the mid-1980s. Currently China has a dozen or so centres for women's
studies, though these have still not achieved an independent disciplinary
status. Women's studies researchers such as Li Xiaojiang, a young literature
teacher, have argued strongly for such a development (Li and Zhang 1994:
148) but so far university authorities have resisted such a radical change.
The first non-governmental institute of women's studies was set up in
1985 in Zhengzhou University, Henan Province, by Li Xiaojiang. Since
then university departments in Beijing, Nankai and Wuhan have followed
suit, setting up lecture series on women's issues, organising conferences
and meetings. The ACWF also set up its own Women's Studies Institute.
Parallel to these developments, numerous informal groups of women prepared to look critically at the position of women in Chinese society began
to proliferate in the universities from the mid-1980s.

Unlike the official research bodies attached to the ACWF which adopt
a Marxist approach to women's oppression, these non-governmental institutes explore alternative theoretical frameworks.[8] The introduction of
classic feminist publications by authors such as Betty Friedan and Simone
de Beauvoir into China have exposed women intellectuals to some of the
theoretical approaches and ideas common in Western feminist thinking
(Li and Zhang 1994: 148). Given the abstractness of some postmodern
feminist theorising and the concomitant problems of translation, it will
take some time for contemporary debates among Western feminist theorists
to filter through into wider discussion in China. However, the gradual

encounter with non-Marxist feminist theory will provide new ways of exploring gender oppression and ideas for alternative policies for addressing this.

The conference played an important role in galvanising this spate of research into women's studies. Numerous books were published in the run-up to the conference on women's issues in China and on Chinese women's reactions to the preparatory meetings.[9] The ACWF, universities and various research institutions launched research projects to discover more about the situation of women. Foreign universities, aid agencies and governments encouraged joint projects between Chinese and Western scholars, leading to publications in the form of books and articles. For example, the Beijing Agricultural Engineering University set up a gender section in 1994 and then undertook a joint project on rural women's health with a British university. The conference underlined the need for the recognition of gender studies as an academic discipline in its own right and for the development of gender research specialists (Qi 1997: 13).

The emergence of these new women's organisations as well as the more independent women's studies research institutes poses a challenge to the ACWF both theoretically and organisationally. At the theoretical level, the university-based gender researchers are more open to venturing beyond a narrow Marxist interpretation of gender oppression and to identifying perhaps wider manifestations of gender subordination. At the practical level the groups provide another channel for the articulation of women's interests and to that extent might be perceived as challenging the authority of the ACWF. In so far as these groups have organised around issues, they draw attention to the inability of the ACWF to address evolving needs. The Women's Hotline and the Jinglun Family Centre, for example, both respond to needs which have been beyond the organisational remit of the ACWF.

The relationship between the ACWF and these new organisations is still being defined, leading to some ambivalence on both sides as to how best to work together. Some cadres within the ACWF have welcomed the activities of these new organisations, particularly where they addressed issues that the already overstretched ACWF could not itself take on or where they engaged with groups of women that the ACWF has not traditionally focused upon, such as intellectuals and women entrepreneurs. Some cadres, however, have been less favourably disposed towards the new women's groups, viewing them as a potential challenge to the authority of the ACWF and/or as underlining the inadequacies of the ACWF. Despite this ambivalent relationship, the pluralisation of women's organisations has encouraged the ACWF to reflect further upon its relationship with the party and its members. In turn this has provoked important discussions as to its most appropriate format, be it as an independent organisation, a ministry or a women's affairs' department. One of the most open discussions along these lines took place at the Sixth Annual Congress of the ACWF in September 1988, when some delegates criticised the ACWF for too closely resembling the government and called for greater autonomy.[10]

Impact of the Fourth World Conference on the Status of Women

The final factor which has led to a rethinking of the ACWF's relationship with the Party has been the Fourth World Conference on the Status of Women.[11] We can observe at least four ways in which the conference has contributed towards a redefinition of the ACWF's relationship with the CCP, namely, organisational prestige, exposure to global gender issues, experience of foreign women's NGOs and juxtaposition of gender and party interests and priorities.

While a prime motive underlying the governmental decision to host the conference was to enhance China's international image, particularly in the wake of Tiananmen, there is no doubt that the participation of ACWF cadres in high-level governmental discussions and overseas meetings as well as the perceived success of the conference have enhanced the prestige and confidence of the organisation, particularly vis-à-vis other mass organisations such as the ACFTU and CYL. Through participating in preparatory committee meetings abroad ACWF cadres have gained experience in international affairs to an extent unprecedented in the history of the organisation and unrivalled by other mass organisations. Compared with the ACFTU and CYL the ACWF now enjoys a vast network of international contacts, has experience of operating at both governmental and non-governmental levels and has a much better understanding of the workings of the UN. Furthermore, in hosting the NGO Forum the ACWF has entered the vocabulary of non-governmental women's networks, despite the fact that its credentials as an NGO are ambiguous.

For the ACWF the preparations for the conference as well as the actual event itself provided an opportunity to discover some of the predominant themes in global gender discourse. Exposure to less familiar topics such as sexual orientation, sexual harassment, empowerment and reproductive rights enabled women cadres to have a better idea of what issues were driving women activists in other countries, to become aware of the lines of fissure dividing women as well as the nodes of consensus and to have the chance to reflect upon issues that they may never have thought about before. Moreover, the prominence of human rights issues as well as attacks upon China's record in the media and at the UN Secretariat's March 1995 PrepCom Meeting (Mobilisation for Beijing, Summer 1995: 3) prompted not only government officials, with the aid of researchers, to explore this issue in greater depth and prepare an official line for use at the conference but also Chinese women to hold seminars on human rights abuses in China, a subject which is considered highly sensitive.[12] Indeed, the conference underlined the need for developing a core of gender researchers and in 1997 the State Council gave the go-ahead to Beijing University to accept doctoral students to research gender issues (Zheng 1997: 6).

Knowledge and constraints The depth of all this exposure, however, depended initially at least on the quality of translation. Indeed, the conference served to introduce new concepts and terminology. For example, there is no exact translation of 'gender' in Chinese. Hence UN pressure to provide disaggregated data on gender met initially with some resistance from the China Statistical Bureau which was reluctant to acknowledge gender as a socially constructed category. Similarly, the concept of 'empowerment' cannot be easily translated in Chinese.[13]

Through the NGO Forum, ACWF participants encountered a multitude of different NGOs, an important event given the rarity of such organisations in China. With little experience of NGOs, either domestic or foreign, the ACWF must have initially been surprised by the scale of the NGO Forum, the recognition awarded such organisations by the UN and the implicit importance of these groups. The encounter with activists from different countries, both in workshops and in less formal settings, exposed ACWF cadres to the multiplicity and diversity of groups and activities, the diverse styles of discussion and imaginative ways of involving members and taking up issues. All this would have added considerably to the body of knowledge about NGOs within the ACWF and provided much food for thought. To give but one small example, a cadre from a provincial branch of the Women's Federation in southern China related to me how inspired she had felt by the vibrancy and energy of the voluntary groups she met during a preparatory meeting in the Philippines.

By calling itself an NGO, the ACWF was indeed able to enhance its legitimacy as a representative of Chinese women's interests in the international arena, and in particular at the NGO Forum. For example, in a brochure included in a package for NGO delegates, the ACWF describes itself as follows: 'The All-China Women's Federation is China's largest non-governmental organisation to represent and safeguard the rights and interests of women' (ACWF 1995). Indeed, the process of adopting the term 'NGO' reflected not only the foreignness of the concept[14] but also the ACWF's own struggle with its identity. By taking on this new terminology the ACWF's intention was more to lubricate international exchange than to make a political statement about its degree of autonomy from the party. Yet even after the conference ACWF officials I interviewed still expressed their lack of clarity about the referents of the concept 'NGO'.[15]

Such expediency, however, could backfire, particularly given the context of soul-searching within the ACWF already described. The risk is that this terminology becomes part of the self-consciousness of the organisation. This would then sharpen the contradiction between the actual governmental character of the organisation and its acclaimed non-governmental nature, so creating a discursive opening for demands for greater autonomy.

The juxtaposition of gender and party interests was both an inhibiting factor and a stimulus to ACWF cadres reassessing the relationship of the organisation to their political guardian. Already at the Seventh Congress in 1993 it was clear that the conference was to be used to propagate the successes of reform. Given the importance of the conference in bolstering the international position of China, ACWF participants were made aware through preparatory sessions that they should propagate a positive image of the achievements of the CCP in liberating women. Delegates were briefed, for example, on how to respond to awkward questions posed by foreign participants arising from the controversial BBC film on female orphans[16] or on how to deal with questions on Tibet. It would have been very risky indeed for any delegate to speak out on a controversial issue in a way that questioned CCP policy. It should not be overlooked, however, that other governments, the United States to name but one, were also deeply implicated in using the conference for their own political ends, as indeed were some non-governmental organisations. Thus the conference provided a public occasion on which the dual objectives of the ACWF were juxtaposed and where its ultimate subordination to national goals was expected.

The compliant behaviour of the ACWF was displayed most visibly in the lack of open opposition from top ACWF leaders to the sudden decision to move the site of the NGO Forum from the Workers' Palace to the outlying resort in Huairou County. This is not to say that they agreed with the decision but that they did not dare to oppose it. The imminent death of Deng Xiaoping, potential demonstrations against rising unemployment as well as pro-democracy and pro-Tibet activities were but some of the factors informing the party's decision to change the venue. It is also likely that until this point leaders in the CCP had little awareness about the 'anti-' governmental nature of some NGOs. Indeed, it was probably Li Peng's encounter with the advocacy and protest roles of NGOs at the spring 1995 Social Summit in Copenhagen that provoked this unexpected switch of the NGO Forum venue.[17] With the Forum located a good 50 kilometres outside Beijing and a tight security system in place, the CCP managed not only to dampen the lobbying impact of the NGO conference but also to minimise the contact between overseas participants and un-invited Chinese women and organisations. The decision, though, also fuelled an international outcry and exposed the weak position of the ACWF. Thus the continuing subordination of the ACWF to the CCP, which was rehearsed on numerous occasions in the run-up to and during the conference, served to lessen the potential impact of the conference on the organisation but at the same time crudely highlighted the ongoing dilemma within the organisation.

While we have identified several ways in which the conference has contributed and is likely in the future to contribute towards the process of change within the ACWF, we should also recognise some important constraints which in the end limit the potential influence. With regard to the impact of the actual conference, language was perhaps the most obvious constraint, particularly when rapid exchanges in workshops assume a high degree of linguistic competence. The outlook of individual participants and their willingness to absorb new ideas are also important factors influencing how much of what took place is taken in, worked upon and critically digested. Media coverage of the preparatory meetings and the conference itself is clearly an important element determining what messages are transmitted. Given that the official conference received more treatment than the NGO Forum in Chinese newspapers, radio and TV, and that reports on the latter focused on the success of the organisational aspects rather than the content of workshops, it is likely that most women and men in China had little idea about the key debates, axes of opinion or the difference between the two events.

Conclusion

In this paper we have explored the ACWF's attempts to redefine its relationship with the CCP. The changing needs of women in the context of rapid socio-economic transformation, the emergence of new, more autonomous women's organisations and the Fourth World Conference on the Status of Women have combined to stimulate a process of redefinition with regard to the ACWF's relationship with the party and its members.

In seeking a more independent position from the CCP the ACWF will be constrained on the one hand by the party's need to retain control over a crucial organic component of its institutional corpus and on the other hand by its own desire to reap the advantages of a greater proximity to the centre of power than a more autonomous position might permit. However, the party-state's concern to reduce expenditure and so squeeze further the limited coffers of the ACWF coupled with its recognition of the usefulness of the new social organisations as channels of mediation and interest articulation could make for a looser relationship with its appended mass organisations.

Whether or not the ACWF is able to achieve a more independent position, particularly as it increases its own sources of funding, the question still remains as to what degree of autonomy would actually be desirable. If the ACWF continues to identify closely with the party, then it might meet a similar fate to official women's organisations in the former Soviet Union. On the other hand, if the ACWF were to sever its links with the CCP, there is the danger not only that it would not be able financially to sustain its staff, buildings and activities, but also that it would have less access to policy-making processes than it currently enjoys. The question would then be whether a pluralised, fragmented women's movement in China could more effectively promote women's interests than a strong, government-sponsored organisation with contradictory objectives, encircled by small, activist, satellite women's groups. Given the uncertainty of the trajectory of political events in China and the fate of women's organisations in the former Soviet Union and Eastern Europe, it is essential that the ACWF and women's organisations collaborate on contingency plans for the future pursual of gender interests.

Notes

1. For example, there was a debate in the early and mid-1990s among development agencies in the UK about the relative merits of mainstreaming gender (Jahan 1995).

2. The Special Economic Zones (SEZs) were set up in 1979 in China for a variety of reasons. Like export-processing zones in other Asian countries, the SEZs were supposed to attract foreign investment and technology by providing various tax and other concessions. However, they also provided a laboratory for experimenting with domestic economic reforms as well as with the much broader policy of opening up to foreign investment and trade. Should these not prove successful, then any negative impact would in theory be limited to the SEZs, thus minimising any potentially destabilising consequences. Politically they were part of a longer-term strategy for the reunification of China with Hong Kong, Macao and Taiwan.

3. For further details, see Honig and Hershatter (1988) and Woo (1994).

4. For more details of these organisations see Howell (1994a, 1994b, 1995).

5. For more details of these see Howell (1996: 137).

6. All social organisations have to have a '*guakao danwei*,' that is a superior unit to which they are attached.

7. For an interesting account of one of the discussions there see Wang Yongchen, '"Ladies First" in China', in Wang Yongchen, (1995: 8–18).

8. For a discussion of the different understandings of women's studies in China see Ding Juan (1993). On the history of women's studies in the reform era see also Wan Shanping (1988).

9. See, for example, Wang Yongchen (1995), a collection of articles commenting on

Chinese women's impressions of the preparatory meetings. See also Wei Yu (1995) and Qi Wenying (1995).

10. See Howell (1996: 133) for further discussion of this.

11. This section is drawn from a more detailed analysis of the impact of the conference on women's organisations in China (see Howell 1997).

12. For further details see *Beijing Forum, UK Newsletter*, no. 5, November 1995, p. 2.

13. See Qi (1997: 13) for a further discussion of this.

14. It should be noted that translating the term NGO is also problematic. Using the negative '*wu*' would yield a term which is akin to anarchism ('*wu zhengfu zhuyi*'). Similarly, using the prefix of '*fan*' (anti-) would also lead to an undesirable translation for the government. The prefix of '*fei*' which is currently used has no such connotations but also does not signify a distinct referent in China. I am grateful to an anonymous Chinese interviewee for pointing out these nuances to me.

15. Interview with ACWF, Beijing, October 1995 and 1997. Similar confusion has also surfaced in interviews with the ACFTU. Given the broad and loose usage of the term in the English language it is not surprising that its empirical definition and translation is no easy affair.

16. Here we refer to the film 'The Dying Rooms' made by Stephen Mosher et al.

17. It is interesting to note that China was the only member-state to abstain on a resolution to inform relevant NGOs about the reasons for non-accreditation (see *Beijing Forum UK Newsletter*, no. 2, issue 2, 17 April 1995). Some of the non-accredited NGOs included Chinese women's groups (personal communication).

Bibliography

ACWF (1995) *National Organs Safeguarding the Rights and Interests of Women*, China Intercontinental Press.

Andors, P. (1983) *The Unfinished Liberation of Chinese Women, 1949–80*, Bloomington, IN, and Sussex: Indiana University Press and Harvester Wheatsheaf.

Davin, D. (1976) *Woman-Work: Women and the Party in Revolutionary China*, Oxford: Clarendon Press.

Ding Juan, (1993) 'Present State of Research in China's System of Women's Studies', *Chinese Education and Society*, vol. 26, part 4, pp. 85–98.

Dou Lian Feng (1994) 'We Need to Resolutely Promote the Rights and Dignity of Women Workers' (*bixu jianjue tuihu nugong de quanyi he zunyan*), in *Zhongguo Funu*, no. 2, pp. 4–5.

Goetz, A.M. (1992) 'Gender and Administration', *IDS Bulletin*, vol. 23, no. 4, pp. 6–17.

Honig, E. and G. Hershatter (1988) *Personal Voices: Chinese Women in the 1980s*, Stanford, CA: Stanford University Press.

Howell, J. (1994a) 'Refashioning State–Society Relations in China', *European Journal of Development Research*, vol. 6, no. 1, June, pp. 197–215.

— (1994b) 'Striking a New Balance: New Social Organisations in post-Mao China', *Capital and Class*, no. 54, pp. 89–112.

— (1995) 'Prospects for NGOs in China', *Development and Practice*, pp. 5–15.

— (1996) 'The Struggle for Survival: Prospects for the Women's Federation in Post-Mao China', *World Development*, vol. 24, no. 1, pp. 129–43.

— (1997) 'Post-Beijing Reflections: Creating Ripples but not Waves', *Women's Studies International Forum*, March–April, vol. 20, no. 2, pp. 235–52.

Jahan, R. (1995) *The Elusive Agenda: Mainstreaming Women in Development*, London: Zed Books.

Jiang Yongping and Zhang Yanxia (1997) 'The Survival and Development of Women Workers in Non Public-owned enterprises', *Funu Yanjiu Luncong*, no. 3, issue 23, pp. 21–7.

Johnson, K. (1983) *Women, the Family and Peasant Revolution in China*, London: University of Chicago Press.

Kabeer, N. (1994) *Reversed Realities: Gender Hierarchies in Development Thought*, London: Verso.

Li Xiaojiang and Zhang Xiaodan (1994) 'Creating a Space for Women: Women's Studies in China in the 1980s', *Signs*, vol. 20, no. 1, pp. 137–51.

Ma Lizhen and Ji Xiaocun (1990) 'Report about Work Conference on Training Women Cadres for Selection and Promotion', *Zhongguo Funu*, October 1990, pp. 11–13 (in Chinese).

Ma Xiuju (1995) 'Conditions and Preparations for China's Hosting of the World Conference', *Renmin Ribao*, 12 August, p. 4 (in Chinese).

Moser, C. (1993) *Gender Planning and Development: Theory, Practice and Training*, London and New York: Routledge.

Ostergaard, L. (1992) *Gender and Development: A Practical Guide*, London: Routledge.

Qi Wenying (1997) 'Strengthen International Research on Women', *Funu Yanjiu Luncong*, no. 3, issue 23, pp. 11–13.

Qi Wenying (ed.) (1995) *Women's Studies in China: A Selected Bibliography and Resource Guide, From Ancient Times to the Present* (in Chinese), Beijing: Beijing University Press.

Staudt, K. (ed.) (1990) *Women, International Development and Politics. The Bureaucratic Mire*, Philadelphia, PA: Temple University Press.

Stetson, D. and A. Mazur (eds) (1995) *Comparative State Feminism*, London: Sage.

Wan Shanping, (1988) 'The Emergence of Women's Studies in China', *Women's Studies International Forum*, vol. 11, part 5, pp. 455–64.

Wang Jian Jian (1989) 'A Spring Wind Blows - Report of Reforms in Work of Shanxi Province Women's Federation', *Zhongguo Funu*, May 1989, pp. 28–9 (in Chinese).

Wang Qi (1988) 'Three Hot Movements at the 6th Annual Congress of the ACWF', *Zhongguo Funu*, November 1988, pp. 8–10.

Wang Yi, Zhu Ying and Sun Qi (1991) 'Reflections on Participation of Basic-level Women's Federations in Political Organs of Suzhou City', *Zhongguo Funu*, January, pp. 20–1.

Wang Yongchen (ed.) (1995) *Voices of Women*, Hainan Publishing House.

Wei Yu (1995) *Women's Education in China*, Beijing: Higher Education Press.

Woo, M. Y. K. (1994) 'Chinese Women Workers: The Delicate Balance between Production and Equality', in C. K. Gilmartin, G. Hershatter, L. Rofel and T. White (eds), *Engendering China: Women, Culture and the State*, Cambridge, MA: Harvard University Press, pp. 279–98.

Wu Ying Zeng, Chen Xiao Lu and Bia Nan Feng (1988) 'Summary of a Forum on the

Reform of the ACWF: Comments by Wu Ying Zeng, Chen Xiao Lu, Bia Nan Feng', *Zhongguo Funu*, February, pp. 22–4.

Yang Xinnan (1988) 'Companies Give Cash Incentives to Support Mothers on Their Payrolls', *Women of China*, no. 12, December, pp. 21–3.

Zheng Bijun (1997) 'Follow-up Action and Theoretical Perspective', *Funu Yanjiu Luncong*, no. 3, issue 23, pp. 4–6.

8

Tackling Violence against Women in Brazil: Converting International Principles into Effective Local Policy

Fiona Macaulay

Violence against women is a topic which has only relatively recently received attention in international arenas such as the United Nations (UN). Both domestic violence and sexual assault, only two of the possible forms of violence perpetrated against women worldwide, had been regarded as off-limits for the application of the universalist and normative principles of human rights instruments that followed the Universal Declaration of Human Rights in 1948. Indeed, violence against women was always seen and understood *in context* as an integral part of a society's social, religious and cultural fabric. This contextualisation, most often locating gender violence in the private sphere which further removed it from scrutiny, has only in the last fifteen years been replaced with a new set of international statements firmly condemning violence against women under any circumstances.

In that same period many countries in Latin America began a transition from authoritarian rule to democratic government. Women very often took the lead in grass-roots opposition to the military regimes, embarrassing them domestically and internationally about their human rights record, demanding the minimum means for subsistence and survival in a time of hyperinflation and economic chaos, and making a number of specifically feminist demands (Jaquette 1994). In Chile, for example, the women's movement slogan *¡Democracia en el país y en la casa!* (Democracy in the country and at home!) explicitly linked the experience of authoritarian rule to that of male power and dominance in the home, thus making the personal political. In the transition period, the newly elected democratic governments installed in the region in the late 1980s and 1990s were keen to prove themselves committed players in the international field and to demonstrate their real commitment to the social issues over which members of the new administrations had so harshly criticised the previous military regimes. Conscious of women's leading role in the democratic opposition to military rule, they were also concerned to attract electoral support from women and other 'new' social sectors. Brazil, Chile, Argentina and other countries quickly committed themselves to a number of international human rights instruments, and to trade and co-operation agreements as a form of insurance against future potential violent regime reversals, and as a means of integrating themselves into an international system of democratic norms, values and practices (Whitehead 1996). Among these was the 1979 United Nations Convention for the Elimination of all Forms of Discrimination Against Women (CEDAW). The ground was therefore ripe in many ways for women activists in each country to press their governments to make a reality out of one of their paper commitments to women, and to take concrete action to combat violence against women.

Brazil was one of the first countries in the region to do so, and has also played a key role in regional and international forums, such as the Inter-American Women's Commission and the Beijing Conference, in supporting international policy recommendations on gender equality. The first civilian government took power in 1985 after twenty years of military rule. The Partido do Movimento Democrático Brasileiro (PMDB) had been the 'official' anti-military party and was dominant in the transition to democracy. In this situation, the Brazilian women's movement was able to exert some leverage and the PMDB instituted a number of policies for women, most notably the women's police stations (Alvarez 1990). These were the first in the region and were hailed as an innovation. Now most countries in Latin America have something similar; for example, by 1997, Nicaragua had women's police stations in nine cities and Chile has various specialised stations for sexual assault, protection of children and the family as well as domestic violence against women. Brazil is therefore a country which has attracted regional and international attention for its policies on violence against women and where domestic political actors have shown considerable will to address the problem. However, Brazil's capacity to introduce effective integrated measures is still severely limited by a number of structural and resource constraints. Ratifying an international convention is one thing; turning those principles into day-to-day practice in social policy and in the criminal justice system is quite another. The United Nations Special Rapporteur on Violence Against Women highlights in her report on Brazil 'the general failure of the Brazilian criminal justice system to investigate and prosecute in a non-discriminatory manner crimes of domestic violence against women'. This failure points to the complex and contradictory process of attempting to use legislation and social policy to eliminate violence against women in a political and administrative system such as Brazil's. This contradiction brought her to choose Brazil for her first full country study in July 1996, 'because available data indicate a high prevalence of such violence in the country, but also because of the many existing programmes and activities, both governmental and non-governmental, to combat and prevent such violence' (ECOSOC 1997: 2).

This chapter is concerned with that contradiction, and specifically with the policy implementation gap between the broad principles and declarations made at international level about the importance of combating violence against women, and the reality of attempting to enact such policies on the ground. The chapter begins by tracing the evolution of discourses and declarations on violence against women in international arenas. It then outlines some of the common challenges faced by Latin American countries in putting into practice those principles. Finally, it looks at the specifics of Brazil's experiences, outlines the advances which have been made, and identifies the structural limitations to those gains as well as the opportunities which made them possible.

Evolving International Discourses

The last decade has seen a sea-change within international development and human rights regimes in relation to women's rights and the issue of violence against women (Amnesty International 1995; Kerr 1993; Peters and Wolper 1995). However, the progress made, for example, in the series of UN women's conferences would not have been possible without the tireless backstage work of women's movements which have lobbied governments, held local and regional conferences and drafted the resolutions that have resulted in the current international statements on gender violence. These local and international women activists form part of what has been variously termed an 'international principled-issue network', an international civil society or an international policy network.[1] These networks are vital for sharing information, comparing experiences, passing on good practice and advising on traps and pitfalls to avoid in formulating policy, and on negotiating with decision-makers.

Although the United Nations General Assembly adopted the landmark CEDAW in 1979, it was not until the 1990s that violence against women was placed at the centre of debates on human rights, women's rights and development. Prior to that, the focus was on discrimination, especially with respect to employment, civil, political and economic rights. A concern with violence against women within the private sphere was considered an agenda item pushed by Western feminists, a form of cultural imperialism, and interference in tradition and custom. It was deemed irrelevant to the 'real' concerns of women in developing countries, i.e. poverty and lack of access to basic services.

Although the Nairobi Forward-Looking Strategies adopted in 1985 attempted to address this deficiency by referring to 'gender-specific violence' under the section 'Abused Women' (United Nations 1993: 70, para 288), this still constituted little more than a footnote in the eighty-eight page document. The turning-point came only with the United Nations World Conference on Human Rights (the Vienna Conference) of June 1993. This affirmed explicitly that women's rights are human rights; inclusion in this form in a major declaration moved gender concerns from the arena of development, where policy recommendations are non-binding, into the field of international standards, where the UN's bodies and complaints mechanisms carry more clout with governments. The Vienna Declaration thus opened the door to a much freer debate about gender-specific concerns such as reproductive rights and domestic violence, as well as about customary practices such as female genital mutilation. Moreover, the text stressed the importance of working towards the elimination of violence against women in public and private life and extended state accountability for violence against women to the private sphere of the family and the community, previously a taboo area.

Six months after the Vienna Conference, the UN adopted its most comprehensive statement to date, the Declaration on the Elimination of Violence Against Women which defines the loci of violence as: in the family and home; in the community; at the hands of the agents of the state. This is the strongest rejection of cultural relativist arguments and points up the area of state negligence, as opposed to direct responsibility. It notes that states are *obliged* to exercise 'due diligence' in preventing all acts of violence against women.

Latin America was the first region in the world to co-ordinate and produce its own regional equivalent to the UN declaration. The provisions of the Organisation of American States' own Inter-American Convention for the Prevention, Punishment and Eradication of Violence Against Women actually surpass the UN's. Brazil was particularly active in promoting what is known as the Belem do Pará Convention, adopted on 6 June 1994. The site of domestic violence is defined much more widely to encompass any domestic unit or inter-personal relationship in which the aggressor may have shared the same home as the victim. It emphasises legal reform and the importance of women's access to simple, rapid recourse through the courts. States are urged to set up fair and efficient legal procedures which offer women effective protection and a prompt hearing. It thus takes into account the structural, institutional and public policy dimensions of effectively combating violence against women. Moreover, it also provides an individual right of petition and for non-governmental organisations to lodge complaints with the inter-American Commission of

Human Rights if the state party fails in its obligations. This is particularly important in empowering local women's groups to seek recourse in the face of inaction by their own government and acknowledges the crucial role of women's organisations across the continent.

The 1995 Beijing Platform for Action notes that violence against women is an 'obstacle to equality, development and peace'. In this way it echoes the arguments of a growing body of research within the international development community on the high social, health and economic costs of such violence to the individual and the community (Heise et al. 1994a, 1994b). While the human rights arguments have depended on the principles of universality and the inalienable character of women's rights, the developmental arguments depend on the economistic, cost-benefit, pragmatic logic of international development and financial institutions, in which the consequences and costs of this kind of violence (e.g. health-care, loss of earnings, family breakdown) are characterised as an unnecessary strain on scarce resources. As we shall see, it has been easier for the Brazilian women's movement to persuade the government to sign up to abstract human rights principles, and receive international plaudits, than to tackle a tangible development issue, such as violence, which requires the government to divert resources and modify institutional structures, especially when the domestic budget for social spending is inadequate.

Gender Policy in Latin America

Over the last decade most countries in Latin America have made considerable progress in public policy on gender equality and on violence against women. All have ratified the CEDAW and the national constitutions of around half now expressly prohibit discrimination on the basis of sex or make gender equality an explicit principle. Most are revising now outdated and discriminatory penal and civil codes, and family and labour law. Over the past two decades practically every government in the region has established channels for consultation with women's groups in addition to government machinery dedicated to the advancement of women's rights (Valdés 1995: 185), although the status, resources, political and social legitimacy, and institutional weight of these entities vary enormously. The 1990s in particular saw the formulation of broad, inter-sectoral social policy instruments aimed at ensuring equal opportunities for women, the leader in the field being Chile's Women's Equal Opportunity Plan 1994–2000, drawn up by the country's women's ministry (Servicio Nacional de la Mujer – SERNAM). Many of the legislative, policy and constitutional changes have been brought about by the activities of local, national and regional gender-focused policy networks, which form part of the international principled-issue network mentioned above. For example, 25 November has been established as the Day of Action for No More Violence Against Women in Latin America through the work of such a regional network.

Policy-makers concerned with violence against women have had to confront a number of common issues, although each country has undertaken a different mix of responses (Pimentel 1993). Violence against women in the region is widespread, cuts across social classes and is certainly related to cultural constructions of gender-role identities, for example the notion of *machismo*, that is, a model of exaggerated masculinity prevalent in the continent. Thus, a nationwide survey in Chile in 1992 revealed that one in five women suffered violence at the hands of her partner (Valdés 1995: 191). Identifying the exact scale and location of the problem is more complex; local studies and samples of the problem are available, but there are few reliable national figures or comparative data, due to the common problems of under-reporting and deficiencies in police record-keeping. In most countries, violence against women and sexual assault are typified in law as crimes against morality, social convention and the honour of the family, rather than as crimes against the personal physical integrity and human rights of the woman victim. All penal codes, with the exception of revolutionary Nicaragua and Cuba, still consider the honesty, honour and good name of the woman to be relevant to the characterisation of certain sexual crimes and to determine their punishment. In Peru, as in other countries, a rapist who marries his victim may have charges dropped or a decreased sentence. No penal code classifies rape in marriage as a crime. Several countries have now modified their legislation to eliminate such discriminating laws and provisions from the statute books.

Most measures adopted have been aimed at caring for female victims of assault, for example shelters, telephone services, legal and psychological support. Some preventive community action has been taken, generally carried out by non-governmental organisations (NGOs) alone or in collaboration with government agencies, and consists either of police training, or of raising awareness of women's rights, particularly among low-income women. Special police stations to deal with domestic violence have been set up in several countries, following Brazil's example, and a number of countries have created Women's Defence Councils or Public Defenders for the Family (specialised public prosecutors) (Valdés 1995: 192) The main deficiencies in policy are predictable. There is still a lack of practical support for victims of domestic violence, either to get the abuser removed from the family home or to move the victim into safe accommodation, and provide her and her family with an income. Criminal prosecutions, even when initiated, fail not just due to the peculiar features of domestic violence and sexual assault as crimes, but also due to defects in the judicial system.

All resources are allocated predominantly in the urban areas, leaving virtually nil provision for rural women.

Social Policy and Violence Against Women in Brazil

After twenty years of military rule, Brazil had to construct a democracy (Macaulay 1998: 88). It has a federal system of government, which determines that every tier of government – national, state and municipal – should formulate its own constitution, with the lower tiers subject of course to the higher-level charters. The Brazilian municipalities are among the most autonomous local governments in the world (Macaulay 1998: 95). Many of the practical aspects of implementing most social policies lie within the remit of the twenty-six state governments and the federal district. The penal code and other legal codes are national in reach, while laws passed in the national congress and the federal constitution are considered binding across the country. However, individual states organise their own police and court system, two key elements in the criminal justice system which form an important part of the equation in tackling gender violence. There are therefore a number of policy implementation gaps, which will be discussed below.

Brazil was cited in the 1990s by the human rights group, Americas Watch, as having the highest rate of violence against women in the region (Americas Watch 1991:3). Such an assertion must, however, be treated with a degree of caution, given the paucity and patchiness of data overall, and the different methodologies employed in each country's surveys. It may be that the presence of women's police stations in Brazil prompts a higher level of reporting than elsewhere, although it is certain that the incidents recorded in those police stations represent only the tip of an iceberg. There are no nationally collated data either on murder of women, generally by partners or ex-partners, or on domestic assaults and sexual violence. It has generally fallen to feminist researchers to trawl painstakingly through thousands of police records in order to consolidate data even at state level. In Rio de Janeiro, between 1991 and 1996, 104,182 assaults on women were reported, at ordinary and special women's police stations (Cadernos CEPIA 1995).[2] In 1995 the heads of police stations in São Paulo recorded 130,000 cases of violence against women (ECOSOC 1997: 6). A survey carried out by the Inter-American Parliamentary Group on Population and Development found that 205,219 reports of gender violence had been registered at women's police stations around the country, of which 26 per cent were assaults, 16 per cent threats and 51 per cent sexual offences (United Nations and Ministry of Justice 1998: 34–6). In Rio de Janeiro, 5,098 reports of domestic violence are made a month (*Veja*:

1998: 81). All these figures do is give a blurred snapshot of a partially obscured phenomenon. Lack of hard data is the most fundamental obstacle to designing good, targeted, appropriate policy. As a result, many of the policy initiatives described below cannot fully serve the needs of women victims, and are necessarily proximate and ad hoc measures. Although the costs of domestic violence are very high, certainly higher than that of setting up programmes of prevention and assistance to victims, this has not yet resulted in a commensurate investment in preventive action. The Inter-American Development Bank estimates that domestic violence affects between 25 and 50 per cent of women in the region, and causes a loss of 14.2 per cent of GDP (US\$ 168 billion) per annum in Latin America, and 10.5 per cent of GDP (US\$ 84 billion) in Brazil, taking into account working days lost, the burden on the public health service, and the stress imposed on families (Ministry of Justice et al. 1996).

Domestic and sexual violence was first highlighted in Brazil by women's groups in the 1970s, initially in response to a number of high-profile murders of middle-class women by their husbands. The men were usually acquitted, having argued that they killed 'to preserve their honour'. Legally, no such defence is available, but in practice it was used by defence lawyers, accepted by juries and unchallenged by presiding judges (Americas Watch 1991).[3] It was, however, the advent of a democratic government that gave the women's movement hope of greater institutional influence (Cadernos CEPIA 1994). In 1985 the National Council for Women's Rights (Conselho Nacional dos Direitos da Mulher – CNDM) was set up, a national advisory body attached to the Ministry of Justice. Staffed by feminists, the CNDM was key in mobilising women in the drafting of the 1988 constitution which, perhaps uniquely in Latin America, contains a provision on domestic violence as well as a number of other progressive guarantees of women's rights. An intense publicity campaign to raise awareness and sway politi-cians' opinions resulted in article 226 (para 8) of the constitution which provides that: 'The State shall guarantee assistance to the family, as represented by each one of the persons that makes up that family, by creating mechanisms to deter violence in the framework of the relationships among those family members.' In the same year, the CNDM's equivalent in São Paulo state, the newly established CECF (Conselho Estadual da Condição Feminina), used its influence with the new centrist and democratic government of the state to get the first women's police stations set up. At the instigation of a number of feminist federal deputies, Brazil's national Congress set up a parliamentary committee of inquiry into gender violence from January 1991 to August 1992, followed by another on the abuse of children (Câmara dos Deputados 1993).

However, in the early 1990s, national initiatives became less important.

Shortly after the approval of the constitution, the CNDM was left severely weakened by attempts at political colonisation of the organisation. It lost its staff, budget and direction, and thus the bulk of initiatives on violence against women were initiated from the regions and cities, not from the capital. It was only in the latter half of the first government of President Fernando Henrique Cardoso (1994–98) that they recovered sufficiently to produce a comprehensive equality programme (CNDM 1997), in which was included a chapter on violence against women.[4] This has subsequently been amplified in two joint actions with the United Nations, the national campaign 'A Life Without Violence is our Right', and the 'Community Pact against Domestic Violence', which is intended to create partnerships between the state, the UN and human rights groups (United Nations and Ministry of Justice 1998).[5]

The federal government's remit is chiefly that of legislating, allocating funds, drawing up national strategy and encouraging linkages between the United Nations on the one hand, and local authorities on the other. Brazil still lacks comprehensive legislation typifying domestic violence as such as a crime, although several bills are currently pending.[6] Nor has it allocated the necessary resources to the problem. Since the mid-1990s women's groups have lobbied parliamentarians to revise the penal code to make specific reference to domestic violence. The continuing lack of a law means that the special circumstances of this sort of violence cannot be taken into account by courts, nor are there specially tailored measures available. Domestic violence cases are not recorded as such in police and court files. This draft legislation contains a new definition of what is termed 'family violence', drawing on the UN declaration and the Belém do Pará Convention. The bill also provides for the establishment of shelters for women victims of violence and programmes to rehabilitate the perpetrators. Other bills would reform the penal code to make violence against women a crime against the person, and not against the woman's honour as a collective good, and would criminalise sexual harassment.

These bills have much in common with current initiatives across the region. What differs, however, is the set of institutional opportunities or obstacles confronting women in each country. Brazil is remarkable first for the degree of collaboration between women deputies in a cross-party women's caucus, which enables them to act in concert on these bills, and which has compensated for the institutional weakness of the CNDM, still deprived of adequate staff or resources. Women representatives in turn are the natural allies of a unique feminist lobbying group, CFEMEA, which carefully tracks the progress of all gender-related legislation (Macaulay 1999). The formulation of these bills also depended crucially on the input of national and international members of the feminist policy network.[7]

Following the Beijing conference, specialist groups were formed among the Brazilian feminist and women's activist network, aimed at creating intensive lobbies in order to put legislative and policy flesh to the commitments made at the conference. One such group focuses on violence against women and reforms to the penal code. However, duplication of efforts in this area slowed their progress in Congress. By 1996, there were three bills in parliament on sexual harassment, three on rape, one on sexual assault, and three on crimes against sexual freedom. Now that the executive branch, at the urging of a reinvigorated CNDM, has submitted these same bills, but in unified form, they stand a much better chance of being passed.

Inevitably, expressions of political will are rarely backed up with the necessary commitments, so feminist networks and legislators had to mobilise to ensure a specific allocation of the federal budget for such projects. In 1996, women successfully lobbied Congress to approve around US$ 3 million from the Ministry of Justice's budget to be spent on projects for women's rights, of which the bulk would go to set up twenty-seven shelters for women escaping domestic violence.[8] However, constant monitoring and lobbying is still required to ensure the money is not diverted. As this laborious lobbying process would have to be repeated annually, tactics in 1997 changed and a permanent budget line on violence against women was established under the control of the revitalised CNDM. In 1997 approximately US$ 1.75 million was allocated.

As noted above, women's movements have struggled to get national policy to reflect the recommendations of international instruments on violence against women. Between the federal and sub-national layers of government (state and municipal) there is an even greater gap. For example, for a constitutional provision to become legally binding, it requires complementary legislation, otherwise it remains a dead letter. The long delay in transforming Constitutional Article 226 into a concrete commitment by the government with guidelines and budget allocation meant women activists had to look to their local authorities first for action. The national policy document which set out Brazil's most complete strategy to date for tackling violence against women (Ministry of Justice 1996) lists many policy initiatives which can be carried out only by state or municipal governments with the encouragement but not direct involvement of federal government. On the one hand, without specially allocated funds for violence against women projects, women are reliant on the political vagaries and commitment of state and municipal politicians. It also makes consistency of approach impossible. On the other hand, the sub-national spheres of government in Brazil enjoy considerable political and financial autonomy, which has permitted projects to be implemented first at these levels long before they are adopted by the federal government as a national model.

State and municipal government have structures and powers parallel to those of the federal government and this enables creative initiatives to be tried out without waiting for more sweeping national-level reforms, for example of the criminal justice system. Feminists in São Paulo state in 1991 decided to import and adapt to local needs the United Nations Convention on Women (CEDAW). The Paulista Convention, a statement of commitment to women's rights modelled closely on the CEDAW, was launched in 1992 with the support of eighty municipal authorities representing 60 per cent of the population of the state of São Paulo, who signed up to the convention, in the same way that states parties do to the CEDAW. Following the example of the 1988 federal constitution, most state governments and a number of municipal authorities have incorporated into the text of the state constitution or municipal bylaws (Lei Orgânica Municipal) a commitment to eradicating violence against women and declared the local authorities' obligation to create services for prevention and for assistance to victims of domestic violence, which is in any case a function which falls more naturally to sub-national levels of government. Thus the first concrete projects to help women victims of violence have been set up in the major capital cities of Brazil. One of the first initiatives to extend legal assistance to women victims of violence was the installation in 1984 of the Women's Legal Aid Centre (Centro de Orientação Jurídica e Encaminhamento da Mulher – COJE), linked to the São Paulo state Attorney General's office, followed by the inauguration of the first women's police station in São Paulo.

By the late 1980s, the PMDB's star was in decline, and that of the left-wing Workers' Party (Partido dos Trabalhadores – PT), electorally speaking, was rising, making them a more natural ally of the women's movement. In 1988, they won several important cities, and were able to put into practice their radical principles of participatory government, in which priorities and resources would be targeted at the neediest. Many women in the PT had long supported a feminist agenda, the party has an active women's secretariat whose recommendations on this area have increasingly been mainstreamed into the party's platform, and violence against women ranked high among their priorities. In the 1990s, the PT's elected representatives at all levels (municipal, state and federal government) have been the most active supporters of gender legislation and policy. As a result, women's refuges have mainly been set up under the aegis of the PT municipal administrations in the late 1980s and 1990s.[9] Under PT woman mayor Luisa Erundina, the bylaws of the city of São Paulo committed the city to financing programmes to assist women victims of violence: a shelter was established, and the city's public hospitals provided legal abortion to rape victims for the first time ever. Although the law permitting abortion under certain circumstances had been on the statutes since 1940, women were forced to go to private or backstreet abortionists.[10] Such bylaws and practice have since been adopted by other cities, and the state of Rio de Janeiro.[11] As of 1999, a bill was pending in the federal Congress which would establish in federal legislation the provision of abortion by the public health service. This last case highlights two peculiarities of the Brazilian state and the constraints and opportunities it imposes on enacting social policy. First, the federal system makes top-down application of initiatives very difficult because of the autonomy of the states and municipalities. On the other hand, it offers a space in which practical policy lessons are tested, then replicated, first at municipal, then state, then federal level, in a kind of *trickle-up* effect. This occurs in a second phase after the influence of normative values and principles established at international level has *trickled down*, to national, then sub-national levels. Second, the legal abortion issue illustrates the implementation gap between Brazilian domestic law and actual practice. In effect, women have had to find new institutional tools such as city bylaws, or regulatory legislation, which gives them *de facto* access to a right which was established *de jure* decades ago.

The above also highlights the reliance of the women's movement on the political will of its interlocutors in the centre-left political parties, first of the PMDB, then of the PT. In a 1994 competition conducted by the Ford Foundation and the Brazilian Institute for Municipal Administration (IBAM), all five prizes for 'best practice' in tackling violence against women went to PT administrations (IBAM 1995). Women in the party concur that violence against women is prioritised for a number of pragmatic reasons: these are discrete projects, funded by the municipality, with staff seconded from other administrative areas such as health or legal services. The refuge may be set up at one remove from the municipal authorities so that it may seek funds from other sources, such as international aid agencies. This in turn creates a feedback effect in which international donor recognition of the value of the project further legitimises the scheme among sometimes sceptical or indifferent local leaders. In one city, Rio Branco in the Western Amazon, with a long legacy of social movement activism, the PT mayor was initially resistant to the idea of setting up either a women's secretariat or any other special services for women. However, national and international attention fell on the town following press reports about trafficking in young women in the region, and he set up a centre to assist teenage prostitutes,[12] as well as a refuge for women of violence.

PT administrations have also gone one step further in prevention work and conducted awareness-raising programmes with municipal employees and local police. Two cities, Santo André and Porto Alegre, have also worked with women's groups in conceptualising the public space of the city as one which women occupy and on which they are entitled to make claims, not least to ensure their physical safety in the urban environment. This last ambitious approach reveals a more integrated strategy that goes beyond one-off initiatives such as shelters or police stations. A first step in this direction was taken in 1986 when a Support Centre for Victims of Domestic Violence (Centro de Convivência Para Mulheres Vítimas da Violência Doméstica – COMVIDA) opened as a pilot project in São Paulo, sponsored by the CECF and the state social welfare secretariat. Closed in 1989 at the whim of the government, it reopened at the insistence of women activists, this time in a more institutionalised form, via gubernatorial decree. It had a capacity to house and help fifty women for up to ninety days, supported by a working group composed of the CECF, Attorney General's office, and the state secretariats for justice, public security, employment and social welfare. By 1992 this working group had created a number of integrated centres for victims of violence around the state. In 1994 the PMDB state governor expanded this into a State Policy for the Prevention of Violence Against Women. The only other comparable experience of integrated policy has been in Porto Alegre, the capital city of Rio Grande do Sul state in the south of Brazil, governed since 1988 by three consecutive PT administrations. Local PT women lobbied for a refuge, finally proposed and approved in the municipal chamber, and now attached to the Secretariat for Health, which in turn liaises with the municipal housing offices. This allows women to escape temporarily from the violent situation, apply for rehousing and work, and to file a petition with the courts. The PT were elected to the state governorship in 1998, so it remains to be seen whether they can expand this integrated policy model throughout the state.

Violence against women can be dealt with through health-based approaches (violence as a violation of women's mental and physical well-being), legalistic approaches (violence as a criminal issue), or both. The NGO/feminist sector began by focusing on the former (e.g. shelters) but has lately turned its attention more to state reform of aspects of the criminal justice system (e.g. police stations). The Belém do Pará Convention, and the UN Special Rapporteur's Report, stress the importance now of legal reform, women's access to the courts, fair and efficient legal procedures, effective protection and a prompt hearing. Here Brazil faces serious institutional and structural blockages. Its criminal justice system, that is, the police, the courts and the legal apparatus, is chronically under-funded and understaffed. The courts have enormous backlogs and there are not yet sufficient civil remedies to combine with criminal sanctions, such as a fast-track system of special courts to deal with domestic violence.

The legal basis was put in place with the creation of Specialised Civil and Criminal Courts in 1995, but they do not yet deal with domestic violence. Without protection orders or court injunctions available, women either leave the site of abuse, risking losing their home, or are forced to return to an abusive situation, given the shortage of shelters. This tends to dissuade women from pressing charges: around half of victims do not (*Veja* 1988: 82). Brazil also has a very low prosecution rate: of 2,000 cases of sexual assault and domestic violence reported to a Rio de Janeiro women's police station in 1990, none resulted in punishment; of 4,000 cases reported in the north-eastern state of Maranhão, 300 went to court, resulting in two convictions (Americas Watch 1991). It is estimated that only 2 per cent of those convicted of domestic violence actually serve sentences (ECOSOC 1997: 7).

Brazil's experience with persuading the police to tackle violence against women has been mixed. There are over 250 women's police stations nation-wide, of which 130 are in São Paulo state, a distribution typical of the geographical skewing of services that characterises the Brazilian public sector. Rural and small towns are not served at all. Since their inception, a number of common criticisms have been made of their day-to-day functioning: the lack of training of personnel working in them; the un-reliability of the data collected; the restricted opening hours (only one functions twenty-four hours in São Paulo, although most assaults occur during the evenings and weekends); lack of infrastructure, of staff, and of police cars to attend to calls; and complaints that the attitude of staff was sometimes 'worse than in normal police stations'. Although the stations opened up new career paths to women police officers, they also became a ghetto. Women officers are often allocated unwillingly to the stations, which were seen as performing a soft social welfare function, not a policing role. The stations have no competence over murder or suicide cases. Of over two hundred women police chiefs, only one was promoted while still working in a women's police station. Moreover, the severe underprovision of legal and social services targeted at women to provide advice on social security, employment, child custody, maintenance and matters relating to family law, means that the stations are overburdened with inquiries of a non-police nature, which they are ill-equipped to answer. As positive legislation and constitutional norms accord women new rights and capacities, there is a clear need for legal literacy programmes and legal advice centres. As the police stations multiplied in São Paulo state, the state women's council was unable to monitor the stations, either by contributing to the training of staff, by maintaining the original mission of the stations, or by assessing their performance. The majority of cases of violence against women are also reported to normal police stations, underscoring the lack of specialised provision, the overall demand, and the need for training of police and all other actors in the criminal justice system. The police lack training in basic human and civil rights, much less in women's rights. All that notwith-standing, the women's police stations in certain areas have provided concrete assistance to women, in general where they collaborate closely with other services, such as health and housing, and liaise with the local women's movement via a municipal or state women's council. The women's police station in Brasilia is hailed as one of the best. It employs sixty-five women staff, divided between three detectives, nine desk officers, two psychologists and four shifts of seven police officers. It is well run, led by a senior woman detective committed to her work who had made a name in other areas of police work. A dedicated freephone line receives one hundred calls a day. The women's police stations clearly have great potential, but only in conjunction with political will and resources, liaison with the local women's movement, and close integration with *non*-police services and with the courts.

Conclusions

The range of public policy initiatives to combat violence against women put in place in Brazil since 1985 does not differ so much from other countries in the region – shelters, public awareness campaigns, changes in the penal code, new legislation and so forth – although the women's police stations were considered distinctively Brazilian at their inception. This chapter has shown how women activists in one Latin American country have attempted to convert international discourses on tackling gender violence into a tangible reality in their own country. The 1970s saw a struggle by the international women's movement to get gender violence on the international development and human rights agenda. Patient lobbying of national governments and careful strategising in international con-ferences and organisation gradually created an opening in the 1980s, then a tide of opinion, finally an international consensus in the 1990s. The women's movement now face a second phase of struggle, that of trans-forming these commitments into new laws, budget lines, training of police and judges and outreach to women victims of violence. Brazil has managed what it has due to a broad alliance of women's groups and individuals, both inside and outside government, since the mid-1980s that has been able to identify opportunities, first at national level, then at sub-national level. Lack of women's direct influence at the centre for several years was compensated for by the creativity of women, particularly of the left, in state and municipal governments. This dynamism yet lack of overall direc-tion is attested to in the UN Special Rapporteur's Report on Brazil, which notes of these local women activists and NGOs 'without their activism, none of the reforms that have taken place in Brazil over the last decade would have been possible' (ECOSOC 1997: 29).

The Brazilian women's movement has skilfully used new international discourses and instruments, and globalised principled-issue networks in pushing the national government and some local administrations into action. Many factors impinge on how principled commitment is translated into action: ideology, administrative structure, the organisational capacity of the women's movement, modification and application of legal norms, political parties as legislators and generators of public policy. Brazil illustrates the possibilities of local spaces as arenas for innovation, and responsiveness to local needs. It also demonstrates the constraints imposed by low state capacity, a tendency to respond to social demands with one-off ad hoc policies, and a general failure to think through strategies to deal with violence against women as an integrated social policy, rather than as isolated measures, however laudable in intent. Women need laws and constitutional provisions which enshrine their basic human rights, they need access to legal education, the police service, legal assistance, psycho-logical and social service back-up, and material resources to escape violence, for example women's refuges. The preconditions for an integrated approach have to be delivered at different levels, by different groups of actors. For example, legal changes have been made possible by sustained lobbying by an effective policy community of (mainly) women legislators, and feminist NGOs. The provision of training of police has, however, generally been delivered in a decentralised manner, at the instigation of the national, state-level or even local women's councils, with training conducted largely by NGOs. Awareness of violence has yet to be mainstreamed into the professional training of police, health and social workers. In Brazil the effective collapse of the CNDM in 1989 prevented national-level sectoral collaboration and shifted the locus of service delivery to municipalities and states.

Violence against women is, on the face of it, one of the easier aspects of gender discrimination for state authorities to tackle. The reformulation of this issue at international and regional levels as both a human rights and developmental problem has removed the controversy that still sur-rounds, say, reproductive issues. It can be approached through a variety of discourses ranging from the conservative to the radical, the instrumental to the principled; invoking, variously, women's rights, the strengthening of the family, protection of women and children, reduction of financial burdens on society, modernisation. Projects to combat violence against women are visible, non-controversial and attract external funding from international finance agencies. However, approaching the problem in an inter-sectoral manner and tackling the gendered apparatus of the state are much greater challenges. The women's police stations have had varied degrees of success, because of the failure to address wider, structural questions, such as the effectiveness and accessibility of the criminal justice system in Brazil. However, reform of the police and the courts will be a very long time coming. In short, the issues of domestic and sexual violence, now that they are understood as discrete and important issues, need to be mainstreamed in development planning, both at an international level, right down to the local level in order to close the current policy implementation gap, which still leaves millions of women with no real recourse to justice, to security of person or to a life free of violence.

Notes

1. The first term was coined by Sikkink in relation to human rights networks. The second and third derive from the field of international relations and political science. Sikkink defines an international principled-issue network as 'a set of organizations, bound together by shared values and by dense exchange of information and services, working internationally on an issue' (Sikkink 1993: 415).

2. The majority of these cases may be assumed to be domestic violence, although they are not recorded as such. See Cadernos CEPIA (1995) for a detailed account of the practical problems encountered in attempting to track domestic violence cases through a hugely bureaucratic, overburdened and inefficient criminal justice system.

3. In Brazil only homicide cases are tried by jury. However, research by Cadernos CEPIA (1995) revealed that the 'honour defence' is little used now, and only as a last resort.

4. The National Human Rights Programme launched in 1996 contained some of these recommendations, after women's groups had been consulted on the section on gender policy.

5. This is part of the Programme of Action to Combat Violence Against Women, involving all the agencies of the United Nations, to mark the fiftieth anniversary of the Universal Declaration of Human Rights.

6. Chamber of Deputies, bill no. 132 'Family Violence' presented by PT federal deputies Maria Laura and Marta Suplicy; bill no. 4.429 'Crimes Against Sexual Freedom' presented by the Parliamentary Committee of Inquiry into Violence Against Women.

7. For example, the International Women's and Rights Action Watch, the Latin American Committee for Women's Rights (CLADEM), the Latin American and Caribbean Network against Domestic Violence and CFEMEA.

8. The 'insider' lobbying was carried out by the Commission on Human Rights and the Consumer, Environment and Minorities Commission within the Ministry of Justice, and the feminist PT deputy, Ana Julia Carepa.

9. In Campinas, Diadema, Jacarei, Santo André, São Jose dos Campos, São Paulo, Porto Alegre, Belo Horizonte, Rio de Janeiro, Fortaleza and Rio Branco.

10. Paragraph II of article 128 of the penal code permits termination of pregnancy, performed by a doctor and with the woman's consent, in the case of rape or where the mother's life is in danger.

11. The close working relationship in the city of Campinas between the women's police station and University Hospital of Campinas means that women have access to speedy, legal terminations. In São Paulo, professionals in the health service and women's police stations drew up a '*procedimento padrão*', guidelines for getting women swiftly through the system

12. It has since widened its remit, and won one of the IBAM/Ford prizes.

Bibliography

Alvarez, S. E. (1990) *Engendering Democracy in Brazil: Women's Movements in Transition Politics*, Princeton, NJ: Princeton University Press.

Americas Watch (1991) *Criminal Injustice: Violence Against Women in Brazil*, New York: Human Rights Watch.

Amnesty International (1995) *Human Rights are Women's Right*, London: Amnesty International.

Cadernos CEPIA (1994) 'Violência contra a mulher a cidadania: Uma avaliação das políticas públicas', Rio de Janeiro: CEPIA.

— (1995) 'O judiciário e a violência contra a mulher: A ordem legal e a (des)ordem familiar', Rio de Janeiro: CEPIA.

Câmara dos Deputados (1993) *Comissão Parlamentar de Inquérito Destinada a Investigar a Questão da Violência Contra a Mulher: Relatório Final*, Diário do Congresso Nacional, Ano XLVIII Suplemento ao no. 202 14 December 1993, Brasília-DF: República Federativa do Brasil.

CNDM (Conselho Nacional dos Direitos da Mulher) (1997) *Estratégias da Igualdade*, Brasília: Ministry of Justice.

ECOSOC (United Nations Economic and Social Council) (1994) *Preliminary Report Submitted by the Special Rapporteur on violence against Women*, E/CN.4/1995/42, 22 November.

— (1997) *Report on the Mission of the Special Rapporteur to Brazil on the Issue of Domestic Violence 15–26 July 1996* E/CN.4/1997/47/Add.2, 21 January.

Fórum Nacional de Presidentas de Conselhos da Condição e Direitos da Mulher (1994) *Seminário Nacional: Violência contra a Mulher*, São Paulo: Documentos Fórum 2.

Heise, L. L., A Germaine and J. Pitanguy (1994a) *Violence Against Women: The Hidden Health Burden*, Washington, DC: World Bank.

(1994b) 'Violence Against Women: A Neglected Public Health Issue in Less Developed Countries', *Social Science and Medicine*, vol. 39. no. 9, pp. 1165–79.

IBAM (Instituto Brasileiro de Administração Municipal) (1995) *Primeira Mostra de Experiências Municipais sobre Defesa da Mulher contra a Violência*, Rio de Janeiro: IBAM.

Jaquette, J. (1994) *The Women's Movement in Latin America: Participation and Democracy*, Boulder, CO: Westview Press.

Kerr, J. (ed.) (1993) *Ours by Right: Women's Rights as Human Rights*, London: Zed Books.

Macaulay, F. (1998) 'Localities of Power: Gender, Parties and Democracy in Chile and Brazil', in H. Afshar (ed.), *Women and Empowerment: Illustrations from the Third World*, London: Macmillan.

— (1999) 'Getting Gender on the Policy Agenda: A Study of a Brazilian Feminist Lobby

Group', in E. Dore and M. Molyneux (eds), *The Hidden Histories of Gender and the State in Latin America*, Chapel Hill, NC: Duke University Press.

Ministry of Justice, National Human Rights Secretariat and National Council for Women's Rights (1996) *Programa Nacional de Prevenção e Combate a violência doméstica e sexual*, Brasília: Ministry of Justice.

Peters, J. and A. Wolper (eds) (1995) *Women's Rights, Human Rights: International Feminist Perspectives*, London: Routledge.

Pimentel, S. (1993) 'Special Challenges Confronting Latin American Women', in Kerr (ed.), *Ours by Right*.

Sikkink, K. (1993) 'Human Rights, Principled-issue Networks and Sovereignty in Latin America', *International Organization*, vol. 47, no. 3.

United Nations (1993) *The Nairobi Forward-Looking Strategies for the Advancement of Women*, New York: United Nations, Department of Public Information.

United Nations and Ministry of Justice (1998) *Uma vida sem violencia e um direito nosso: Propostas de ação contra a violência intrafamiliar no Brasil*, Brasilia: Ministry of Justice.

Valdés, T. (ed.) (1995) *Latin America Women: Compared Figures*, Santiago, Chile: Instituto de la Mujer-Spain, FLACSO.

Veja (magazine) (1998) 1 July, pp. 80–7.

Whitehead, L. (1996) *International Dimensions of Democratization: Europe and the Americas*, Oxford: Oxford University Press.

9

Gender, Community, Nation: The Myth of Innocence

Parita Mukta

Violent deeds perpetrated by women on men and women of the 'other' community, as well as on women in close familial relationships, appears to be a phenomenon which feminists find difficult to face at both a theoretical and programmatic level, raising as it does the question of women's complicity, agency and central positioning within processes and structures of violent configurations. In this context, it is valuable to discuss and highlight the analyses and works which have emanated from within Indian feminism in the past decade, whereby a sustained body of scholarship has arisen through which the authoritarian politics which have marked Indian society in this period are analysed with sufficient cognisance given to women's role in propping up and extending neo–fascist tendencies.[1] Some of the most extreme political violence has been visible in the demolition of the mosque in Ayadhya in 1992 (spearheaded by the Vishwa Hindu Parishad and the Bharatiya Janta Party) which was attended by calculated pogroms against Muslim citizens.

The broad context within which the rightist Bharatiya Janta Party (the BJP), together with the extra-constitutional bodies of the Vishwa Hindu Parishad (VHP) and the Rashtriya Swayam Sevak Sangh (RSS), have risen to capture a large section of the political ground, is the globalisation of capital, increased fractures in economic and social life, and the insatiability of democratic political parties to command a popular mandate. The BJP has held power for shorter or longer periods in the states of Uttar Pradesh, Rajasthan, Gujarat and Madhya Pradesh since 1990, and the March 1998 general elections saw this party form the government at the centre (albeit a minority one), which heralded itself as an aggressive regional (and world) power through exploding nuclear devices in Pokharan (Rajasthan) in May 1998.

The ways in which class, caste and religious identities have become embodied in contemporary India in distinctively gendered forms within the rise of the Hindu right require careful analysis. In particular, feminist scholarship emanating from India raises salient questions of women's embeddedness within aggressive and violent political movements aimed against the women and men of subordinate castes and the minority religious communities. This textured layer of writings has explored the history and politics of neo-fascist organisations, the centrality of sexual politics in the hate-filled propaganda of the Hindu right, and the visibility of upper-caste, urban women in movements against the minority Muslim communities. Here, feminist analyses have had to confront the spectre of the imprecation of upper-caste, middle-class women within processes of violent assertions that, in the contemporary period, have become especially visible in the Indian polity since 1984. This body of feminist scholarship attempts to face up to the question of women-as-perpetrators (rather than as victims) of violence. This chapter provides an overview of these events and asks two questions: how 'new' is this phenomenon? How adequate are existing analyses in facing up to the central issue of how a politicised feminist movement relates to and confronts women who preach and practise violence?

In my own research work which draws heavily on women's songs and oral communicative structures, I have been struck by the presence of narrative songs which provide graphic descriptions of the violence of older women in the family to in-coming daughters-in-law, leading to the death of the latter. These narrative songs are extremely popular among women of all social communities and groups, and are familiar to women over forty in the towns and villages of Gujarat and the Gujarat diaspora. This brings me to the starting point of this essay. Women who have not been organically tied to the ideologies and different forms of praxes which have emerged out of contemporary feminisms appear to have no illusions, and do not subscribe to the myth of women's innocence, and indeed take the brutality of a mother-in-law and a sister-in-law as a salient part of the social world. There exist not only well-recited songs of a mother-in-law killing a daughter-in-law, a daughter-in-law poisoned for daring to voice a slight complaint against a prestigious family within which she was married and so on, but a *common-sense* understanding that certain women are capable of inflicting/orchestrating a violent death on other women (in the family). While these songs (written down and compiled within various folk-lore materials from the 1920s onwards) (Meghani 1993: 80, 84, 152) point to an extended and shared cultural sphere within which some women were *recorded as antagonistic and brutal towards other women over whom they wielded authority in the domestic realm*, they are salient on what space (if any) women occupied in the public world of political violence. Much more systematic work needs to be done before one is able to ask hard questions of the historical record, but it appears to me important that these questions are raised so that in terms of both the past and the present, the issue of political responsibility is explored with a less innocent accounting of women's actions. This calls for more complicated explanations of 'patriarchal power', which wields force over all women while at the same time granting certain sections of women authority and privilege over other women and men.

I would argue that it is inadequate to analyse the phenomenon of violence-by-powerful-women-in-the-family within the grid of 'personal violence', for this depoliticises the act and reduces it to that of one motivated by strong personal feelings and personalities, outside the structures of domination and power. Rather, the violent act must be situated within the structure of power *between women* of the household, in the social dynamics between an older sister-in-law, a mother-in-law and a much younger (and more recently arrived) daughter-in-law. The differential power allocated to women situated differentially within the hierarchy of a family leaves those at the bottom of this open to substantial abuse. To extend this argument (and this forms the focus of this paper), the structures of power and domination between women of the upper castes in relation to women and men of the lower castes and minority religious communities require much more careful analyses to inform a demystified ethical and intellectual praxis.

Growing up in the early 1960s in an extended family and close-knit Gujarati community in Nairobi, one heard a great deal of women's cruelty to women, and the indifference as well as brutality of men. There were arenas of violence which remained untouched by the rule of law, and which were sanctioned (through being tolerated) by the male-controlled community organisations. Within the dense networks of women's communicative structures, there existed the complex strategies which attempted to analyse the causes which bred such violence, as well as accommodated it. There were, however, no organisational structures to provide either a political critique of the different forms of violence, or a refuge for those women and children facing abuse. It appears, on the surface, light years away from the period of the 1970s metropolitan feminism, when the question of violence done to women was central to the feminist agenda, and there was a significant increase in the number of refuges for women facing domestic violence.[2] However, the process of silencing, toleration (or intolerance of the basic right to security) and compromises which leave intact the power of domination and violence can be seen in both metropolitan and non-metropolitan contexts, among all social communities and classes. It was, nevertheless, left to the more deconstructive feminism of the 1980s to unpack the category of 'woman' and argue for its non-homogeneity in terms of class, race and sexual orientation. However, the question of violence perpetrated by women continues to destabilise sub-terranean notions of women as objects of patriarchal practices rather than subjects within it, bringing to the fore questions of political agency and the moral responsibility of women positioned in privileged structures (of caste and dominant religious community) who wield brutal power over women and men of subordinate communities.

In this chapter, I explore the centrality of women in reproducing structures of family, community and nation–state and I argue that it is women's embeddedness within processes which perpetuate certain forms of social and community structures, and their imprecation within identities which are group-based (around family, caste, religion, community, nation) that make for certain women taking up cudgels in defence of these systems of power. These systems of power, while being overtly 'patriarchal', provide specific spaces for women in relation to women, men and children of that (and other) family, caste, religion and community. My analysis is focused on an exploration of the society of the Indian sub-continent, though there is ample evidence to demonstrate the workings of very similar power structures in societies as varied as those of the ex–Soviet bloc and South Africa.[3]

Gender, Caste and Caste-violence: Defending Privilege

The centrality of women in the reproduction of a hierarchical (and politicised) (Kothari 1970) caste structure, specifically through the system of arranged marriages, is now accepted as a standard sociological truism. Dr Babasaheb Ambedkar, the *dalit*[4] author of the constitution for modern independent India, pointed out in 1916 in his 'Castes in India' that the 'prohibition, or rather the absence of intermarriage' remained the 'essence' of caste and he traced the 'Origin of Caste' to the 'The Origin of the Mechanism for Endogamy'. Whatever the historical complexities to the evolution, spread and consolidation of castes over the epochs of (differential) agrarian settlements, Ambedkar was surely correct in his proposal that the 'annihilation of caste' was predicated on the freeing of women and men from the system of caste-based marriages, and that the survival of castes could no longer be guaranteed once this latter foundation was removed (Ambedkar 1989: 8, 14, 67). The control over women's sexuality, and a rigid disciplining of inter-caste marriages has provided the main bulwark to the continuity of caste structures. An early feminist interpreted this with a stirring call for a close (and necessary) alliance between women of all social communities and the *dalit* struggle for social emancipation from upper-caste oppression (Omvedt 1975). While the theoretical and analytical importance of the inter-twining of caste and patriarchal structures is valid here, for it provides the political basis for joint struggles on a common front, political events since the 1980s have demonstrated that upper-caste women are well-positioned to defend and uphold caste privilege, which they enjoy together with men of the caste, and that *as upper-caste women they face the prospect of lower-caste assertion with as much fury and fear as do men of this section.*

The visible and public assertions of urban, upper-caste women in the reconfiguring of political culture and political violence are phenomena of great significance in contemporary Indian politics. Not only has this lent more depth and force to authoritarian movements, inserting women into the public domain of a violent contestation for retention and enlargement of privilege, but it has also politicised the inner fabric of family and community life within this reinvented middle class, shifting familial and civic culture in profound ways. The reconstruction of gender, caste and religious identities (with visible women at the helm) has been a salient feature of middle-class political assertions in India, and the state of Gujarat in western India was in the forefront of some of these movements. Gujarat has led the way in some crucial assertions by upper-caste women against the disadvantaged castes, and against the minority Muslim communities, whereby a small, but publicly significant section of women have formed a crucible for some of the worst excesses of anti-lower caste and anti-Muslim movements. The year 1981 marked the beginning of the 'anti-reservation' agitation, and culminated in the 1985 movement which proved a watershed in upper-caste agitation. This was a movement against the extension of affirmative action legislation which granted to members of 'other backward castes' reserved seats in institutions of higher education, and in government employment. This anti-reservation agitation must be situated within the caste-based politics of Gujarat, where in March 1985 a resounding victory was won by the Congress under Madhavsinha Solanki (a chief minister who was not of the 'upper-caste' Baniya–Patidar–Brahman triumvirate), who moved quickly to institute and enlarge the eligibility of those entitled to 'reserved seats' in educational institutions. Violence shook the state of Gujarat from the middle of March to August 1985, particularly in the cities of Ahmedabad and Baroda, but this spread through to the rural areas of Central and Northern Gujarat, destabilising the elected government and toppling the elected chief minister. The city of Ahmedabad was put under army rule for almost five months, and a state of siege existed in *dalit* and lower-caste neighbourhoods, with vigilante groups forming in various areas. This acute crisis both of constitutional politics and of the stability within civil society was exacerbated by the entry of the opposition party, the Bharatiya Janta Party (the BJP), into the fray. The BJP is wedded to the creation of an authoritarian Hindu nation-state, and it is significant that an agitation which had begun as one against affirmative action for lower castes quickly became communal in the tussle for power between Solanki and his opponents, with violence directed against the Muslim communities (Engineer 1985; Iyengar 1985).

Upper-caste women took the lead in setting up Vali Mandalis (Parent Associations) which mobilised support over the major city of Ahmedabad to close down institutions of higher education in protest against the extension of affirmative action legislation. In the violent struggles which followed, upper-caste women were militantly active in asserting and acting out of a specific agenda which maintained the privilege of this section, and which inserted women as crucial mediators within this struggle. They organised meetings, demonstrations and stoppages of educational institutions, often coming up against police in their street activities, this gendering of politics in itself fuelling the energies of the larger body of anti-reservationists. The women involved had a clear perspective of what was at stake, arguing that the positive discrimination policies did 'injustice' to the upper castes, since the lower castes and the *dalits* had 'no brains, no atmosphere to stand first in class' (Women and the Media 1985: 1730–1).

The implications I wish to draw out from this are not solely that power structures (in this case caste) have the ability to draw in groups of women within their workings against disempowered groups even at the same time as they grant them a subordinate status within this; but, rather, that within the multiple identities inhabited by women, large numbers of them have chosen, in contemporary times of acute political crises, to reconstitute themselves as *powerful and privileged women vis-à-vis* those seeking a formal recognition of their disadvantage, and structural ways of rectifying this. It is not that these women put 'caste' above 'gender' and submerge their gender interests to the cause of caste domination, but that a more complex caste-gendered politics is taking place whereby in the ideologies they espouse, the demands that they articulate and the actions that they take on their own behalf, the women are carving out a political space for themselves as a critically important and gendered section of the upper castes (and classes). Indeed they have marched into the public domain as protagonists against lower-caste men and women.

The modern age of visible feminisms has witnessed the recognition of the importance of women in political struggles by movements of all persuasions. This is an ironic spill-off from the success of a vibrant and dynamic women's movement in India, with strong historical and contemporary roots in the anti–imperialist, workers' and socialist movements. The recognition of women's strength in bringing about significant shifts in the policies and practices of state as well as non-state institutions is one reason why men of militantly rightist movements have encouraged and capitulated women into the forefront of these agitations, resulting in upper-caste women gaining significant agency within these movements. Upper-caste women fronted the aggressive manoeuvres of the anti-reservation movement which toppled the elected state government and unleashed violence against the *dalit* communities. An all-women investigative committee led by independent feminist journalists, who also had involvement in women's groups, found that the assumption that women would not be harshly treated by police and the army encouraged women to be positioned in the front-lines of agitational activities. They reported:

> It seems likely that women are being used to neutralise the law-enforcing authorities during demonstrations as well as during riots. Are the women aware of this? Even if they are willing agents, are they conscious that if the assumption is proved false in even one instance, they are the ones who are going to receive the first blows/bullets? (Women and the Media 1985: 1727)

The spectacular growth of women's political presence in the post-1992 rightist movements makes the second question asked by the women's committee a little naive: 'Is it right for women to use society's supposed perception of their vulnerability even to support causes they care about? (Women and the Media 1985: 1727)? The analysis moved from seeing women as 'being used' (by men in political movements), to concede the agential capacity of women ('even if they are willing agents'), only to draw back into an intellectual mould which presumed gender to be the over-arching mode of social and political existence ('is it right for women to use … '). The frameworks then existent within sections of the women's movement had not yet come to terms with the necessity for seeing certain groups of women as centrally bound to violent caste assertions. This was left to the post-1990 period.

The perception of upper-caste women who toured all over the state of Gujarat to gather support for the anti-reservation agitation and 'fight for our rights' (Women and the Media 1985: 1731) points to the engendering of caste politics whereby upper-caste women worked to reconstitute the dynamics of a caste-gendered dynamics. This was further demonstrated in a grim fashion in the capital city of Delhi during the anti-Mandal agitation during late 1990. This too was an agitation aimed against the extension of the positive quota system within lower-level government employment to backward castes, and was spearheaded by young women and men, of whom 200 attempted to commit suicide as an act of public protest. The horrifying incidents of attempted suicides (which led to the death of 112) included a visible number of young women. 'Thirty percent of total suicide attempts were by young women and girls. Some of them said clearly that girls are no less brave and heroic than boys' (Kishwar 1991: 55). The deaths of these young women, and their entry into the public domain as martyrs for the preservation of caste hierarchy, is critical here for it breached incontrovertibly the notion of women's pacifism; annihilation of one's body in the defence of privilege, 'merit', the nation, was yet another example of the harnessing of middle-class passions into a violent street mobilisation which not only overthrew an elected government, but transfigured popular perceptions of 'rights' and 'justice', overturning the previous political discourse on disadvantage to posit the upper castes as victims of governmental policies.

Let me emphasise a point which is relevant to long-term theorisation here. In the rightist political upsurgences that have swept through the Indian sub-continent in the past decade and a half, women have not acted always, or most of the time, *as women* in political movements, but as upper-caste women, women who support the BJP, or women who oppose affirmative action for lower castes and so on. The cleavages between women who demonstrate their political allegiance to aggressively militant casteist and communal structures (and those feminists who are attempting to evolve a feminist practice which is attentive to the related questions of caste privilege, communalism and, under-girding all this, economic disparities) are becoming increasingly evident, and necessitate a sharper analysis which places gender relationships within the (reconstituted and reconfigured) space of community, caste and state politics.

The 'newness' of this phenomenon is in the *public, political centrality* accorded to women within these movements (some of which space has been wrested by women themselves), and in the *scale* of women's direct involvement within these. These movements are without a doubt innovatively modern, reflecting the forces of an assertive rightist indigenism that provides the counter-façade to the process of globalisation, and has *nationalised* the ideology of 'family', retranscribing traditional (often feudal) norms of family (community) loyalty and allegiance on to a communalised national space. There is an urgent need to address the knotty question of the relationship between the workings of gender, caste and state politics in order to 'map out' the continuities and discontinuities in the specificities of engendered caste within dominant assertions.

The grim utilisation of one's life in the service of a specifically configurated nation-state – as in the immolations which took place in Delhi – were a testimony to a shift in the civic culture of urban middle-class India, which valorised deaths within its own body polity, showing the suicides of young women and men (some as young as twelve) to be heroic and worthy of emulation. The lineages of contemporary neo-fascism in India, with upper-caste women as central articulators of 'our' rights, and young people zealously embracing the mantle of death against the perceived threats posed by those attempting to shake off ascribed disadvantage, were becoming apparent. This was soon to be transmuted into a valorisation of death and destruction wreaked on Muslim communities in an unprecedented way in independent India.

Women and Hindu Nationalism

The forces of Hindu nationalism have consolidated themselves remarkably since 1984, with a dangerously heightened ability to mobilise street violence against the minority religious community, as well as against democratic movements struggling to defend the rights of people displaced by inappropriate developmental projects. The public phenomenon of women in violent upsurges following the demolition of the mosque at Ayodhya on 6 December 1992 has led one author to coin the term 'feminisation of violence' (Banerjee 1995: 216). This phrase highlights the central importance of women within the newly emerged politics of contemporary communalism, spearheaded by the paramilitary groupings of the Shiv Sena in Bombay, the extra-constitutional organisations of the Vishwa Hindu Parishad together with the Rashtriya Swayam Sevak Sangh, and the political expression of the Bharatiya Janta Party.

The upsurgence of the Hindu right has taken place precisely in an age of market liberalisation and increased globalisation, after a decade of a dynamic progressive feminist movement in India which has shown a highly public face through its political interventions, and after fifty years of economic development which has seen a substantial increase in the number of female students in higher educational institutions. The bitter struggle over economic resources in an era of inflation and high prices has gone hand-in-hand with the struggle over capture of political power, witnessed in an acute conflict over the constituent features of who is deemed to be a legitimate member and citizen within the Indian nation-state. The terrifying attempt to marginalise and make illegitimate the claims of the minority Muslim communities has once again had militant women in the forefront of this assertion.

There are three significant ways in which militant Hindu women have put a very specific stamp on the communal movement, indelibly marking the violence endemic in this movement both as gendered and actively sanctioned by a vocal female community:

1. Through the stridently female voices of Rithambhara and Uma Bharati, two ostensibly religious figures who have played a crucial political role in reconstituting a specifically violent Hindu identity. They speak not only in the angry voice of female guardians of Hindutva, but they have also taken upon themselves the role of constructing and vivifying a

highly aggressive Hindu masculinity. Both Rithambhara and Bharati (in public speeches) have goaded Hindu men to shed their (supposed) emasculation and rise up against the masculine male.

2. Through the organisations of women's branches of RSS and VHP, both of which have provided storm troopers for the resurgent Hinduism of present times.

3. Through their public involvement in the demolition of the mosque, through their public national tours, and through their sanctioning of violence not simply against the mosque in Ayodhya (which was demolished), but against women and men of the Muslim communities. This extended to their uncritical stand vis. burnings of Muslim properties, killings of Muslim women, men and children in Bombay 1992–93 and rapes of Muslim women in the city of Surat in December 1992.

I will discuss each of the above in turn.

Re-ordering a violent Hindu masculinity In a prescient article written before the demolition of Babri Masjid at Ayodhya, Tanika Sarkar pointed to the emergence of a strikingly militant Hindu femaleness, where the emphasis was on the 'trained, hardened, invincible female body' and where the women worshipped their weapons in particular. Sarkar's argument that the 'new communal phase enables the women's self-constitution as active political subject in dangerously unprecedented ways', importantly linked up with the attraction of an assertive and aggressive femalehood for upwardly mobile women of trading and service sectors who faced questions of domestic violence in the form of dowry death and marital violence, as well as sexual violence in the public sphere of work and employment (Sarkar 1991: 2061).

That violent nationalisms which stress aggressive masculinities and which are directed against members of a different community is attested to by the brutal experiences of the former Yugoslavia (*Feminist Review* 1993: 45). The political point here is that a hyper-aggressive Hindu masculinity will relate to women in general (including women it is in close familial relationship with) in ways which demonstrate its power and dominance. The women of the Hindu right, thus, who have been instrumental in shaping the currently resurgent Hindu masculinity bear a fraught relationship to the forces of Hindu male assertions which can affect and brutalise the upper-caste Hindu woman herself. A close reading of the evidence suggests that the public 'exceptional' women of the Hindu right – Rithambhara and Uma Bharati, the female demagogues who preach a return to primeval violence through which the Hindu male can prove his virility – remain relatively secure in their public world of hate-filled propaganda, while there has been an increase in violence faced by both lower-caste and upper-caste women in states such as Rajasthan which have been dominated by the BJP since 1990 (*Communalism Combat*, November 1997).

The increased incidents of reported rapes, particularly against college-going young women, the shielding of rapists connected to the political structure by the chief minister and the top echelons of the BJP, the distancing from this issue by fire-brand women such as Uma Bharati who propound a strong femalehood which defies male violence but who succumb to male party line when faced with actual cases in a particular constituency, has caused dissonance among local party activists in the women's wing of the VHP. The preaching of female power cannot be reconciled easily with the acceptance of violence towards women from within the socially constructed and homogenised 'Hindu' community, and the rift between the rhetoric of female power directed against the lower castes and Muslim communities, and the actuality of violence faced by caste women in the urban towns and rural areas of Rajasthan, are being negotiated in complex and often opportunistic ways by militant Hindu women. It is likely to create a necessary fracture within an ideology and praxis which is not self-sealed.[5]

However, while women of the Hindu right might well be forced to pay heed to violence perpetrated by privileged Hindu men on women from different caste communities, in order both to secure their political following and by virtue of the glaring social realities which face them within their own social milieu, the crucial point is that there is no critical self-examination nor any ambiguity in the minds of the militant Hindu women as to what they think should be meted out to Muslim communities in general. The public exhortations to Hindu men to prove that they are 'man enough' to stand up against the perceived depredations of the stereotypical lustful Muslim men of neo-fascist propaganda demonstrate an unequivocal voicing of *intentional* violence against a gendered subject of dubious historical (or contemporary) veracity. The violence of the majority religious community is sanctioned by pointing to the vicious portrayal of the Muslim male as a sexual predator who threatens and rapes the Hindu woman (Basu 1995:162–4). The construction of the pure Hindu warrior who is willing to lay down his life for the motherland is predicated on the construction of the Muslim male as rapist and/or polygamist, as well as on the dangerous and sinister notion of the Muslim woman as 'sexually available, desirous of the dominator, or sexually dominable through force' (Baccheta 1994: 217).

The complex reordering of Hindu masculinity, goaded and engendered by public female voices, thus has had wide ramifications on the forms and features of contemporary communal violence that has seen unprecedented levels of killings, rapes and torching of members of the Muslim as well as

Christian communities (*dalits*, tribals) in independent India. The acceptance of these vengeful preachings in the female voice by a wide section of urban, caste society in India can be seen by the constant replaying of Rithambhara's cassette which, while constituting a new form of political culture, 'naturalised' this by its continuous hearing within everyday public spaces.

The rise of the woman warrior The woman's wing of the RSS, the Rashtrasevika Samiti (Women in Service of the Nation), and the VHP's Mahila Samiti as well as the Vahini, have been crucial in consolidating and extending the reach and influence of these anti-democratic and hate-filled organisations. While this is critically important for the spread of illiberal and anti-minority practices among a wide section of middle-class Hindus, it also ensures that womanhood and motherhood are harnessed into the project of nurturing, equipping and sustaining a new generation of Hindu warriors: male and female. Sarkar's comment that 'the right aims at nothing short of transforming the upper-caste/middle-caste leaders of Hindu society individually and collectively', whereby 'it is an inch by inch, person by person mode of advance' (Sarkar 1995: 182, 187), is crucial, for it points to the refiguring of whole sections of civil society (indeed its very foundations) along communal lines. This is of as much importance as the militant street mobilisations and capture of political power within local and national state structures that the Hindu right has so successfully demonstrated in the last seven years.

The violent communalism of the interior, 'private' sphere of the 'family' and 'community' through the assertions of women who are linked up within the rightist networks provides a density and depth to the present political project of Hindu neo-fascism which it had lacked before. In this sense, then, the Hindi right has, in important ways, managed to achieve a remarkable degree of gendered unity on a communal platform that, while it creaks under the weight of its manifest fissures internally (see above), requires the necessary existence of a demonised community for its very existence. The tensions and threats that this poses for a democratic, secular women's movement are clear. It is also obvious that as long as the democratic, secular women's movement continues to speak out against the violence done to members of the minority religious community (which it has done in fine and principled actions), the question of a strategic alliance with women on the Hindu right on the issue of the violence of rightist men against caste women (as in Rajasthan) is an extremely fraught one.

The icon of the Hindu female warrior, which draws upon mythical and religious symbols replete with notions of blood, anger and strength of an enraged female body, together with the violent spaces that an angry femalehood has carved out for itself in anti-Muslim acts, has also greatly problematised the liberal (cultural and political) project of 'gender empowerment', that has signally failed to explain the 'empowerment' of women within a newly configured national space whereby these women go on a rampage against a specifically constructed enemy community. It is to this that I now turn.

Women sanctioning violence against Muslims The strident, screaming voice of the female ascetic (Rithambara) who urged the assembled crowd of men and women to 'give one more push' and 'put the Babri Masjid to rubble' on 6 December 1992 has undoubtedly put the issue of female agency centre-stage. Rithambra's voice unleashed a reign of violence against Muslim communities in significant urban areas. This saffron-clad figure had rehearsed this violence in public speeches up and down the country, thus subverting the rule of law and the workings of a democratic polity.

Rithambhara's voice and person symbolised and made visible the *centrality* of rightist Hindu women in this particular violent phase of militant mobilisation. The local, regional and national networks of the branches of the VHP and RSS, which had mobilised male and female cadres prior to the demolition of the mosque, have also been reliant on female personnel and female strength. There is little doubt that the cadres of the VHP and RSS were cognisant of the ultimate objective of the onslaught: to 'teach the Muslims a lesson' and make them subordinate citizens in a Hindu nation-state. In this sense, the militant Hindu women were violently complicitous in the actions perpetrated against citizens of the Muslim faith in the cities of Surat, Bombay and elsewhere following the demolition of the mosque on 6 December 1992.

However, while the concern to understand the various means by which a vociferous section of upper-caste womanhood has lent its weight to contemporary communal violence has encouraged the growth of concerned feminist scholarship on the subject, which has moved beyond viewing as objects of patriarchal (and state) violence, one needs to be vigilant against the other tendency which homogenises this section of women and sees them as the practical and ideological 'shock-troopers' within each bout of (recent) fury and hatred that has accompanied communal violence. Thus, the particular acts of torchings, killings, pillage and rapes that were witnessed in the country following the destruction of Babri Masjid also saw some significant acts of solidarity and provision of shelter in particular by women who provided refuge to victims of communal violence, at considerable danger to themselves (Sarkar and Butalia 1995: 305). Public acknowledgement of these courageous acts of neighbourhood women, however, was silenced by women and men of the rightist political parties

(Sarkar and Butalia 1995: 305). The censuring of information which provides counter-propaganda to the Hindu right's claim that *all* 'Hindus' are joined together in a 'community' against 'the Muslims', and the non-acceptance of the acts of preservation, is profoundly perturbing. Together with the wide-ranging public works which the democratic and secular left (including the women's movement) continues to do, there needs necessarily to be the counter-articulation of humane and sane voices on the ground, which will act to prevent and contain the levels of violence such as those witnessed recently.

While the periods of communal violence saw the withdrawal of support to neighbours, friends and colleagues in shocking acts of disassociation within a charged political ethos, there has not been a complete rupture of relations in residential areas, trade arenas, working spaces and the more public domains of employment, education and civic urban life. The protection and enhancement of this, ensuring the channelling of political energies into domains which engage the citizenry in democratising of conjoint working and living, are of equal importance to the (related) question of the defence of lives.

Conclusions

The questions exercising Indian feminism today are three-fold:

1. How and in what ways to face up to and challenge the women of the Hindu right
2. How and in what ways feminist understandings and praxes can confront (both within themselves and vis-à-vis the external society) central issues of caste privilege and communal divisions
3. How and in what ways a reconstituted feminism which has taken seriously the other salient social oppressions in society can, in the long term, point to meaningful alternatives to social relationships bound by gender, caste and communal privilege.

Remaining alert to the inter-linkages of social oppressions may, at times, mean ignoring the simplistic primacy accorded to 'gender' in favour of a more complex and difficult negotiation of caste and communally engendered domains, in order to map out ways of further breaching the fissures which lie at the heart of the dilemma facing women of the Hindu right in their own internal construction. Given, however, that the women of the Hindu right are both informed and willing agents within the larger ambit of an anti-Muslim violence, then one must face up to the question of (some) women's guilt in directing, coalescing and crystallising the forces of violence.

The continuum between the active female instigator who claims to speak for her (Hindu) sex, the legitimacy accorded to the violent political con-figuration by the women's wings of the rightist organisations, the gleeful pillage of consumer goods by a middle-class Hindu womanhood in a time of communal rioting, and the silencing of ordinary, humane voices on the ground, have all, in various ways, raised the spectre of female capacity to wreak violence on the lives and property of minority communities. A sharper analysis of events and their meanings is necessary if one is not to become politically disabled in assuming too great a hegemony wielded by rightist organisations over women and men in times of caste and communal riots – or, conversely, in assuming (over-optimistically) that rightist women can be politically wooed away from their anti-lower-caste and communal depredations on the platform of gender rights. The evolution of more informed strategies is necessary to confront the different forms of violence perpetrated by women, as caste-gendered and communal subjects. This necessitates more grounded analytical frameworks, as well as an expansion of perspective which incorporates the complicity of women – as dema-gogues, ideologues, hecklers, side-supporters, looters, carriers of kerosene – each of which positions them differently in the political nexus of the national state–locality–neighbourhood. One has thus moved substantively beyond the analyses of 'male violence' and the violence of the state, to confront the violence-perpetrated-by-women in rightist assertions.

Notes

1. Tanaka Sarkar and Urvashi Butalia's *Women and the Hindu Right: A Collection of Essays* (1995), was one of the first influential collection of papers. The edited volume by Kumari Jayawardena, *Embodied Violence: Communalizing Women's Sexuality in South Asia* (1996) provided a second set of consolidated readings on the centrality of gender to the communal, neo-fascist project. The critical point to note is that the theoretical and political points raised in these contributions were exercises in intellectual endeavours to situate and contextualise the phenomenon of the 'woman as communal subject' in Tanika Sarkar's innovative article with the same title in *Economic and Political Weekly* (1991).

2. I had been involved, with others, in setting up and running the Asian Women's Refuge and Resource Centre in the London Borough of Brent between 1980 and 1982. The Indian sub-continent has a longer history of paternalist welfare provision for outcast widows and so on, beginning at least in the modern period from the time of Gandhian nationalism, and the more contemporary feminism actively set up women's refuges in the late 1980s in urban cities.

3. For comparative material on the former Yugoslavia, see special issue on 'Thinking Through Ethnicities', *Feminist Review*, no. 45, Autumn 1993; and Hassim 1993).

4. *Dalit* translates as the 'oppressed', and it is used here to denote members and communities who come from the stigmatised section earlier defined as 'untouchables'.

5. Paola Baccheta's conclusion, from her study of the extreme rightist group, the RSS, is that 'the gendered fractionalisation of Hindu nationalist discourse is ultimately

a function of its unifying praxis' (Baccheta 1994: 161). This needs to be read together with the evidence from the city of Jaipur in Rajasthan that 'On their own initiatives, the Vahini women [the women's wing of the VHP] have contacted activists of the anti-rape movement in Jaipur and with their support have started independent investigations into complaints of rape' (*Communalism Combat*, November 1997).

Bibliography

Ambedkar, A. (1989) 'On Caste', Part 1 in *Dr. Babasaheb Ambedkar: Writings and Speeches*, vol. 1, Bombay: Government of Maharashtra.

Baccheta, P. (1994) 'Communal Property, Sexual Property', in Hasan (ed.), *Forging Identities*.

Banerjee, S. (1995) 'Hindu Nationalism and the Construction of Women', in Sarkar and Butalia (eds), *Women and the Hindu Right*.

Basu, A. (1995) 'Feminism Inverted: The Gendered Imagery and Real Women of Hindu Nationalism', in Sarkar and Butalia (eds), *Women and the Hindu Right*.

Basu, T. (1993) *Khaki Shorts and Saffron Flags*, Delhi: Orient Longman.

Engineer, A. A. (1985) 'Communal Fire Engulfs Ahmedabad Once Again', *Economic and Political Weekly*, vol. 20, no. 27, 6 July.

Feminist Review (1993) special issue, 'Thinking Through Ethnicities', no. 45, Autumn.

Gopal, S. (ed.) (1991) *Anatomy of a Confrontation: The Babri Masjid-Ramjanmabhumi Issue*, Delhi: Penguin Books.

Hasan, Z. (ed.), (1994) *Forging Identities: Gender, Communities and the State*, Delhi: Kali for Women.

Hassim, S. (1993) 'Family, Motherhood and Zulu Nationalism: The Politics of the Inkatha Women's Brigade,' *Feminist Review*, no. 43, Spring.

Iyengar, S. (1985) 'Gujarat: Violence with a Difference', *Economic and Political Weekly*, vol. 20, no. 28, 13 July.

Jayawardena, K. (ed.) (1996): *Embodied Violence: Communalizing Women's Sexuality in South Asia*, London: Zed Books.

Kishwar, M. (1991) 'Instigators of Hysteria', *Manushi*, nos 63–4, March–June.

Kothari, R. (ed.) (1970) *Caste in Indian Politics*, Delhi: Longman.

Meghani, Z. (1993) *Radhiadi Raat*, Bhavnagar: Prasar.

Omvedt, G. (1975) 'Caste, Class and Women's Liberation', *Bulletin of Concerned Asian Scholars*, vol. 20, no. 16, 20 April.

Sarkar, T. (1991) 'The Woman as Communal Subject', *Economic and Political Weekly*, vol. xxvi, no. 35, 31 August.

— (1995) 'Heroic Women, Mother Goddesses: Family and Organisation in Hindutva Politics', in Sarkar and Butalia, (eds), *Women and the Hindu Right*.

Sarkar, T. and U. Butalia (eds), (1995) *Women and the Hindu Right: A Collection of Essays*, Delhi: Kali for Women.

Women and the Media (1985) 'Impact of Ahmedabad Disturbances on Women', *Economic and Political Weekly*, vol. 20, no. 41, 12 October.

10

Women and Peace in Northern Ireland: A Complicated Relationship

Ruth Jacobson

The Peace Process, 1994–99

Although the thirty-year conflict in Northern Ireland has sometimes seemed insoluble, the events of 1998 gave its inhabitants unprecedented hope for a peaceful future. Multi-party negotiations initiated in late 1994 by the joint IRA and loyalist ceasefires had survived successive crises to produce the historic 'Good Friday Agreement' (henceforth 'the Agreement') of 10 April 1998. This was followed in May by the Northern Ireland Referendum, where 71.2 per cent voted to adopt the Agreement and its commitment to an eventual resolution of the conflict through exclusively non-violent and democratic means. The June elections for the Northern Ireland Assembly opened the way for a power-sharing executive to come into place in the spring of 1999 as the essential next step towards peace.

These advances need to be set against the backdrop of a much broader 'peace process', involving manifold initiatives to bridge entrenched divisions and fears. This momentum was sustained through 1998, despite some appalling incidents of violence.[1] The withdrawal of army patrols from many areas and reductions in sectarian killings reduced the shadow of fear throughout Northern Ireland (although the political progress also served to throw light on the brutal conduct of both loyalist and republican paramilitaries against their own communities in the form of 'punishment' beatings). During the later part of 1998, however, the political situation became increasingly tense. Although the elected Northern Ireland Assembly was convened as envisaged, disputes over the issue of decommissioning[2] created an impasse in the further implementation of the Agreement. This impasse blocked the creation of the Northern Ireland Executive (akin to a Cabinet). As it continued into the spring of 1999, the vital underlying element of the Agreement, that of trust between its signatories, began to be affected (Deaglan de Breadun, *Irish Times*, 22 April 1999).

By mid-1999, there was still a commitment among the political leadership to reach an eventual resolution of the impasse and, more generally, a mood that there could be 'No Turning Back'. Nevertheless, there was a more pessimistic opinion that the peace process could not survive the strains of the imminent 'marching season' (see below), particularly in the light of escalating loyalist attacks. On the other hand, there was some hope of a political breakthrough before July or, at the least, of 'parking' the entire process over the summer.

Identifying the complications This case study will concentrate on the earlier period of momentum between 1996 and 1998. By this point, the conflict had cost 3,601 deaths directly attributable to political violence (see Table 10.1). Northern Ireland's population in 1992 was only 1.5 million, meaning that a considerable proportion of families have had direct experience of bereavement, injury, emotional and economic loss. The nature of the conflict has resulted in a gendered distribution of suffering; thus, while the deaths have been overwhelmingly male, it is widely felt that the burden of preventing major breakdowns in social and family life has fallen disproportionately on women, often at enormous cost to their well-being (Morgan 1995). It might therefore be assumed that women as a whole must have a proportionately higher stake in securing an eventual political settlement which ensures no more armed violence and that this applies particularly to women's involvement in the peace process.

TABLE 10.1 Counting the cost: 1969 to 1998

Total deaths	3,601
Male deaths	3,279
Female deaths	322
Male deaths as % of total	91.1
Female deaths as % of total	8.9
Affiliation of victims (as % of total)	
Civilians*	56.4
Security forces (army, RUC)	27.9
Republican paramilitaries	12.6
Loyalist paramilitaries	3.2

Note: * defined here as not in active service or in reserves

Source: adapted from M. Fay et al. (eds) (1998), *Mapping troubles-related deaths in Northern Ireland 1969–1998*, 2nd edition, INCORE, University of Ulster

I will argue, however, that the relationship is complicated because it can be demonstrated that women have constructed their identities, including that of 'mothers', in ways which have *not* always been conducive to peace. While only a few women have exercised their agency actually to inflict violence,[3] considerably larger numbers have seen 'our children's future' as their reason for supporting activities which have a virtual certainty of provoking violence, such as Orange marches through highly contested areas. Moreover, they have used their electoral voices to oppose the Agreement, despite its potential to achieve a non-violent resolution of the Northern Irish conflict.

This argument is not intended to diminish the record of women's contribution to peace in Northern Ireland. They have always been significant presences in peace movements; for example, Women Together for Peace was founded in 1972 at the height of 'the Troubles'. Since the ceasefires, they have made unprecedented breakthroughs into the public and political process. The advent of Marjorie 'Mo' Mowlam as Northern Ireland Secretary of State, of the Northern Ireland Women's Coalition (NIWC) and of some other women delegates changed the face of the previously all-male negotiating table. Moreover, at those points when political leaders were refusing even to acknowledge the presence of their opponents, women from the communities they claimed to be representing have been coming together, meeting in shabby community centres to struggle over the intricacies of different electoral systems.

Against this background, the situation in Northern Ireland may appear as a demonstration of the 'maternalist' position within feminism which rests on seeing the condition of womanhood as peaceable and stressing the values commonly associated with motherhood (Pettman 1996: 107). Writers such as Ruddick (1989) and Brock-Utne (1985) have argued that those engaged in 'mothering work' have distinct motives for rejecting war which run in tandem with abilities for resolving conflicts non-violently. The visible face of violence in Northern Ireland has been overwhelmingly masculine, whether of masked gunmen cradling their weapons or ranks of besuited and bowler-hatted marchers shielded by armed police. Other than the women actually involved in paramilitary activities, 'normal' women were supposed to engage only in grieving or on making 'their men' stop the violence (Rooney 1995).

In looking at the period prior to the ceasefires, Morgan points out that the numbers of paramilitaries or peace activists has been very small while 'the great majority of women in Northern Ireland have had little such direct involvement' (Morgan 1995: 11). As a result, 'to describe women as "peacemakers" in Northern Ireland says little of value. Some women have made a notable contribution to reducing physical, structural and cultural violence – as have some men. But equally their actions have often served to reproduce the divided community rather than challenge it' (ibid. 17). In marked contrast to the maternalist position, she finds that the more accurate assessment is that 'women have been both peace makers and peace preventers and that the range of their attitudes and responses has been as wide and varied as that of men' (ibid.).

This case study has been based on developments in Northern Ireland since the ceasefires, and it will reach a slightly different conclusion from Morgan's. There have been many strands of the peace process where women have made a distinctive contribution that has not been mirrored by men. At the same time, it will argue the need for a more probing examination of the multi-dimensionality of women's actions in these more recent years in order better to encompass the characteristics of women's agency in this particular conflict. Its first section will deal with the terminology and principal characteristics of the Northern Ireland conflict and with the research methodology adopted. The central section takes up the problematic nature of women's actions in the context of disputed marches and of the electoral events of 1998. A conclusion attempts to look at the relationship between women and peace from the perspective not of 'shared motherhood' but of capacities for change.

The Northern Ireland Conflict[4]

Given the size of its population, there has been an enormous literature on the Northern Ireland conflict. One tendency has been to prioritise only one element, whether of 'tribalism, religion, imperialism, class, discrimination, inherited enmity, or simple irrationality' (Quinn 1993: 102). There are, however, many less uni-dimensional analyses which confirm Ruane and Todd's observation that 'The conflict is between historic communities constituted and differentiated by multiple rather than single dimensions of difference', whether of religion, class or history (Ruane and Todd 1996: xiv).[5] The conflict is inseparable from the historical and contemporary involvement of the British state in Ireland. While religious ideologies per se have not been the principal driving force, religious affiliation has been and remains very largely the touchstone for locating oneself and others in everyday life. 'Protestant' and 'Catholic' also remain standard in academic work (see, for example, Boyle and Hadden 1994; Sales 1997) and will be retained here, but combined where relevant with the terminology of political identity, as set out in Table 10.2.

Feminist research over the decades has uncovered the gendered aspects of the conflict, such as the way in which levels of 'political violence' have masked other forms of violence. For example, the accessibility and use

TABLE 10.2 Political identities and their electoral expression

Unionism	Committed to maintaining Northern Ireland's integration into the British state; overlaps with and is reinforced by a strong adherence to the Protestant faith; condemns armed violence from all paramilitary sources but strongly supports what is seen as 'legitimate' use of state force against threats to security.
Electoral voice	Historically, the Ulster Unionist Party (UUP) which is now in competition for the Protestant vote with the Democratic Unionist Party (see below).
Loyalism	Same commitment and Protestant base as unionism but, in its most extreme form, endorses use of paramilitary violence and advocates even stronger state security measures.
Electoral voice	Democratic Unionist Party (DUP).
Nationalism	Committed to achieving the ultimate end of a united Ireland along with substantial change within the institutions of Northern Ireland but prepared, if unavoidable, for this to take place by long-term means; very largely restricted to Catholic population. Rejects all forms of paramilitary violence but also criticises use of state violence as exercised against the Catholic population.
Electoral voice	Social Democratic and Labour Party (SDLP).
Republicanism	Denotes: (a) membership of/active support for the (Provisional) IRA or other paramilitary groups aiming for the total removal of the British state in the shortest possible period; until recent ceasefires, this to be carried through by 'armed struggle' rather than the political route. Rejects the legitimacy of the British judicial and security establishment; (b) a minority which supports the same long-term aim, but without endorsement of violence.
Electoral voice	Sinn Fein (SF), ostensibly operating autonomously but generally seen as the IRA's 'political wing'; maintained the legitimacy of the armed struggle until the ceasefire period.
Other political affiliations:	
Alliance, Workers Party, Northern Ireland Women's Coalition, Protestant Unionist Party (PUP)	These take differing positions on constitutional questions but reject any form of paramilitary violence; although they do not have enough electoral support to be major actors, they can exercise considerable influence in specific contexts.

of guns may be related to the incidence of fatal assaults on women (McWilliams and McKernan 1993). This kind of research has also explored diverse facets of conflict, including those within the women's movement itself (Ward 1986), and has drawn attention to violence against minority groups in Northern Ireland, such as 'travellers'. Recently, there has been more attention paid to constructions of gender within Protestantism and loyalism (Hyndman 1996; Sales 1997).

Researching women and peace This chapter is based on a larger programme of research which started in mid-1996 and has carried through to the post-election period of later 1998/early 1999 (see Jacobson 1997 for details of the first phase). The programme's primary research aim has been to identify and assess the contribution of women's organisations to the political process during that period and there is, of course, no necessary connection between making a political input and being a peace-maker. However, I found that the activities of both women's formal organisations and less formal groupings all carried with them explicit or implicit messages about their concepts of peace, security and conflict, so that the line between 'political' and 'non-political' becomes blurred.

Between July 1996 and mid-1998, I made eight field trips (amounting to a total of thirty days spent in Northern Ireland), during which I interviewed six women's organisations, some more than once, at various stages within the peace process.[6] Because responses to the conflict from outside Northern Ireland have been characterised by an imbalance in the interest shown in the perceptions of Protestants themselves, I made a particular effort to ensure that the organisations and groupings interviewed spanned a range of positions from within the Protestant community. However, the research does not represent a comparative study of 'Protestant versus Catholic'. The research methodology triangulated documentary material, observation of events surrounding contested marching routes and, where compatible with my researcher status, participation in 'pro-peace' activities such as International Women's Day events and campaigning sessions.

It is a truism of Northen Irish society that there is a constant process of 'placing' people when meeting them in terms of religious affiliation through details of names, addresses, schooling, sports, even knowledge of particular songs. As a researcher, there has been no way of avoiding the tensions of 'outsider' status, which has only been partially compensated for by building up longer-term relationships with a number of organisations. This has allowed some progression from cautiously expressed generalisations about 'the Troubles' to pain-filled accounts of what 'their' terrorists did to 'our' family, of having your door kicked open in an army raid or having to take constant measures to avoid letting slip that your husband was working for the British forces. Since much of this was given on the basis of confidentiality, there will in general be no specific attribution. It is also not implied that any material cited is 'typical' of all women in Northern Ireland; it is used only to indicate the widely shared view of the particular group under consideration.

Violence, separation and security   Northern Ireland as a political entity was created in 1921 as a result of the partition of the island of Ireland. Those counties where the majority population was Protestant were retained within the British state as an integral part of the United Kingdom under the monarchy; they also acquired devolved powers in the form of the Stormont government, so-called after its location in Stormont Castle. For much of Northern Ireland's existence as a disputed entity, the demographic balance has been 2:1 in favour of the Protestant population but it has now shifted to approximately 60–40 (1992 census). Its constitutional status, also referred to as 'the national question', remains fundamental to the conflict, whether expressed violently or not. The vision of the founders of the Stormont regime had been of 'A Protestant state[7] for a Protestant people'; this was to be ensured through their control of local government, judiciary and police force, the Royal Ulster Constabulary (RUC). For the majority Protestant population, the period of unbroken rule by the Ulster Unionist Party (UUP) in Stormont from the 1920s through to the 1960s delivered 'peace' in the form of law and order. The Catholic minority lived with being seen as 'dangerous, alien and potentially treacherous' (Roulston 1997: 43). Successive regimes in the British Parliament remained unconcerned about Stormont's manifold abuses of its devolved powers, such as the manipulation of electoral borders in order to exclude Catholic voters and systematic discrimination in employment against Catholics (Sales 1997).

It is generally accepted that 'the Troubles' started during the late 1960s (see, for example, Cockburn 1998). It was only then that Stormont rule met its first severe challenge from protest marches organised by the Northern Ireland civil rights movement whose demands were for fair allocation of housing, jobs on merit and – despite the prominence of women activists – 'One Man, One Vote' (Jacobson 1997:3). The RUC reacted with brutal force against marchers who were largely, but not entirely, Catholics and did not restrain the wave of attacks by Protestant mobs on Catholic areas in Belfast. These attacks set off flight to safe (i.e. not religiously mixed) areas of housing. Between 1969 and 1972, as many as 60,000 people were driven from their homes, 80 per cent of them Catholic, representing the largest enforced population movement in Europe since World War II (McKittrick 1994: 39).

The British government eventually sent in army forces ostensibly charged with the protection of the Catholic population, but these also meted out brutal treatment, noticeably on 'Bloody Sunday' in 1972, when thirteen civilians were killed. These developments shifted the focus of the conflict from civil rights to issues of survival. The search by endangered Catholic populations for a security refused to them by Stormont and the British state led to the revival of the Provisional IRA.[8] This was met by escalation of Protestant paramilitary activities, whose claims were based on their protection of Protestant neighbourhoods. In March 1972, the Stormont administration was disbanded and direct rule from Westminster imposed; intended as a temporary measure, this was to remain the situation until 1998.

These events combined to produce the deeply entrenched patterns of physical, economic and social separation which now characterise most areas of life in Northern Ireland. By the late 1980s, only 7 per cent of the population lived in 'mixed' areas, with most public sector and much private housing exclusively Protestant or Catholic (Jacobson 1997). Less than 5 per cent of the school-age population attend integrated schools. Given this degree of separation, it is not surprising that marriages between Catholics and Protestants are as low as 6 per cent in many areas and have never risen above 12 per cent overall (Morgan et al. 1996). Although the implementation of Fair Employment legislation has substantially reduced overt discrimination in the public services and large employers, this has not been applied to smaller employers (Sales 1997: 163). Meanwhile, structural patterns of disadvantage remain for the majority of the Catholic working class and poverty brought about by deindustrialisation is also marked in many Protestant communities.

Tensions around security are inseparable from the contested status of the RUC. Although applications to join the police force from Catholics have risen since 1994 (Hamilton et al. 1995: 151), the force remains 90 per cent Protestant and is widely, and understandably, distrusted by the Catholic community (Hamilton et al. 1995). The limited restoration of 'normal' policing has not been adequate to overcome this distrust, particularly in the context of contested marches (personal observation). The Protestant community on the whole continues to see the (armed) RUC as their 'legitimate defenders', although this has altered somewhat, with loyalists also claiming RUC bias. In the lead up to the Agreement, the SDLP called for substantial restructuring of the RUC, while SF continued its long-standing demand for its total disbandment; unionist politicians countered with resistance even to largely symbolic measures, such as changes in uniform.

A society at war? There are a number of important accounts of what living 'on the front-line' of conflict has meant for women in Northern

Ireland (for example, Edgerton 1986). Yet if one is looking at Northern Ireland society as a whole, it is clear that the actual physical violence has been largely concentrated into very specific geographical areas. For example, neighbourhoods within North and West Belfast, such as the Falls Road, accounted for 40 per cent of *all* sectarian deaths in Northern Ireland up to 1993 other than those among the security forces (Pollak 1993). Yet around two-thirds of Northern Ireland's population do not live anywhere in these 'conflict zones'; instead, they are spread out in small towns and villages. In such areas, it has been far more possible for most people to live lives which have not been dominated by violence.

In fact, it appears that decades of conflict have not produced a highly involved population overall. In examining political attitudes, it was found that 'only relatively small minorities of the general population chose to identify the pathological aspects of Northern Ireland as exerting a formative influence on their views' (Miller et al. 1996: 80). Morgan and Fraser (1994) have demonstrated that, for women in these areas, the overriding preoccupation over the decades has been with family and, latterly, with paid work. Where they have had any free time, it has been devoted to church and voluntary activities which have not crossed the community divide. Thus, in the early 1990s, the leader of a church organisation could explain why she would not even consider attending an inter-faith service to mark the Women's World Day of Prayer services in these terms: 'I would not feel comfortable in this situation, nor would I encourage women to do this' (cited in Morgan and Fraser 1994: 79). It is, however, essential to recognise that families associated with the security forces or the justice system faced an ever-present threat (Jacobson 1997).

This management of conflict by avoidance made it easier to construct a picture of 'the other' which encompassed the attributes of bad motherhood. During interviews, Protestant women who are now involved in cross-community work recall being convinced that 'all Catholic women were hopeless mothers, because their priests kept telling them to have more children' while their Catholic counterparts had not been able to believe that Protestant mothers were 'real Christians'. Moreover, middle-class women rarely if ever had to face the daily realities of lives lived within conflict zones. Here, over and above the army/police presence, women were aware that their personal conduct might be subject to paramilitary scrutiny; for example, if seen in the company of other men while their husbands were in prison. Such patterns of difference and separation could not simply dissolve with the advent of the peace process.

The Politics of Passage

At the start of my fieldwork in mid-1996, the IRA ceasefire of 1994 was no longer in operation and there was at best the sense of a fragile suspension of violence. The Northern Ireland elections of 30 May 1996 had been held in order to make it possible to re-establish multi-party negotiations but very little progress was being made. Everyone was apprehensive about the imminent 'marching season'.

Northern Ireland society is distinctive in the number of organisations which mount regular parades, particularly during the 'marching season' of July. Most marches are also accompanied by flute and drum bands, principally made up of young men (see Jarman and Bryan 1996 for details). The largest organisation is the Orange Order, founded in the late eighteenth century. During its history, it has opposed Catholic emancipation and, until recently, membership was barred for anyone married to a Catholic. For close-knit communities, the Orange Lodge (meeting hall) has been a focal point; anyone, male or female, disassociating themselves from its activities would incur disapproval and suspicion. Even though women can only play support and welfare roles within the Orange Order, older and middle-aged members of the women's section have positive memories of material help and social activities (personal interviews).

There is much historical evidence that Orange and associated marches have been deliberate manifestations of Protestant power over the Catholic minority (Ruane and Todd 1996: 109). Catholic women frequently mention memories of fear for their menfolk and of being confined inside their houses while listening to anti-Catholic songs and slogans. Recent years have seen a much more direct Catholic resistance to the passage of marches, but there are dozens of sites across Northern Ireland where a local accommodation has been reached. Under certain conditions, however, strips of road have acquired an intense symbolic significance.

This had become the case for part of the Garvaghy Road in the predominantly Protestant Portadown area. The dispute centres over the right of Orange marchers to return from a church service at Drumcree along the Garvaghy Road, part of which goes through a Catholic housing estate whose residents were determined that there should be no more marches outside their homes. To stave off confrontations, the RUC blocked the passage of the marchers with barricades while negotiators attempted to find a solution but both sides refused to compromise. As a result, other Orange members, marching bands and loyalist supporters began to flood into the area immediately around the church, creating what came to be known as 'the siege of Drumcree'. The RUC eventually made an about-face on the basis of avoiding major loss of life and allowed the march to go down the Garvaghy Road, to the fury of its Catholic residents and the nationalist community as a whole (Jacobson 1997).

The public image of the siege had been of a sea of men hurling abuse and threats at the police barricades. However, throughout the period, there also had been contingents of women, albeit overlooked by media interested only in the prospect of violence. When noticed, the women were dismissed as 'tea and sandwich makers'. Yet to see their presence as the result of coercion or as misguided determination to 'stand by their men' undervalues these women's potential for self-determining agency and resistance on the basis of their convictions. These women were neither immediate *agents* of violence nor were they in any sense engaged in peace-making since they could not have been unaware of the way in which the denial of passage was inflaming *Protestant* opinion and stretching the security forces to the limit. Indeed, in early July, Protestant protest escalated across the region until it amounted to a civil insurrection. For two days, free movement throughout the province was suspended; there were blockades between the international airport, the ferry ports and other vital routes, as well as on many local roadways.

Simultaneously, in Belfast, conflict was escalating around another strip of road which links the Ballynafeigh Orange Lodge to the city centre, passing over the Ormeau Bridge into the Catholic and predominantly republican Lower Ormeau Road. (It has therefore come to be generally known as the Ormeau march.) In the recent past, Orange marches along this route had been accompanied by obscene language and gestures and, even more notoriously, triumphal taunts from marchers male and female. On the eve of the scheduled march, the tension on both sides of the bridge was palpable. Women from the Lower Ormeau neighbourhood talked to me of their plans to block their side of the bridge with prams while those around the Ballynafeigh Lodge were preparing to brave police barricades.[9]

The fall-out of anger and fear from the Drumcree and Ormeau episodes provoked widescale rioting in Catholic areas and this in turn led to a tragic echo of the 1960s. Protestant and Catholic families had taken advantage of the ceasefires to move beyond the confines of separate housing estates to find better accommodation; many of these cases were single mothers. Thus, Catholics who had moved into majority Protestant areas or vice versa found themselves under attack by their neighbours, with bricks through windows, threats and actual incidents of firebombing. A total of 600 families were forced to flee. Figures are not available as to the breakdown of this total into Catholic and Protestant; however, eye-witness accounts[10] repeatedly reported the presence of women from both communities as participants in intimidation against the 'outsiders'.

On the other hand, Protestant women publicly disassociated themselves from the conflict over Drumcree. In letters to the press, and in radio and TV interviews, they emphasised how associating the protest around the Drumcree church with the maintenance of 'Protestant rights' constituted a distortion of their personal faith. Along with the NIWC, they called for meaningful negotiations to de-escalate the situation, rather than the accusations and counter-accusations which the mainstream political leadership were making. During the height of the civil unrest, women care workers and nurses pleaded with those mounting the barricades to let them through to attend to their elderly and disabled clients in the name of non-sectarian humanitarianism (Jacobson 1997).

However, the group of loyalist women I interviewed in the immediate aftermath of the Drumcree and Ormeau marches were adamant that the security forces were right to have used all means at their disposal to ensure the passage of the marchers. They expressed regret that the situation had afterwards deteriorated so badly, but insisted that this was the cost of drawing attention to the encroachments on their 'Protestant rights'. In particular, they claimed an essential place for marches in retaining their young people's cultural identity. Any negative impact on Catholic residents along the routes was dismissed as a fabrication of 'trouble-makers'. For understandable reasons, it was not possible to find women who admitted actually to having taken part in intimidation, but interviewees did condone road blocks, which they saw as the only way to demonstrate their resistance to what was going on.

After the violence of July 1996, there were some unanticipated compromises over marches. Northern Ireland entered an extended period of negotiations, where cross-community initiatives continued, but more cautiously; as one woman activist commented:

> Repairing the bridges torn down in the flood of sectarianism we witnessed this summer of '96 will take tremendous courage and goodwill on the part of everyone ... Do we stand in the relative safety of our own community, gaze into open wounds inflicted by 'the other side' ... [o]r do we acknowledge that it has been difficult for all of us, reflect on and accept the consequences of our action – collectively? (Greer 1997: 3)

In view of the progress made in the political process since these events, it is tempting to regard them as manifestions of 'the bad old days'. However, Drumcree continued to loom over the progress of negotiations in 1997 and 1998. As noted, by 1998, women's voices were making themselves heard. It is therefore necessary to examine their conduct as political representatives and voters.

Casting Votes 'For Peace'?

Gendered constructions of the public/private divide in Northern Ireland have led to a startling absence of women from all forms of political representation, particularly when compared with contemporaneous development within Western Europe (Miller et al. 1996; Fearon 1996; Porter 1998).[11] Against this history, the advent of the Northern Ireland Women's Coalition (NIWC) in early 1996 was groundbreaking. The NIWC was instigated by a cross-community group of women who were aware of the fact that the May 1996 Northern Ireland elections were going to perpetuate the absence of women. They hurriedly constituted themselves as a formal electoral player which could mount a campaign, adopting the slogan 'Wave Goodbye to the Dinosaurs'. Their election manifesto stated: '[T]he Women's Coalition is dedicated to drawing together the different views, ideas and options to achieve a workable solution. Over the years of violence women have been very effective in developing and maintaining contact across the various divides in our society ... In doing this women have seen themselves as agents of change.'

Remarkably, despite their lack of infrastructure and funding, the coalition achieved their objective of winning sufficient votes under the complex system adopted for the 1996 election to entitle them to seats at the negotiating table. Yet this still amounted to only slightly over 1 per cent of the total vote and they encountered substantial criticism from some of the few women who were already in the public sphere. The SDLP local councillor and activist, Brid Rogers stated: 'The problem with Northern Ireland is how to accommodate two clashing aspirations. To do this you need a clearly worked out idea of how that will be done ... [T]here are women who have worked their way up through political parties despite the difficulties. Now they're facing another woman for the same vote' (*Irish Times*, 17 May 1996). In less temperate terms, Iris Robinson, a prominent activist in the DUP stated: 'They are doing their best to destroy anything that smacks of Unionism or Protestantism. Thank God only 7,000[12] idiots voted for these women' (quoted by David McKittrick, *The Independent*, 25 April 1997).

Between 1996 and 1997, the NIWC made an important input into political forums in the face of consistently derogatory attacks on their sheer presence there *as women* over and above their political stance. During the negotiations of 1997–98, their representatives were not major players, but they acted as a conduit between otherwise intransigent parties and ensured at least some attention to gender issues. Two representatives have also been elected to the Northern Ireland Assembly. However, it still has a very specific electoral support base which benefits from the particularities of the proportional voting system (Roulston 1999). Women from a variety of backgrounds in Northern Ireland recognise the contribution the NIWC has made; one typical comment was that 'Before they [the NIWC] came along, the nearest women got to the negotiating table was to polish it!' However, this cannot be extrapolated to mean that they also found a shared identity which overrode other affiliations, as was to be made evident by voting patterns for the referendum and the Assembly elections.

The promise of the 1998 Agreement   At the time of its initial publication, the Agreement was widely acclaimed as 'achieving the impossible' in the way its proposal could be endorsed by both sides: 'The beauty of the agreement is that both nationalists and unionists have sound reasons for believing that they are right about the long term ... There are incentives for each bloc to accommodate the other precisely in order to make its vision of the future more likely' (O'Leary 1999: 66). Retrospectively, there is more acknowledgement of how the acceptance of the Agreement rested on the deliberate vagueness of conditions around decommissioning which was to create the impasse of 1999.

In the context of this case study, however, it is necessary to link the implicit message of the Agreement with women's reactions. Its opening statement reads as one with which anyone seeking peace in Northern Ireland could agree: 'We must never forget those who have died or been injured, and their families. But we can best honour them through a fresh start, in which we firmly dedicate ourselves to the achievement of reconciliation, tolerance, and mutual trust, and to the protection and vindication of the human rights of all' (Good Friday Agreement 1988: 1). All the signatories made an absolute commitment to exclusively democratic and peaceful means of resolving differences on political issues, and stated their opposition to any use or threat of force by others for any political purpose, whether in regard to the Agreement or otherwise (ibid.: 1). The promise here, used for subsequent campaign slogans, was that the Agreement would 'take the gun out of politics' and open the way to an eventual resolution of Northern Ireland's statehood without recourse to violence.

The decision as to whether to accept the Agreement was to be put to

TABLE 10.3   1998 referendum results in Northern Ireland

Electorate	1,175,403
Turnout (%)	80.98
Percentage of Yes votes	71.12
Percentage of No votes	28.88

the electorate in the 22 May referendum. Three out of the four majority parties (the UUP, the SDLP and SF) and all the smaller political parties represented at the negotiations advocated a 'Yes' vote. The DUP had always regarded the negotiations as a 'sell-out' to republicanism and urged 'No', despite having no feasible alternative other than increased security measures. Voters with established political affiliations therefore had some clear guidelines; however, the situation became tense as divisions escalated within the UUP itself and when the leadership of the Orange Order also decided to endorse the Agreement.

Women were, of course, fully aware of all these tensions while they mulled over the Agreement (a copy was sent to each household) and discussed it together and with me in interviews conducted during the run up to the referendum. Catholics and Protestants alike commented on the NIWC's achievement in gaining the inclusion of a statement in the Agreement pledging to promote 'social inclusion, including in particular community development and the advancement of women in public life' ('Rights, Safeguards and Equality of Opportunity', clause 1). At the same time, there was considerable disquiet coming from different locations.

For both middle- and working-class Catholic women, the sheer location of the proposed Assembly raised fundamental fears; a frequent statement ran along these lines: 'Just the name "Stormont" reminds me of those days when the RUC could do what they liked in our communities ... I know this time it's supposed to be different, but I can't help having my doubts.' For virtually all Protestant women interviewed, the prospect of the SF leadership participating in the Assembly was abhorrent: 'I know they are supposed to have given up violence, but the thought of them sitting down to make our laws sends shivers down my spine.'

During the pre-referendum campaigning,[13] it became all too clear that, despite the euphoria of April, the result of the referendum would not be a foregone conclusion. Technically, a statistical majority of the total votes would be sufficient for adoption of the Agreement. However, the complex power-sharing provisions for the Assembly meant that it was crucial to convince at least 60 per cent of the Protestant electorate to vote 'Yes'. My interviews reflected a sense of motherhood shared with those victims of political violence and their families who appeared on television and in the press to urge a 'Yes' vote.

Some women, however, remained adamant about their intention to vote 'No',[14] perceiving the Agreement's provisions as the first steps on the 'slippery slope' to non-voluntary integration into an Irish state. One was prepared to admit past wrongs:

I know that bad things were done to them [Catholics] in the past, and I'm willing to play my part in putting them right so that we have no return to those days. But, that doesn't mean that I want to stop being British, being proud of my flag and my culture ... I'm *not* [with great emphasis] Irish and never will be ... and I don't want my kids to be, either.

The referendum did provide the necessary majority and was acclaimed with heartfelt relief. Yet a closer analysis of the voting figures confirms the divisions within Protestantism. Experienced analysts estimate that as many as 97 per cent of the Catholic population had voted 'Yes'. This means that the Protestant 'Yes' vote might only have amounted to 51 per cent of the votes cast and could not have been above 58 per cent (Borooah 1999). Exit polls suggest that there might have been a slight gender gap within these figures, with more Protestant/unionist women making the decision to vote 'Yes' than men, but this still cannot account for the size of the 'No' vote (personal communication). It must therefore be assumed that, at the least, a substantial percentage of women Protestant voters did not 'vote for peace'. Instead, they must have voted 'No' or abstained.

The divisions between Protestant pro- and anti-Agreement voters were confirmed by the Assembly elections in June 1998. Although the UUP managed to get sufficient seats to be the leading Protestant 'Yes' party in the Assembly, the number of seats gained by the anti-Agreement DUP bolstered its claims to be the 'true defenders' of the Union. This intensifed pressure on the UUP leader, David Trimble, to insist on prior IRA decommissioning before SF be allowed to take up the two seats on the Executive to which their electoral support entitled them. The subsequent impasse and the distrust and sense of insecurity referred to at the start of this chapter are inseparable from women's electoral choices.

Gender, Peace and Change

This case study rests on research carried out over a period when the momentum of the peace process has varied from full speed, through crisis to impasse. Interviews carried out in April 1999 reflected the fact that women's groups were, on the whole, deeply troubled by the language of 'No Surrender' being bandied about on all sides. Quite a few women commented on the reluctance to hand in weapons with the phrase: 'It's because the boys don't want to lose their toys.' At the same time, the overriding concern was not so much with gender but how the progress made to date towards a democratic political process could be maintained. Even groups of loyalist women who had condoned controversial Orange marches in previous years were not clear as to what they should be doing in the forthcoming marching season.

In this case study, I have argued that the history of the Northern Ireland conflict does not produce convincing evidence of a categorical preference for 'peace-making' among women as mothers. On the contrary, their positions have ranged from irredentism, through a general 'politics of avoidance' and an absolute commitment to non-violence, even at personal risk. This conclusion should not, however, overshadow the capacity for *change* which people in Northern Ireland have demonstrated. Indeed, some of the most noticeable changes have been undergone by men, such as former paramilitary killers now leading entirely non-violent community-based initiatives. I would like, therefore, to suggest that a more fruitful approach is to look at the gendered conditions and constraints affecting change. These may even appear trivial at first; after the first ceasefires, Protestant women from Northern Ireland made the short trip to Dublin for the first time in their lives and returned with their convictions about the nature of the Irish Republic at least a bit disturbed (personal communication). Others affect fundamental issues of how we live today. As Cynthia Cockburn observes in her fine study of women's movements in conflict situations (including Northern Ireland), the women involved in peace-making initiatives were not 'on the whole, pacifists. What they are looking for is an opening to justice, so that words can replace weapons sooner than might otherwise be the case' (Cockburn 1998: 8). It is in these cumulative processes that Northern Ireland's best hopes for the future lie.

Notes

1. Such as the bombing of Omagh in August 1998 by a group which was not observing the ceasefire, killing twenty-eight people.

2. The actual wording of the Agreement was that parties linked to paramilitaries must be committed to 'work constructively and in good faith' towards achieving decommissioning of all weapons by April 2000. This was meant to apply to *all* armed paramilitary groups but the dispute has been focused on the IRA. The UUP (see Table 10.2) demanded the destruction of substantial amounts of weapons and explosives before the IRA's political representatives, Sinn Fein, could take up the places they had gained in the executive on the basis of their share of the Assembly elections vote.

3. In 1992, there were twenty-two women serving prison sentences for IRA paramilitary activities. Loyalist paramilitaries had banned women from 'active service' in 1974 but there is still a strong likelihood that women continued to be involved in some support roles, including the 'luring' of targets (see Bruce 1992).

4. Even the geographical terminology is contested: republicans generally prefer to refer to 'the north of Ireland' while unionists and loyalists often use the historic name of 'Ulster'. Northern Ireland will be adopted here as the language of all the official documentation.

5. For an introductory account of this kind, see in particular Dunn (1995).

6. Interviews were carried out with the following: activists and elected representatives

from these political parties operating in Belfast and Derry/Londonderry: SDLP, Sinn Fein, NIWC, DUP, PUP; members of the women's section of the Orange Order in Belfast; women members of the Lower Ormeau Concerned Community Group (LOCCG) representing nationalist and republican residents in an area strongly opposed to Orange marches; members of the cross-community Women in the Churches project (including some women ministers); members of Women Together for Peace involved in anti-sectarian activity around the Harryville Church; women from the Antrim Family Centre, engaged in setting up cross-community initiatives around childcare.

7. Properly speaking, of course, Northern Ireland has never been a 'state' in its own right but it has had a unique status within the United Kingdom polity.

8. This is the correct title of the principal organisation contesting British rule through the armed struggle; alternatives in use in Northern Ireland are 'the Provos' and 'the boyos'. Over the course of the conflict, other smaller republican groupings such as the Irish National Liberation Army (INLA) have carried out bombings and attacks. As at April 1999, INLA and other breakaway groups which reject the Agreement, such as the Real IRA, are not on ceasefire but they do not have any input into the negotiating process.

9. In the event, the march went off without violence only because the British army physically blocked Catholic residents in their homes to allow the passage of the march.

10. There were extensive reports in all sections of the Northern Irish press: see *Belfast Telegraph, Irish News, Newsletter* for the period 12–14 July 1996.

11. Since 1920, only three women have served as MPs for Northern Ireland's Westminster constituencies. During its entire fifty years' existence, the total percentage of candidates for election to the Stormont government never rose above 4 per cent.

12. In fact, the figure was approximately 10,000 votes.

13. During which Rhoda Paisley, the daughter of the DUP leader, designed a special tie for her father to wear emblazoned with 'No'.

14. It is, of course, entirely possible that their actual votes were different although the final figures would tend to suggest that they did not change their minds.

Bibliography

Borooah, V. (1999) 'No Change', *Fortnight*, December/January.

Boyle, K. and T. Hadden (1994) *Northern Ireland: The Choice*, London: Penguin Books.

Brock-Utne, B. (1985) *Feminist Perspectives on Peace and Peace Education*, New York: Pergamon.

Bruce, S. (1992) *The Red Hand: Protestant Paramilitaries in Northern Ireland*, Oxford: Oxford University Press.

Buckley, S. and Lonergan, P. (1983) 'Women and the Troubles 1969–1980', in Y. Alexander and A. O'Day, *Terrorism in Ireland*, London, Croom Helm.

Cockburn, C. (1998) *The Space Between Us: Negotiating Gender and National Identities in Conflict*, London: Zed Books.

Dunn, S. (ed.) (1995) *Facets of the Conflict in Northern Ireland*, London: Macmillan.

Dunn, S. and V. Morgan (1994) *Protestant Alienation in Northern Ireland: A Preliminary Survey*, Centre for the Study of Conflict, University of Ulster.

Edgerton, L. (1986) 'Public Protest, Domestic Acquiescence: Women in Northern Ireland' in R. Ridd and H. Callaway (eds), *Caught Up in Conflict: Women's Responses*, London: Macmillan.

Fearon, K. (1996) 'Introduction', *Power, Politics, Positioning: Women in Northern Ireland*, Democratic Dialogue Report no. 4, Belfast.

Greer, D. (1997) *Community Relations Journal*, Winter 1996/97.

Hamilton, A., L. Moore and T. Trimble (1995) *Policing a Divided Society: Issues and Perceptions in Northern Ireland*, Centre for the Study of Conflict, University of Ulster.

Hyndman, M. (1996) *Further Afield: Journeys from a Protestant Past*, Belfast: Beyond the Pale Publications.

Jacobson, R. (1997) *Whose Peace Process? Women and Political Settlement in Northern Ireland, 1996–1997*, Peace Studies Papers, Third Series, Department of Peace Studies, Bradford University.

Jarman, N. and D. Bryan (1996) *Parades and Protests: A Discussion of Parading Disputes in Northern Ireland*, Centre for the Study of Conflict, University of Ulster.

McKittrick, D. (1994) *Endgame: The Search for Peace in Northern Ireland*, Belfast: Blackstaff Press.

McWilliams M. and J. McKernan (1993) *Bringing it out into the Open – Domestic Violence in Northern Ireland*, Belfast: HMSO.

Miller, R. L., R. Wilford and F. Donoghue (1996) *Women and Political Participation in Northern Ireland*, Aldershot: Avebury.

Morgan, V. (1995) 'Peacemakers? Peacekeepers? – Women in Northern Ireland 1969–1995', professorial lecture, INCORE, University of Ulster.

Morgan, V. and G. Fraser (1994) *The Company We Keep: Women, Community and Organisations*, Centre for the Study of Conflict, University of Ulster.

Morgan, V., M. Smyth, G. Robinson and G. Fraser (1996) *Mixed Marriages in Northern Ireland*, Centre for the Study of Conflict, University of Ulster.

O'Doherty, Malachi, (1998) *The Trouble with Guns*, Belfast: Blackstaff.

O'Leary, B. (1999) 'The Nature of the British-Irish Agreement', *New Left Review*, no. 233, January–February, pp. 66–96.

Pettman, J. J. (1996) *Worlding Women: A Feminist International Politics*, London and New York: Routledge.

Pollak, A. (ed.) (1993) 'A Citizen's Inquiry: The Opsahl Report', Dublin: Lilliput Press.

Porter, E. (1998) 'Political Representation of Women in Northern Ireland', *Politics*, vol. 18, no. 1, 25–32.

Quinn, D. (1993) *Understanding Northern Ireland*, Manchester: Baseline Books.

Rooney, E. (1995) 'Women in Political Conflict', *Race and Class*, vol. 37, July–September, pp. 51–6.

Roulston, C. (1997) 'Northern Ireland: Women on the Margin: The Women's Movements in Northern Ireland, 1973–1995', in L. West (ed.), *Feminist Nationalism*, London: Routledge.

— (1999) 'Women's Political Participation: What Difference Did it Make?', paper presented at the Political Studies Association Conference, University of Nottingham, 23–25 March.

Ruane, J. and J. Todd (1996) *The Dynamics of Conflict in Northern Ireland: Power, Conflict and Emancipation*, Cambridge: Cambridge University Press.

Ruddick, S. (1989) *Maternal Thinking: Towards a Politics of Peace*, Boston: Beacon Press.

Sales, R. (1997) *Women Divided: Gender, Religion and Politics in Northern Ireland*, London and New York: Routledge.

Ward, M. (ed.) (1986) *A Dangerous, Difficult Honesty: Ten Years of Feminism in Northern Ireland*, Belfast: Women's Book Collective.

Wilford, R. (1996) 'Representing Women', *Power, Politics, Positionings: Women in Northern Ireland*, Democratic Dialogue Report no. 4, Belfast.

11

Revealing Silence: Voices from South Africa

Teboho Maitse (in conjunction with Jen Marchbank)[1]

My aim with this case study is to explore the association between nationalism, the struggle for national liberation, apartheid, traditional culture and male violence against women. As such, I examine the relationship between gender and the struggle for national liberation in South Africa. Essentially, I am questioning whether nationalism and national liberation from racist oppression and exploitation of a people means that African men can exist as self-possessed autonomous beings only through the continued subordination of women. Explaining that African political violence was a response to conquest, dispossession and the authoritarian nature of apartheid is too simple. To understand how men who were dehumanised by apartheid failed to understand, even on the eve of South Africa's political transformation, that violence against women was a violation of their (women's) human rights is a very complex prospect. Male violence against women during the process of struggle for national liberation explains nationalism and national liberation's inability to change men's attitudes towards women. Nationalism and national liberation did not shift the unequal power relations between men and women, but they entrenched men's power (Nzenza 1988).

The fundamental purpose here is to hear the voices of African women.[2] To do this, I will draw on my doctoral fieldwork carried out during late 1993/early 1994 which included in-depth interviews with women who had experienced violence at the hands of male partners. Some of these interviews were with women who had been delegates to the December 1993 conference of the African National Congress (ANC)[3] Women's League; other women were contacted via women's refuges and from networking with women contacted via the ANC conference. In all, I carried out seventy-four interviews. These included educated and uneducated women, employed and unemployed, political activists of long-standing and those who were not personally involved in activism. Through these interview, I aim to illustrate both common and diverse themes, for I am of the opinion that 'life histories of women ... their stories tell more' (Browne 1987: 17). In these narratives, where women tell the same story, I will use a few women's voices to represent others, but the names are not their own.

Setting the Scene

In South Africa male violence against women occurs within the framework of a male-dominated society, in which men of all ages are socialised to define their power in terms of their capacity to effect their will, especially over women (Mabena 1990). This unbalanced system of gender socialisation became an integral part of a society where young men were taught to be assertive and masculine, and women, particularly African women, were expected to be subordinate and submissive. Young African men grew up to see their mothers and other women living under the domination of their fathers and other adult males. Apartheid compounded this dynamic through the creation of 'powerlessness' and 'impotence', which generated feelings of an 'inferiority complex' among African men (Biko 1978; Campbell 1992). African men of all ages had to deal with their 'inferior' status, their 'emasculation' in society and their position in the workplace where they were treated as 'minors'. This 'inferior' status contradicted African men's socialisation and the sense of power that nationalism and the struggle for national liberation afforded them as a powerful group that had control over women. Inevitably, it was within the seclusion of their own homes that the 'emasculated' men could expressly reassert their masculinities (Campbell 1992). For African women, then, 'home' took on a deceptive duality; as a sanctuary, haven and a place of safety on the one hand, and a potential prison and torture chamber on the other (Hanmer et al. 1989; Stanko 1988).

To illustrate the way apartheid, nationalism and the struggle for national liberation condoned and promoted violence against women, I have examined the interview data under the following headings: the payment of lobola[4] and marriage arrangements; women's views on men's violence; the changes taking place in South Africa and whether women thought these changes could end male violence towards women; and the way that nationalism plays itself out in gendered relationships.

The Specific Nature of Women's Oppression and Exploitation under Apartheid

Women in South Africa, irrespective of race, were subjected to a patriarchal and capitalist society, as women are the group most victimised by sexist oppression (hooks 1984: 43). However, in South Africa racial domination divided women into colour categories, and African women were subjected to a unique form of oppression and exploitation. They were subjected to a patriarchal system, which was reinforced by the apartheid laws, and were subjected to male authority in the home. Further, women were forced to do the drudgery of unrecognised and unpaid work for the family, which was accepted as a natural sexual division of labour. In addition traditional laws and the Native Administrative Act of 1927 regarded women as perpetual minors (Ramphele 1993) who could not own property nor enter into any contract.

African women were not regarded as fully-fledged South African citizens; their recognition as citizens was contingent on getting married, changing their names, and becoming wives and mothers. Thus it was not women as ordinary human beings who became citizens; it was their reproductive systems. Within marriage a woman's reproductive system officially belonged to a male citizen, whose duty it was to make certain that a woman reproduced future 'citizens'.

African men served as an extension of the state apparatus, because while the state oppressed all people in public, the men were legally empowered to oppress and exploit women in private for their own and the state's maintenance of hierarchical and oppressive patriarchal structures. Moreover, the control African men and the state had over women was a way of ensuring that a woman stayed in a monogamous relationship, while the number of women a man slept with was of no consequence. Most importantly, this form of dual control over women was aimed at sexuality, because women, particularly African women, were always at the mercy of men in the sense that white and black men could rape or beat them and they had no recourse to any court of law. The state indulged African men's employment of mythic African cultural 'norms' to defend their unsociable behaviour towards African women while white men raped them because of the perception that they were always ready to have sex.

The Ideological and Political Construction of the African Family

South African 'proper' families are constituted along patriarchal, hierarchical and heterosexual lines enforced by a fusion of African 'heathen' culture and European 'civilised' culture, maintained by the church, the state and society. Within the African societies of South Africa, family equalled women. Apartheid's economic and political developments interfered with the conjugal stability between African men and women, intensifying women's reproductive and productive duties. It is common knowledge that every time men (migrant workers) came home for a vacation they expected their wives to conceive. Occasionally, if the woman did not conceive by the end of her husband's vacation, men were known to rent rooms in the township so that their wives could visit them to *uku thatha isisu* (be impregnated). Fidelity was expected of women as men's property.

The apartheid system maintained the disarrangement of the African traditional family through economic, political and social interventions. Inevitably, during the phase of struggle for national liberation, the family assumed a dichotomous position; it became both a private and public institution. On the one hand, the family was a haven from the harsh brutalities of apartheid, and a site to inculcate and imbibe cultural values. Women became transmitters and emblems of African cultural norms, while men assumed the position of custodians of that culture (Anthias and Yuval-Davis 1989). It was within the family that the next generation was taught about beliefs and obligatory customs for the continuation of the African race. Thus society not only maintained the existence of family, but also secured the continuity of the distinctive characteristics of Africanism. However, political mobilisation was also based on the perception that apartheid was destroying the African family (Cock 1992), yet during the struggle for national liberation gender relations were not problematised.

Nationalism, Tradition and Gender

Nationalism as a concept to form identity is a powerful tool, particularly when people are denied any control over their lives, and their way of life is demeaned. However, nationalism can be a very flexible concept of identification by the oppressor or the oppressed, because it implies a unity and identification of different ethnic groupings irrespective of the class or gender to which individuals belong. Nationalism fails to acknowledge overtly that within the 'nation' there are two categories, men and women, whose relationship to each other is that of exploiter and exploited (Thiam 1986). Maria Mies argues that nationalism does not protect women from 'various forms of male violence, rape, wife-beating, harassment, molestation and sexist jokes. In this system both direct physical and indirect structural violence are commonly used as a method to "keep women in their place"' (Mies 1986: 27).

'Tradition' becomes men's exclusive prerogative which they use in defence of their subordination of women, because one of 'the fundamental aspects of our culture is the importance we attach to Man. Ours has always been a Man-centred society' (Biko 1978: 41). African men invoke their tradition and are unaware that similar arguments have been made and are still being made by men the world over. Men cling on to culture as a way to reclaim African history which colonialism reduced to barbarism and superstition (Biko 1978). Unfortunately, many women do not contest these arguments because women share cultural understandings as well as nationalistic feelings with men. Women, however, are denied the right to call on tradition to refute oppressive traditional practices of the past (McClintock 1993; Maitse 1996; Nhlapo 1992). As a result, nationalism and tradition are often used to construct images of femininity, womanliness and motherhood; for example, the 'mother of the nation'. Thus, women as transmitters of national culture and as symbols of national oppression are used to generate collective anger and hatred towards the oppressors and sympathy for the oppressed nation.

Nationalism and the struggle for national liberation in South Africa gave women a false sense of equality. Nationalism united all the people, regardless of ethnicity and gender. By virtue of its unification of the oppressed peoples, the struggle for national liberation afforded women a temporary respite from focusing on the harsh brutalities of their lives in the home. The presumption that national liberation would usher in a gender-equal society concealed from women the expandability of nationalism and national liberation (Karis and Carter 1972). As a result, the brutality of an oppressive regime became the focal point of their lives.

In South Africa, nationalism enabled African men to reclaim both the imaginary and real status they had prior to colonisation and apartheid; nationalism fed men's nostalgia of a 'perfect' past wherein they owned both the land and women (Arendt 1950). Nationalism authorises men not only to behave aggressively towards 'others', but to direct their aggression systematically, and not infrequently with calculated cruelty towards those constructed as 'others', especially those over whom they have exclusive ownership, or who are deemed inferior. South African literature on nationalism and the national liberation struggle has often reinforced gender invisibility (Walker 1982) despite the fact that women have spent long periods in jail, have fought, organised, mobilised and died in the resistance against settler colonialism (McFadden 1992).

However, the question is, in the day-to-day lives of these oppressed men *who* constitutes the 'others'? Often the oppressor does not live in close proximity to the oppressed victim. Is it possible for women to become 'others' (Wallace 1979), because of their expected subservience to men? Fanon (1967) maintained that violence against 'others' is liberatory, he also said that to get rid of his anger and frustration 'the colonised man will first deposit his aggressiveness against his own' (Fanon 1967: 40).[5] Fanon approved of the use of violence against one's 'own' by making a tacit justification for it. Fanon did not say so but his reasoning that men could have and do have the right to unleash their frustrations and anger against their 'own' during the process of struggle is an affirmation that 'nationalism has a deeper and more profound influence on men' (King 1973: 256).

Thus I conclude that the 'othering' of nationalism is not only confined to the oppressor, but to all those who are constructed as other, 'those who think, behave or act differently, but are constantly present "others" in day to day life, women' (Korac 1993: 256).

Women Speak

To discover how women explained violence against women I employed interviews. These reveal and illustrate the ways in which apartheid, nationalism and the struggle for national liberation condone and promote violence against women. These interviews also revealed the extent, severity and harm caused to my respondents and their ability to survive. Sometimes the recounting of experience was painful (see Maitse 1996). However, here I intend to discuss not their experiences of violence but their responses in relation to lobola, apartheid, national liberation and nationalism, for these were issues reported to me by my respondents as causes and supports of male violence towards women.

Firstly, all women interviewed agreed that male violence against women was due to how men perceived women. One argument frequently presented was that violence was a by-product of apartheid and that lobola, as well as African culture, enhanced the perception of women as men's possession, because both culture and lobola forbade women to discuss what happened within the four walls of their own homes. Given this, the following discussion focuses on lobola and nationalism, apartheid and national liberation.

Lobola and nationalism   Prior to apartheid, industrialisation and formalised capitalism, lobola (bride-price) for an African wife was cattle, the number of which was determined by the wealth of her prospective husband's family. Lobola was determined by characterising the wife-to-be as a mule-cow. The desirable woman was depicted as persevering, docile, understanding and physically strong with an udder big enough to nurse all the children born to the couple (Kenyatta 1938). The advent of urbanisation and capitalism ushered in a new phase, whereupon cash payment for a wife was now based on the woman's beauty, chastity and education, and from my respondents' reports it is clear that the amount demanded for lobola was influenced by economic circumstances including the inflation rate. This cash transaction for a wife further reduced a woman's status to that of a commodity.

Aside from the different definitions of culture, depending on the women's languages,[6] economic and educational status, all respondents who had had lobola paid for them (sixty-three in total) were unanimous in stating that 'lobola is a fundamental part of African culture'. However, women gave contradictory statements about lobola because, regardless of their view that lobola signified their subservience to men, part of them still wanted their husbands to pay it:

ELIZABETH: It certainly made me feel proud because he paid twelve heads of cattle to my family.

NOMSA: You feel superior to your friends, because it is such an honour to have someone pay for you.

Likewise, some thought that the payment of lobola would make their husbands or his family appreciate them, or curb his violence:

THEMBI: I … do not think men should pay for a wife. Rather, I think that a man should fork out a lump sum for a deposit towards a house, furniture or something. Not for another human being. [Then she contradicted herself thus] When we got married lobola was not an issue, it only became a problem when we returned home [from exile] because both our parents were making various demands on us. Although our marriage was shaky I started thinking that maybe things would work out if he paid lobola.

Lobola, however, is a social control upon women and illustrates sexual roles. Woman after woman mentioned virginity as a prerequisite on which the price tag for lobola was based. In addition, tradition taught girls how to please a man sexually and older women to guard the virginity of younger women. Lobola also casts women as passive and voiceless, making girls into easy prey for men.[7]

Women spoke of lobola in different ways. The majority of urban respondents drew similarities between lobola and nationalism while in the rural areas the majority view was that lobola compensated parents for their daughter and showed appreciation for the woman. Others emphasised family bonding, arguing that lobola enables the woman and the man's family to formalise relations, and to ensure that the grandchildren born out of the marriage belong to both sides of the family. Over half of the forty urban women interviewed also stated that the significance of lobola was to show a man's appreciation to the girl's family; unite Africans; reflect a man's gratitude to the girl's parents; and to compensate the girl's family. Fourteen respondents, while recognising its payment as an old African custom, also maintained its payment meant the end of freedom for the girl, as she was now viewed as purchased goods:

MEISIE: Really, I think that lobola signifies the end of the woman's individuality and freedom, because once she is paid for she is no longer allowed to have a mind of her own.

The view that lobola allows men to treat women as commodities was not uncommon. Yet all the women interviewed stated that lobola was a fundamental part of African culture. As such, it was remarkable to discover that although some women were aware of the consequences of lobola, they did not propose that it should be done away with, perhaps because the positive aspects of lobola, as a means to unite Africans and defeat apartheid, were also expressed, linking together nationalism and lobola:

> Lobola signifies the ability of black people to formalise relationships that unite them despite the divisions that apartheid has imposed on us, because we need each other to defeat apartheid. (representative of six women's views)

> REBECCA: Well, the significance of lobola is that it enables us to bond as an oppressed nation, and to unite against the enemy. What I'm trying to say is that in this country whites perceive themselves as a nation, but they call us tribes, so lobola and the struggle are what connects us. Lobola makes it possible for us to become one nation.

These quotes illustrate an understanding of nationalism's need for cohesiveness, and the need for oppressed people to utilise any means, particularly culture, to affirm and authenticate their lives (Cabral 1973). Associating lobola with nationalism suggests that these women (some political activists) needed an acceptable reason to explain lobola. Furthermore, it is my contention that the association of lobola and nation-building suggests a strong connection between culture and national consciousness. That no one questioned this connection reinforces Seidman's observation that during times of crisis lobola attained the status of: 'The national heritage, an essential element of stable social relations. Without the exchange of women to tie together lineage groups, society would crumble' (Seidman 1984: 433).

Women contrasted the symbolic meaning of lobola with its significance, in the sense that the payment of lobola on its own did not unite people, because families were united only through the rituals that were performed after lobola was paid. While these women tried to adhere to the ancestral meaning of the significance of lobola, drawing similarities between lobola and nationalism was a deviation from its historical purpose. In addition, I was extraordinarily dismayed that no-one discussed the divisive nature of lobola in that it permits the grading of women (based on virginity) which both authorises and encourages abuse because men are not compelled to marry women whom they sexually violate. Likewise, with lobola, male violence against women is normalised; the need for social cohesiveness compels women to collude with men due to fear of individual reprisals and breaking up of community cohesiveness. Both the apartheid laws and

African tradition (see Seidman 1984; Lazreg 1994) deemed that all men regardless of age had authority over women; as such, this communal inferiority prevented women, especially mothers-in-law, from intervening in domestic violence.

However, lobola was not the only issue charged with responsibility for violence against women. The matter of apartheid was raised by many in my interviews and it is to this that I turn next.

Apartheid and male violence Apartheid was discussed both on its own and in conjunction with other factors; for example, some linked apartheid with their experiences of lobola:

> TSHOLO: I think that in part his violence is a byproduct of apartheid, maybe apartheid frustrates him very much, and then when he becomes frustrated he becomes rude and violent to people closest to him. But also lobola has granted him the sole right to my body. I am his possession, so really both apartheid and lobola encouraged his violence.

> DINEO: My views are that apartheid made our men violent, I mean the disempowerment of African men by the whites did their heads in and of course lobola and African culture helped, especially the need to cling to that culture.

However, not all women blamed apartheid, relating male violence to socialisation across all cultures:

> GRACE: I think my husband's behaviour was not different from the general behaviour of men the world over. I was his possession, period.

> LINDIWE: I certainly do not subscribe to the school of thought which says that African men's violence towards women is a byproduct of apartheid. I essentially believe it is socialisation ... men the world over are socialised into believing that they have the power to control women and that is the most fundamental reason men use violence towards their wives. But then in this case apartheid seems to complicate things because black men say that they have been emasculated.

It is understandable why some women perceived male violence to be a byproduct of apartheid. It is a well-known fact that the apartheid regime abused the human rights of blacks; as a result, the racist and inhuman policies of apartheid were often blamed for turning African men into violent machines. But if we want to use apartheid as the explanation for African men's violence towards African women we have to question why this violence was unleashed only on women rather than on the men who were the oppressors. Is it because, historically, the oppression of a race has often been seen as an oppression of men? (Biko 1978; Fanon 1965). Thus, if we view oppression of a race as oppression of one gender, it explains the failure of the anti-apartheid nationalist movements to recognise that the apartheid regime directed its harshest and most demeaning forms of brutality towards women as reproducers of the African race.[8]

Apartheid seemed to offer excuses for and tolerance of male violence. I found that there was less concern among the husbands of my respondents to hide their violence from others, be they family or 'comrades' (the term used to refer to a fellow-member of the ANC):

THEMBI: Once my husband hit me in the office in [name of country withheld], there were other comrades there and I remember one senior comrade saying 'Come, you should not do that in public.'

As such, these men had neither fear of reprisals from the law enforcement agencies nor fear of losing society's respect. Apartheid laws that portrayed African men as the most violent in the country compounded the control they had over women. Such a portrayal made it difficult for the African community to recognise or condemn the violent behaviour of some of their men. Apartheid also designated a specific territory for African men over which they had absolute control; consequently, these men knew they would not be reprimanded, or lose status, for abusing their wives.

National liberation and silenced women Women also spoke of nationalism and the struggle for national liberation as the fundamental sources of male violence, some recognising and apologising for the fact that their views included an inherent critique of the nationalist movement:

CLAUDIA: I know that this sounds reactionary. Frankly, I have no qualms in stating that the struggle for national liberation and nationalism enabled him, in fact condoned his and all men's violence to women. You know, we were just added on to the struggle; the agenda was already set and it was men's agenda. What I mean is that being a member of any liberation movement does not necessarily protect women from male violence. In fact, the struggle encourages the violence because women do not have any forum to discuss anything that directly affects them, because in the first place the women's organisations are not independent of the male-dominated organisations. Women's organisations have to further the aims of the overall struggle for national liberation, rather than women's liberation. So women do not discuss issues that affect them because that is not what the struggle is about.

REBECCA: I would say that the struggle for national liberation masked male violence against women. I mean, look at it this way, the struggle was primarily about employing violence to achieve our liberation, so it would have been difficult to isolate violence against women and make it into a big issue. Anyway, who would have done that? Not women. We did not have a language.

Forty of my seventy-four interviewees were able to draw the connection between nationalism, national liberation struggle and violence against women. Their ability to connect male violence with the struggle for national liberation serves as an example of the benefits men derive from the 'liberating influence of violence' (Fanon 1967), inasmuch as women, being men's possessions, become 'others'. In addition, these narrations explain how both the culture of lobola and the struggle for national liberation enforce the silence about male violence against women. Further, women stated that participation in the struggle did not afford them the space to talk about issues that affected them as a gender.

SHEILA: I really think that the struggle encouraged men in general to use violence against women; this is their way of retaining power over us. Just to give an illustration of what is going on right now in this country: who cares that a gang of young men abducts and gang-rape a woman? Nobody. You know I regard this jackroll business as a form of terrorism similar to the one where the AWB [an extremist white organisation] takes black men and kills them. You know when that happens you find everybody wanting to do something about it, but then when women are gang-raped by their own people nothing is done. So you know what is classic about this country? It is that women have always been in the forefront of the struggle for national liberation. But when it comes to issues that directly affect us as women we are nowhere to be seen, and this is because the struggle for liberation promised us a better future by not problematising male violence towards women. Also, at other times, the very people who are violent towards us are our very own comrades in the struggle. So, there is the fear that we are not supposed to challenge our own people because national unity is of paramount importance. As a result, women do not complain about male violence because it is not perceived as something anti-social. I certainly never complained about my husband.

NONDUMO: This is a difficult question because a lot of men do beat their wives, and it is something we never ever talk about. You know why? It is because of the need to focus on the struggle, because as Africans we need each other, men and women, to defeat apartheid. So, we all have to stick together. We cannot afford to be divided because that weakens our struggle. Male comrades beat us and they know that we will not talk about their violence, or leave them because we do not want to be called sell-outs.

LULU: I remember once I wanted the Women's Section [of the ANC] to discuss men's violence to women in VOW (*Voice of Women*) and [name of person withheld] said the publication did not deal with such issues.

While Lulu's response cannot be judged as a true representation of how male violence towards women was perceived throughout the ANC, unquestionably this response (among others) confirmed my conviction that the struggle for national liberation did not protect women from male violence. Moreover, some women did not want male violence against women to be made into an issue, and I wondered whether their refusal to discuss it was due to a fear they would be forced to confront or acknowledge their own experiences of male violence. The similarities between both the community in exile and that at home in their tolerance of, and the excuses they advanced for, male violence against women amazed me, particularly the unwillingness to intervene when a man beat his wife. I concluded that the unwillingness of the African National Congress to acknowledge that some of their members were violent towards women was symptomatic of how 'People ... in power ... deny ... the problem. Because, if they admitted the truth they would have to ask some very fundamental questions about the nature of the relationships between men and women' (Wilson 1983: 82).

While participation in the struggle conscientised women about racial oppression, it failed to conscientise them about gender oppression. Compared to the oppression of a whole race, male violence towards women did not warrant the same kind of focus as that directed towards ending racial oppression.

It is important to point out that women were not at fault for not challenging gender oppression; they were under the impression that national liberation was akin to gender equality. Women's views suggest that nationalism and the struggle for national liberation embody gender power, which is male power. The ethos of the nationalist movement is to achieve self-determination. However, that ethos does not in any way include the self-determination of women as a gender. Inevitably, women's position in society prior to and during colonisation and post-liberation is never discussed. Nationalism does not espouse women's issues, as gender oppression is assumed not to 'exist'.

Women's responses also suggest that men derived support for their violence from culture, apartheid and the struggle for national liberation. This indicates that, in a society struggling for self-determination, and where men of one racial grouping experience some kind of sexist attitudes from both men and women of the dominant group, the oppressed group is bound to confuse and excuse male violence towards women as a reflection of the hostility and frustration that African men carry towards their oppressors. Consequently, there is always a reluctance to accept that the oppressed race can also be brutal in its actions, because the violence is often attributed to others. Evidently, racial oppression countered with nostalgia for a utopian past, as well as outrage and a sense of injury that the utopia no longer exists, implant in the oppressed people a consciousness of solidarity (Biko 1978; Fanon 1967).

As such, issues that affect women or male attitudes towards women are often not problematised because to challenge abusive attitudes would demand that women challenge not only their oppressors but their 'own' people too. In conclusion, the failure of the liberation movement to problematise male violence against women was also exacerbated by the fact that women did not only experience sexist or abusive attitudes from African men, but from all men. Oppression dehumanised and belittled the African people regardless of their gender; therefore, there was a need for some kind of cohesiveness. Since black men were not seen as the oppressors of 'others' but as the oppressed, it would have been difficult for black women to isolate men of one race as the most abusive because this action would have confirmed racist perceptions of black men as violent.

Conclusions

Violence towards women in countries that are, or were, engaged in the struggle for national liberation is often linked to nationalism and masculinities, because nationalism promotes and validates masculinities in its popular images of nationalist struggles which are predominantly male (Enloe 1983, 1993; McFadden 1992; Mies 1986; Russell 1975; Wallace 1979). As a result, nationalism projects women as passive objects and as victims of legalised oppression. In addition, nationalism grants men the privilege to 'take their past for granted: [and to] look back to it for guidance, confirmation, inspiration' (Spender 1982: 15). I maintain that if during the process of the struggle for national liberation and after liberation from an oppressive and racist regime, women are still beaten, raped, molested, humiliated and tortured by men, then there is something discordant with the ethos of nationalism and the struggle for national liberation.

In this discussion, some women blame apartheid, traditional culture and nationalism for male violence. It is crucial to specify that 'traditional' culture and nationalism were used to counter apartheid's denigration of rituals and modes of behaviour, hence some women drew similarities between nationalism and lobola. However, it is fallacious to suggest that it is only African men who were affected by apartheid. To believe that apartheid policies threatened the personal identity of a mass of men is to lose sight of the fact that despite their oppression African men were the engineers of the liberation movements. In addition, to propound the belief that apartheid made African men passive and powerless runs counter to a masculine sense of self because this perception provides a strong foundation to excuse men's violence as induced by apartheid. While it is acknowledged that the apartheid system dehumanised people, apartheid also afforded men immense control over women. Similarly, the struggle for national liberation and nationalism allowed African men to close ranks and make women invisible. The truth is, we all know that often men do not aggress against the source of oppression. In many respects the perfect victim is always a woman, because what men often need is someone to overpower and control without too many negative social consequences, that is someone who cannot challenge their physical strength, someone who can reaffirm some of their 'lost manhood' (Campbell 1992). Until such connections between gender and nationalism are changed, the 'new' South Africa will not mean peace for women. Women maintained that political changes alone in South Africa would not necessarily mean change for women. Speaking at the birth of the 'new' South Africa in 1994 Katlego said:

> I firmly believe that the change taking place in this country at the moment will not change men's attitudes towards women. You see we have never challenged our cultural perceptions of what it is to be a man and a woman in this society. We have never made men take any responsibility for their violent actions, because political organisations have never intervened at a level of consciousness raising in an effort to make men responsible for their violence … It is fashionable to say that a 'new' South Africa will be non-sexist, but how can we achieve that if men do not acknowledge that they are violent towards women? So I suppose for women to experience meaningful change men must examine themselves as well as admit the horrible things they do to women. In addition, women have to be involved … if we leave it up to men, they will conveniently forget about women's rights. They will perpetuate the old customs, which condone violence against women.

Notes

1. This chapter is based upon Teboho Maitse's Ph D thesis, *Women's Experiences of Male Violence in the Context of the South African National Liberation Struggle* (University of Bradford, 1997).

It was edited by Jen Marchbank in consultation with Teboho Maitse. Responsibility for the presentation of this research lies jointly with both women. The authorial 'I', however, refers to Teboho Maitse.

2. I myself am an African woman who has been a political activist for several decades.

3. The ANC led the national liberation movement and formed the government of South Africa after the historic 1994 election.

4. Marriage among educated and uneducated Africans is structured through the system of lobola. Lobola is a form of patriarchal control and it divides women from each other. This practice controls women because a woman's submissiveness and virginity determine the bride-price. It is recognised that there exist debates regarding the exact meaning of lobola.

5. Steve Biko offers a different argument, maintaining that, in South Africa, black men's violence against their own was a symptom of their anger against the apartheid regime. In his own words 'Deep inside his anger mounts at the accumulating insult, but he vents it ... on his fellow man in the township' (Biko 1978: 28).

6. The women in this study spoke eleven different languages.

7. Similarly, Christianity requires women to take responsibility for men's behaviour, because it places emphasis on the need for women to retain their virginity. From personal experience, I recall being told over and over again that the best dowry a woman could give to her husband is her virginity (Chigwedre 1982).

8. It is no secret that African women were sterilised and were also injected with Depo Provera without their knowledge or consent.

Bibliography

Anthias, F. and N. Yuval-Davis (eds) (1989) *Woman–Nation–State*, London: Macmillan.

Arendt, H. (1950) *The Origins of Totalitarianism*, London: Harcourt Brace Javanovich.

Biko, S. (1978) *I Write What I Like: A Selection of His Writings*, ed. A. Stubbs, London: Bowerdean Press.

Browne, E. (1987) *When Battered Women Kill*, London: Collier Macmillan.

Cabral, A. (1973) *Return to the Source: Selected Speeches by Amilcar Cabral*, ed. Africa Information Service, London: Monthly Review Press.

Campbell, C. (1992) 'Learning to Kill? Masculinity, the Family and Violence in Natal', *Journal of Southern African Studies*, vol. 18, no. 3.

Chigwedre, A. (1982) *Lobela: The Pros and Cons*, Harare: Books for Africa.

Cock, J. (1992) *Women and War in South Africa*, London: Open Letters.

Cooper, A. (1982) *Wives for Cattle: Bride Wealth and Marriage Payments in Southern Africa*, London: Routledge.

Enloe, C. (1983) *Does Khaki Become You? The Militarization of Women's Lives*, London: Pluto Press.

— (1993) *The Morning After: Sexual Politics at the End of the Cold War*, Berkeley: University of California Press.

Fanon, F. (1965) *A Dying Colonialism*, London: Penguin Books.

— (1967) *Wretched of the Earth*, London: Penguin Books.

Hanmer, J., J. Radford and E. A. Stanko (1989) 'Policing Men's Violence: An Introduction', in Hanmer, Radford and Stanko (eds), *Women, Policing and Male Violence: International Perspectives*, London: Routledge.

hooks, b. (1984) *Feminist Theory: from Margin to Centre*, Boston: South End Press.

Karis, T. and G. Carter (eds) (1972) *From Protest to Challenge: A Documentary History of African Politics 1882–1964. Vols 1–4*, Stanford, CA: Hoover Institution Press.

Kenyatta, J. (1938) *Facing Mount Kenya: The Tribal Life of the Gikuyu*, London: Secker and Warburg.

King, R. R. (1973) *Minorities Under Communism: Nationalities as a Source of Tension among Balkan Communist States*, Cambridge, MA: Harvard University Press.

Korac, J. (1993) 'Serbian Nationalism: Nationalism of my Own People', *Feminist Review*, no. 45, Autumn.

Lazreg, M. (1994) *The Eloquence of Silence: Algerian Women in Question*, London: Routledge.

McClintock, A. (1993) 'Family Feuds: Gender, Nationalism and Family', *Feminist Review*, no. 44.

McFadden, P. (1992) 'Nationalism and Gender Issues in South Africa', *Journal of Gender Studies*, vol. 1, no. 4.

Mabena, L L. (1996) 'The Political Mobilisation of South African Women in Exile: A Social Analysis of African National Congress Women in Exile in Tanzania', M Phil, University of Bradford.

Maitse, T. E. (1996) 'The Past is Present: Thoughts from the New South Africa', in D. Bell and R. Klein (eds), *Radically Speaking: Feminism Reclaimed*, Australia: Spinifex.

Mies, M. (1986) *Patriarchy and Accumulation on a World Scale: Women in the International Division of Labour*, London: Zed Books.

Nhlapo, T. (1992) 'Culture and Women Abuse: Some South African Starting Points', *Agenda: A Journal about Women*, no. 13.

Nzenza, S. (1988) *Zimbabwean Woman: My Own Story*, London: Kalia.

Ramphele, M. (1993) *A Bed Called Home: Life in the Migrant Labour Hostels of Cape Town*, Cape Town: Dave Philip.

Russell, D. E. H. (1975) *The Politics of Rape*, New York: Stein and Day.

Seidman, G. W. (1984) 'Women in Zimbabwe: Postindependence Struggles', *Feminist Studies*, vol. 10, no. 3, Autumn.

Spender, D. (1982) *Women of Ideas and What Men Have Done to Them*, London: Routledge and Kegan Paul.

Stanko, E. A. (1988) 'Hidden Violence Against Women', in M. Maguire and J. Pointing (eds), *Victims: A New Deal?*, Milton Keynes: Open University Press.

Thiam, A. (1986) *Black Sisters Speak Out: Feminism and Oppression*, London: Pluto Press.

Walker, C. (1982) *Women and Resistance in South Africa*, London: Onyx Press.

Wallace, M. (1979) *Black Macho and the Myth of the Superwoman*, London: John Calder.

Wilson, E. (1983) *What is to be Done about Violence against Women?* London: Penguin Books.

Part III

Conclusion

12

Globalisation, States and Women's Agency: Possibilities and Pitfalls

Susie Jacobs

This chapter takes up several themes – globalisation; the erosion of the state; the questions of nationalism and of ethno-nationalism – discussing them from a gender perspective. In examining these topics, it attempts to make connections between discourses that tend to remain separate. It suggests that serious analysis of women's movements and the impact of feminisms has been sidelined in many discussions of globalisation. Associated topics such as debates over the death of the state also require more thorough gender analysis, especially as the demands women have made have tended to be of national states. Valuable feminist work on nationalism exists, yet does not always appear to be incorporated into mainstream work on new nationalisms and local movements. A more complete analysis of globalisation and gender would examine not only trends promoting global flows and connections, but counter-movements such as ethno-nationalism as well. Despite these cautions, globalisation has enhanced the prospects for women's organising and more micro-level resistances; this is, however, only one possible outcome and should not – as is the tendency in the literature – be treated as already determined.

The chapter is structured as follows: the first, and larger, part examines three topics – globalisation, the state and nationalism – giving an overview of some general themes as well as gender implications. There follows a discussion of ethno-nationalisms and gender, incorporating a discussion of gendered agency. The penultimate part of the chapter explores the seeming inconsistency that women's agency is often constrained; yet some exercise it in violent actions against male and female 'others'. Despite all this, as the last section notes, women's movements are gaining in strength, if unevenly, and are becoming internationalised.

Definitions and Conceptions of Globalisation

Debates concerning the extent and the implications of globalisation are current within several social science disciplines. The term 'globalisation' itself is often used loosely to mean growing global inter-connectedness and the increase of open-ended global flows. The term tends to be employed differently by different authors, reflecting differing theoretical orientations, disciplinary concerns and different political stances. Some, for instance, emphasise the compression of time and space (Harvey 1989), usually seen as closely linked to the development of new transport and communication technologies. As Stivens notes (1998), the Western discussions of global-isation, themselves following on from prior discusssions of modernity, are preoccupied with a shift from an industrial to an informational world, seeing the circulation of seemingly empty and universalist signs in a world system of flows and their recasting into different configurations of meaning (Featherstone and Lash 1995). Kiely remarks, however, that time-space compression is not equivalent to the destruction of time and space; such compression is experienced differently in different parts of the world (Kiely 1998: 4). It might be added that it is experienced differently by different groupings even in the same territory.

Other uses of 'globalisation' concentrate more strongly on the aspect of westernisation, seeing the spread of economic, cultural, managerial and other institutions across national and cultural boundaries. This view, usually associated with anti-imperialism, concentrates on globalisation as a (capitalist-led) economic force with concomitant effects in terms of consumption patterns, weakening of state protectionism (see below) and cultural change. McMichael provides a clear statement of this viewpoint. The globalisation project includes market-based rather than state-managed development; centralised management of market rules by the G-7 states; implementation of these policies by the IMF, the World Bank and the WTO; the concentration of market power in trans-national corporations; and the subordination of societies to these global forces (McMichael 1996: 177).

Thus, some accounts are more optimistic than others concerning the eventual effects of globalisation. Most writers do recognise that processes may take place unevenly across the globe. And most, despite other differences, see globalisation as taking place simultaneously at economic, cultural and political levels.

Globalisation and gender Discussion of gender issues in globalisation studies tends to be patchy or tokenist (Jacobs 1997a). In the mainstream literature on globalisation, gender and feminism tend to be treated in one of two ways: either they are mentioned only in passing, or else they are treated in sweeping terms as one of the new social movements at the forefront of cultural globalisation.

Albrow's work has the merit of recognising conflicts between states' attempts to maintain traditional gender relations and the civil rights legislation they also enact. However, he also concludes that sexual relations in a global age are conducted on the basis of equality (Albrow 1996: 152). Less nuanced, Waters writes, 'Globalisation encompasses such possibilities as … the emergence of universal feminist sisterhood from the confines of localized and nationalized patriarchies' (Waters 1995: 163). This statement is over-generalised and overlooks divisions within feminism/s. At least since the 1980s, feminism has been marked by a good deal of dissension, brought on in part by assumptions of universalism on the part of of many Western feminists. Although, more recently, various feminist strands and coalitions have been more cognisant of difference, both of politics and social positionings, it remains the case that many movements with otherwise similar aims, particularly in the South, eschew the term 'feminist', preferring to be termed 'women's movements' (see, e.g., Basu 1995). Nor, in general, does the literature attend to the possibility of backlash against feminist currents and organisations.

Feminists, in contrast, deal with globalisation, but as a concept problematic for gender analysis (Stivens 1998). And these discussions tend to remain separate from (or, unacknowledged by) the general globalisation literature. They are usually also more pessimistic about the consequences of globalisation. There exists a body of work on gender, globalisation and economic matters This is seen in, for example, terms of the effects of: structural adjustment and liberalisation policies (see Aslanbegui et al. 1994; Elson 1995). Others have analysed the increasing impoverishment of women in many contexts, North and South, as well as the complex and contradictory trends of increased female employment in manufacturing (see *World Development* 1999). Women may gain better wages and conditions in some manufacturing contexts while losing paid employment, and being pushed back into the informal sector, in others. Feminist political scientists have also been active in discussion of globalisation (see, e.g., contributions in Kofman and Youngs 1996). Along other lines, feminists have also discussed the growth in female-headed households (e.g. Chant 1997), itself a global trend, and the failure of feminist strategies to make concrete gains, including the reform of customary law, especially in patrilineal contexts (Agarwal 1994; Basu 1995: 17).

Another aspect of globalisation can be seen in the internationalisation of social divisions – for example, class, ethnicity/'race' – usually analysed as appertaining to nation-states (Shaw 1994). This may occur both through diasporic migrations and through economic and political processes – for example, the existence of Export Processing Zones – creating similar types of divisions across national boundaries. Analyses which are critical of the impact of globalising processes are most commonly applied to the erosion of community structures (Scholte 1999). Gray (1998) points out that the dominance of the market has effectively destroyed many local communities[1] and leads to social fragmentation. Less commonly, class divisions are analysed in terms of globalisation (see Wilkin 1999). Bauman points out that many lose in economic as well as social terms in the global marketplace. Thus 'the winners' from globalisation may be seen as an emerging trans-national professional or upper-middle class, which accompanies an already internationalised bourgeoisie.

Most mainstream analyses do not see gender divisions as one aspect of emerging global stratification/s; nevertheless, globalisation is likely to have gender-specific effects. Women are generally less geographically mobile than men, although there are exceptions, in national as well as class terms. Female migration, including some long-distance migration, is common in parts of Latin America as well as the Philippines (Chant and Radcliffe 1992). Rural to urban female migration is common in newly industrialising settings, including parts of South-East Asia. The sexual traffic in women and children is hardly new, but has acquired wider scope with inter-nationalising trends. A small, professionalised female elite of women is more mobile than many; industrial and other workers may migrate from rural to urban areas. However, in general, some correlation between 'the local' and female rootedness still exists; moreover, rootedness in locality has, at least in the past, often been linked to sexual reputation and respectability. 'Mobile' women, especially if without their families, are often seen as having lost respectability and may be seen as sexual prey. It is possible that the mass of women – female casualised labour in new global scenaria – may come to represent the 'local'. It may also be the case that some women, more tied in with localised kinship networks than is (often) the case for men, may prefer to avoid the movement and migration accompanying globalisation. Bauman writes of the 'growing misery and desperation of the grounded many and the new freedoms for the mobile few' (Bauman 1998: 72). Women are disproportionately represented among the 'grounded', those subject to the constraints of globalisation with few of its benefits, and tied to localities.

Globalisation and the question of the state   Within discussions of globalisation, the 'fate' of the nation-state is a matter of much debate; to what extent do globalisation processes undermine the nation-states which have been so central to modernity and to developmental projects?

Differences of opinion and analysis are of importance in discussing the demands which might (still) be placed on the state by various agents and groupings, including feminists.

Some (e.g. Hirst and Thompson 1996) hold that changes have not been as great as posited, as many international trends in capitalism have been long-standing; thus, social democratic-type alternatives are still a possibility.

Another grouping, termed by Held (1998) 'hyper-globalisers', argues that processes of globalisation are making analyses of the nation-state of less importance. Whereas in the past the global scene was the theatre of inter-state relations, in the contemporary world, all three legs of the sovereignty 'tripod' – economic, military, political – are broken beyond repair (Bauman 1998). In this view, individual states have declining capacity to determine economic policies. This is due both to the growth and increasing power of transnational corporations, and to the rapid escalation of flows of money, technology and information. These render state boundaries of decreasing relevance, at least in economic terms.

Although they agree that globalisation is occurring at a rapid pace and that this undermines aspects of state power, in other respects 'hyper-globalisers' differ. One grouping is broadly optimistic concerning the prospects afforded for improved communications, inter-dependence and global action (e.g. Robertson 1992; Waters 1995). A second stance is far more critical of the social and political effects of globalisation. States which are already weak, especially developmental states, may become further weakened (see Rai 1996) and have less capacity to effect policy of whatever sort, including reformist policies. Bauman notes that it is the *demise* of state sovereignty, not its triumph, which accounts for the current popularity of statehood; new claims to statehood are facilitated by the fact that many governments today are not expected to fulfil what have been considered normal functions of state bureaucracies (Bauman 1998: 64). Further, he argues, the 'new world [dis]order' requires *weak* rather than strong states. Global finance, trade and information depend upon fragmentation for their untrammelled mobility (p. 66). Gray (1998) adds that collapsed states now pose far greater threat to civil liberties, at least in some contexts, than does excess of state interference.

Others argue that although changes are proceeding in global economic and political structures, discussions of state power in terms of a simple 'decline', misunderstand the complexity of the processes occurring. Held and McGrew (1998) argue that there exists no simple diminution of state power. Economic globalisation, for instance, has often been initiated by states which have pursued policies of deregulation (Held 1998). In military terms, no lessening of power is evident. In some arenas such as policing, state power may be increasing rather than decreasing (Anderson 1995: 99).

Mann (1997) (cited in Held and McGrew 1998) notes that states in the developed world are now more powerful than their antecedents: so too, however, are demands placed upon them. The apparent simultaneous weakening and expansion of power of nation-states is symptomatic of an underlying structural transformation. James Anderson, from another viewpoint, notes that political processes are changing qualitatively as well as quantitatively; that is, changes cannot be seen simply in terms of centralisation at higher (for example, federal) levels or devolution to smaller, regional bodies. Instead, a 'new medievalism' of overlapping authorities may be developing.[2]

Globalisation processes, in any case, are not experienced uniformly by all nations. States and governments remain powerful but now share the global arena with an array of other political actors: inter-governmental agencies, international agencies, regional bodies. Thus debate rather than a consensus exists concerning the power, influence and autonomy of individual states. At a minimum, it is agreed that it has now become difficult to buck international economic trends.

(More on) gender and states The future of the state form has much resonance for gender analysis. Throughout the world, women have struggled for citizenship rights, hindered by various institutions and means, from the imposition of 'customary' law (usually, as constructed within colonial frameworks, for instance in southern Africa and India) to inequality within welfare institutions, and lack of equal rights to property. Feminists have argued that the citizenship rights for women must be part of any 'democracy'.

It remains common for analyses implicitly or explicitly to pose the question of whether the (masculine) state is/has been 'good' or 'bad' for women. On the one hand, highly authoritarian states which have shut down other forms of organisation (for example labour organisations; civil rights movements) sometimes find it impossible to 'close down' women's networks because of the informal manner in which they are constituted (Waylen 1998b). On the other hand, governments have often been seen as intruding upon areas of privacy or autonomy and have been agents of oppression.

However, some states, especially reformist and bureaucratic state socialist ones, have also enacted laws which attempt to weaken pre-capitalist male-dominated structures and practices (see Molyneux 1994; Tetreault 1994). As noted, women in both more- and less-industrialised countries have lobbied states for (*inter alia*) reforms in marriage and family law; for more widespread education and health provision; for equal pay and protection at work; for maternity leave rights; for rights for control over reproduction; and for controls over male violence.

And many women are advantaged through welfarist measures, as noted above, although these can also increase state surveillance, as Rowbotham (1986) notes. Despite the fact that there are disadvantages to as well as benefits from welfare measures, women are disproportionately affected when these are cut back, for instance through SAPs (structural adjustment programmes) or other measures of financial stringency or market-led reforms.

In contrast, many women of dominant ethnic/racial groupings (often defined as 'white') are unaware of the daily reality and/or threat of state violence and coercion faced by some minority group women and men. Threats of violence, and its actuality, stem not only from racist/rightist popular movements but also from various state authorities, in particular the police. Feminists 'of colour', have done crucial work in pointing out, in forcible terms, the omissions of much feminist theorising concerning the nature of constraints on women's lives and the involvement of state agencies of welfare and of social control in these (see, e.g., Mirza 1997). For many racialised 'others' (and 'others' vary in historical and contemporary circumstance), state-based oppression may structure women's lives as much or more than that from individual men. And those who face repression, including violence, from men within their own homes or families, are in most circumstances unable to turn to the state for protection. Lack of examination of the multi-faceted nature of the state aids the analytical erasure noted above.

The state (or, particular states) cannot be seen as unambiguously 'good' or 'bad' (Randall 1998; Waylen 1998a). In most instances, women do not have unitary interests in any case, although they may have many interests in common. Additionally, the state is not a unitary institution (Alvarez 1990) but consists of different relations, practices and bodies.

Thus the question of the benefits of state policies and actions is not answerable in general terms; specific analyses of situations, taking into account historical, cultural and political contexts, are necessary. Difficulties of generalisation do not end there, since the same policy may have both 'negative' and 'beneficial' effects (see, e.g., Jacobs, 1997b on the varied effects of land reforms) even for one group of women. However, the above caveats do not indicate that asking 'big' questions is a misplaced ('wrong') activity, even if, as in the above example, they cannot always be answered. Nor do macro-level questions necessarily entail making universalist assumptions.[3]

The extent to which states are, or remain, capable has particular gender implications. This is the case especially since demands of women's movements have often been addressed to state governments. Cox, discussing how globalisation affects the internal structuring of states, remarks that one effect is that power may become concentrated in those agencies in touch with the global economy – for example treasuries, banks, the prime minister's office – whereas agencies identified with domestic concerns (industry, education, health) may become subordinated (Cox 1992). This observation is of import for gender analyses; the great majority of women are far from power centres such as national treasuries while many are more identified with and affected by – and possibly employed by – agencies concerned with education, health and some industries. In a similar vein, globalisation is significantly complicating where power is located. States may become more accountable to corporate or private interests than to their citizens or to a world community (Peterson and Runyan 1999; see also Mittelman 1996). Thus, just as women may be making more gains in national legislatures (or international parliaments), power is further shifting to bodies such as the World Bank, the IMF and the European Commission. Aside from the question of women's representation in these bodies without public accountability, it is ironic that women remain associated with the 'private' sphere of home and family while the more powerful corporate private sphere is highly masculinised. In contrast, Peterson and Runyan argue, the state appears more feminised and as representing domestic and welfare issues (Peterson and Runyan 1999: 104).

Nationalism

Nationalisms and states Closely connected with questions of gender, the state and globalisation, is work on nationalism; most nationalisms have state formation as a main aim. However, writings on nationalism have often been semi-divorced from those on the state. With the proliferation of new (and older) ethno-nationalisms which have occurred with globalisation (see below), discussion of nationalism regains urgency.

Classical analyses of nationalism, particularly within Marxist discourses, discussed the relation between class, nationalist movements and the rise of (bourgeois) nation-states. In the post-war period, the proliferation of different types of nationalist movements from wars of liberation in former colonised societies, or those subject to US-style military domination, to new 'neo-nationalisms' within Europe, east and west, posed analytical problems. In particular, appellations such as 'progressive' (and by implication, regressive) became far more questionable. Nairn (1997) made the point that nationalism in terms of its general political tendency, is Janus-faced; looking at once backward to an idealised society of the past and forward to a new one.

Analyses from the 1960s/70s, to some extent in response to the above developments, have concentrated on examination of nationalism as a belief-system. Gellner's influential work (e.g. 1983) discusses the myths that nationalists (or nationalist leaders) create, concerning primordial unity. Benedict Anderson (1983) coined the useful term 'imagined community' in discussing the origin of nationalisms in Europe.

More recently, much-needed attention has been paid to the links between nationalisms and ethnicity/'race': are nationalist movements necessarily racist? Anthony Smith (1979) argues that nationalism does not always involve the idea of superiority, whereas racism does; elsewhere (Smith 1991), he elaborates a distinction between 'civic-territorial' and 'ethno-genealogical' models, with the former being far less prone to racist ideologies. In practice, however, nationalism tends to draw upon both civic and ethnic elements (Brah 1993). Others argue that racism derives from nationalism (see Nairn 1977). Miles (1987) emphasised the similarities between the two belief-systems: 'race' is no less imagined than is nation, although racism/s often have no specific political or territorial objectives.

Gender and nationalism A growing body of feminist work has analysed nationalism and nationalist movements in gendered terms. This work has established that nationalisms are profoundly contradictory for female ad-herents. Gender relations have often been a crucial focus of nationalist movements; this is also the case for revivalist, religious fundamentalist and ethnically based movements. Nationalist ideas often draw heavily on notions of the nation as a family, and invoke an ancestral past. These ideas invoke powerful constructions of women's place and their nature, as well as constructions of gender relations which are believed to be 'traditional' (Hobsbawm and Ranger 1984) It is a common finding of analyses of nationalism that, once movements come to power, gender issues become seen as secondary.

Women are implicated in nationalism in a number of ways: as biological reproducers; as reproducers of boundaries of national groups (for example, through marriage restrictions); as transmitting national cultures; and as active participants in national struggles. Additionally, women are symbolic figurations of the nation and embodiments of male honour (Anthias and Yuval-Davis 1992; Yuval-Davis 1997). They both represent cultural and psychic boundaries and help to inscribe them through ritual and cultural practices (Brah 1993, 1997).

Some women, then, participate in nationalist movements as part of a gendered mobilisation (see Molyneux 1998); others become mobilised through participation. Still others support nationalist movements as part of a wider social movement. Whatever women's actual participation, they often hold a particular place in nationalist thought, as 'bearers of the collective' (Yuval-Davis 1980). The Janus-faced nature of nationalism is commonly resolved through gendered symbolism. In a common process of splitting, men are often seen to represent forward-looking progressive aspects of nationalism while women, represented as bearers of national tradition, implicitly carry its backward-looking aspects (McClintock 1993).

However, nationalist movements also provide positive benefits for women. Both nineteenth-century and anti-colonial nationalist movements were sometimes liberationary, or at least espoused ideals such as legal equality for women, the right to work, to become citizens (Jayawardena 1986; Rowbotham 1992). Although women are often involved in action/ support through the needs of the movement, through the process of mobilisation they may come to question male domestic and sexual controls (Rowbotham 1992; Saraswati 1998). Enloe (1990) argues that nationalism has provided some women with a positive space, learning that colonisers were not inherently superior people, and a space to become international actors. However, women are frequently treated as ciphers; as symbolic rather than as active participants in nationalist struggles (J. Marchbank personal communication, 1998).

Links Between Globalisation, Ethno-nationalism and Gender

The recent period has seen the proliferation of movements often termed 'ethno-nationalist'. Why should globalising processes have spawned such movements? Globalisation has been associated with the increase of multiple or 'hybrid' identities. As Hall notes, the 'other' has been imported into all societies through migration, tourism and the impact of the media, making the sense of strangeness difficult to maintain (Hall 1992). Globalisation may increase awareness of social 'difference', even creating a longing for it (Kahn 1995). Thus, globalisation may directly undermine a search for boundedness; however, it may at the same time stimulate a desire for boundaries.

The increasing impact of global culture, especially the arrival of television, and the widespread belief that globalisation brings homogeneity (i.e. Americanisation), all stimulate attempts to define local cultures (Anderson 1995: 95). Thus, a common analysis is that, in circumstances of globalisation, people may seek security in known group identities, or ones constructed as 'traditional' – for example ethnicity, nation, religion. Ethnonationalisms tend to share the characteristic of wishing to return to a more bounded world, one in which meaning is attached to local practices and representations.

It is important not to conflate 'the local' with ethno-nationalisms. Islamist movements, for instance, are not ethnically based although they may wish to counter globalisation; Scottish nationalism is, at least at present, an example of civic nationalism (that is, nationalism based on residence). Nor do ethno-nationalisms have only, or even predominantly, social-psychological motivation. Many of the internal or civil wars that have proliferated (see Jacobson, Jacobs and Marchbank, this volume) have some basis in economic and social inequalities, sometimes of a racial/ethnic type (see Chossudovsky on Rwanda 1999).

Ethno-nationalist movements can take various forms, including conventional nationalism as well as religious and culturalist forms. Some, although not all, have been marked by extreme nationalism and accompanying racism/s and xenophobia, including anti-black racism, anti-Semitism, anti-Chinese racism and anti-Islamic hatred. Such movements often (although, not invariably) have in common with older nationalisms the formation of images and fears concerning stereotypical 'others'. Appadurai's powerful analysis shows the extremes that such fears can take in circumstances of globalisation. Seemingly, he argues, the bodies of ethnic 'others' and suspected enemies 'within' must literally be turned inside out in a grisly verification of their human status (Appadurai 1999).

Where ethno-nationalisms occur – including ones where such rage, such uncertainty and fear of impurity are expressed – they are not counters to globalising processes (even where they see themselves as such) but are integral to it. In the same way, the Holocaust and modernity, seemingly irreconcilable, were all part of *one* process (Bauman 1989, 1998).

The gendered representations of new ethno-nationalisms are similar to those of previous nationalistic discourses. However, in the current proliferation of wars and militarisms, such neo-nationalist notions have been carried through in rather different conditions – of which the more generalised risk and insecurity of post-modernity and of globalisation are important (Bauman 1995; Gray 1998). As outlined, one such response is a scenario in which the body – always gendered – becomes the central site of ethnic violence.

Another is to envisage a world in which women are firmly tied to homes and localities, and in which men's sexuality and authority are not (or, are less) threatened. As noted, where women become geographically mobile they often lose respectability and are associated with prostitution and sexual trafficking. To counter such possibilities, women are usually allocated (at least, symbolically) a particular social space but a highly controlled/circumscribed one; their inhabiting such spaces without complaint is (sometimes) awarded with approval. Thus such a reaction tries to contain the anxiety that women might become more mobile, more part of 'public' worlds, less subject to constraints on sexuality/ies.

In practice, as discussed, relatively few women are likely to be able to benefit from the opportunities globalisation presents. However, the *possibility* that some women may become detached from their localities/ kin, and may cease to represent 'home', may constitute a further source of insecurity. Lived communities (where communities still exist) are in actuality now less often composed of households with heterosexual families (whether monogamous or polygynous) at core (Castells 1997). More single-person households exist, and more women head households, whatever their proclivities in this matter, due to male migration, death and (especially) desertion. Thus even the most frantic drawing of ethnic/community boundaries will encircle social 'matter' in rapid states of change.

Agency and complicity The following section revisits the topics of gendered complicity and action touched upon in the Introduction. It first takes up the problem of agency; then examines some forms of complicity in ethno-nationalism and other forms of gendered violence. Lastly, it discusses the necessity for seeing both the growth of women's movements and the backlashes against them within one frame.

In this volume, several chapters begin to explore an area little discussed within feminism: some women's participation in movements which violently oppress other women and men, usually people belonging to vulnerable minority groups of a racialised, class or caste nature. While it is the case that fewer women than men participate in forms of violence, exploration of the above issues emphasises that women by no means always play nurturing, supportive, maternalist roles. The Introduction touches on the problem of 'naming' such participation; should it be termed, for instance, 'co-responsibility', incitement, complicity? I maintain, with Mukta, that it is quite possible for women to be complicit.

'Complicity' may range from women's contempt for men not showing bravery in war/military action, to women urging men on to rape or murder ethnic/religious others (Sarkar and Butalia 1995); to passivity in the face of atrocities; to participation as camp guards; to committing acts of mass atrocity and murder (African Rights 1995). At the same time, it is the case that women's agency often takes different forms than men's, since women are typically subject to more social restriction. To argue that women cannot be complicit, assumes that they have little agency.

The problem of agency The agency/structure debate is one that has long formed an important strand of sociological debates. Within the last years (e.g. Long and Long 1992) these debates have entered those on development policy and planning. Fierlbeck (1997) contributes to discussion of the problem of choice and agency, drawing on Molyneux's (1985) distinction between agency and the context in which agency can be said to be properly exercised. Fierlbeck points out that women who wish to remain valued members of groups or cultures may have difficulty in justifying choices which do not encompass expected gender roles – hence, there is little possibility of refusing marriage or motherhood (Fierlbeck 1997). Jackson, on the other hand, advocating a more actor-oriented approach, argues that 'motherhood' is not an historically unchanging institution and that any institution may express alternative visions. 'Choices are not entirely constrained ... neither are choices and innovations entirely beyond the influence of acting individuals' (Jackson 1997: 162).

It is true that many analyses fail to examine individual actions in practice, and sometimes seem to rule out the possibility of action. However, a focus on action in turn tends to imply a discursive shift to methodological individualism rather than to discussion of how wider processes and individual actions interact. Kandiyoti (1988), for instance, commenting on her well-known conception of the 'patriarchal bargain', now reflects that the emphasis on bargaining highlighted that the crucial issues to be explained were what influences relative bargaining power within and beyond the household, and what constitutes agency (Kandiyoti 1988: 135). She comments that in her initial conception, evidence of hegemony remains concealed because its effects are relabelled and omitted from analysis (p. 145).

Some analyses also overlook that many individuals act but fail to achieve their wishes/desires/goals – both because of the actions of other individuals and because of more structured forces (the latter, the result of past human actions). Whether choices are 'free' or 'constrained' depends upon a whole complex of factors: type of society and state; geographical positioning; age; class positioning; family connections; ethnic and racial/ised position; gender; personality; particular social and cultural norms; luck ... to name but a few.

The following, for instance, is one example of participation/co-responsibility in violence; that of female infanticide in India. In this example, violent actions occur frequently but do not constitute a 'movement'. Murthy (1998) discusses the practice, with reference to north India. She conducted interviews with midwives to ascertain how their participation in acts of infanticide – of which they expressed disapproval – came about. Reasons given by the midwives for acquiescing to such requests (usually, coming from fathers) included: their own poverty; promises of large payments (apparently almost invariably reneged upon); the caste power of many of the families requesting infanticide (the practice being more widespread in higher castes); dependence upon higher-caste families for work; the power of wealthier men in the village. Hence, many elements of caste and class as well as gendered power and coercion underlie the participation of midwives in infanticide. It is worth noting, however, that analysis of power does not *substitute* for analysis of action, although it is necessary to set the context: for example, not all people, even if impoverished, react to the exercise of coercion or to caste/class power in the same way. An interesting feature of Murthy's study is that midwives stressed the responsibility of the state to make female infanticide visible, for example, by publicising statistics and mounting campaigns against it. The implication is that, with the backing of powerful institutions, they would find it easier to act themselves.

Most people in most circumstances, as noted, do have some possibility of action; however, some people's choices are more restricted than are others. Although most men also face heavy constraints (most) women tend to be more socially constrained than (most) men – they have less economic security, are more subject to family commitments and are subject to restrictions concerning bodily autonomy, freedom of movement and political participation. As Held (1995: 178) phrases it, women tend to suffer from 'nautonomy' (lack of autonomy) in many sites of power: the body; the economy; culture; civil society; violence and coercive relations. One of the constraints women face, in many societies and social contexts, is that they are more heavily sanctioned for displaying overt action against social norms than are men of the equivalent (class, racial, caste) status; the exercise of power and will is often in itself seen as unfeminine, particularly within Western settings. For the latter reason, women's actions often appear as more covert than those of men, especially high-status men. This observation also applies to many forms of resistance, which may be individualised and semi-covert.

Jackson rightly criticises the terminology used to discuss action: for example, 'resistance' has negative implications, rather than evoking positive action (Jackson 1997: 163). In similar vein, the term 'action' tends to have positive implications (people act to improve themselves in some sense; to express solidarity; to create). However, actions can and often do have negative as well as positive consequences, both for the actor and for other subjects.

The remainder of this chapter examines two responses to globalisation noted above, in the context of discussion of gendered consequences and women's agency: women's participation in violence, in circumstances of the growth of ethno-nationalisms; and (more briefly) the growth of inclusive citizen-based (for example, feminist) networks.

Complicity, Bystanders and Atrocity (or, What is Empowerment?)

The question raised here is how and to what extent gender analysis is altered by recognition of women's complicity in a range of unpalatable

actions. Women do participate in mass atrocities, as noted in the Introduction, even if with less frequency than do men. What may be a more
common female role, however, is to become a 'bystander', engaging in
actions not requiring overt violence. Following the Nazi Holocaust, and
the resurgence of new, similar if smaller-scale ones, much attention has
been paid to passive complicity as well as to processes through which
bystanders become active, although little of this work deals with gender.
Straub (1992), for instance, discusses the complex set of psychic processes
involved in the development of mass persecution and atrocity. Certain
elements – othering, scapegoating, needs for acceptance, and distancing of
the self – are highlighted. It is the latter aspect which appears incongruous
to many; in many societies, women are viewed as more relational beings
than are men, so that distancing of the self from others is itself 'unfemale'
– certainly in Western conceptions. It then becomes difficult to comprehend
women's involvement in persecution.

It is common for women to be subordinate members of kin, household,
community and ethnic groups, although achieving some respect as wives/
mothers within these. From this positioning, many women enact maternalist roles to protect others, or even society as a whole (for example, at
Greenham Common or in the Plaza de Mayo in Argentina). Others,
however, attempt to consolidate membership by encouragement of or
participation in actions against 'others'.

Women may take part in covert ways, or more overtly. Whether or not
their actions are visible, women who do participate may be taking part in
great violence – massacres; incitement to mass rape; genocide. The question
of 'participation' in mass violence and atrocity is a fraught one; as indicated,
such participation often occurs under duress, whether direct or indirect. At
this level, the alternatives people face are constrained indeed, and may
involve their own deaths/torture or that of their families, and some people
indeed choose to die themselves rather than to inflict torture on others.

Women who are in a position to choose more freely to join in such
actions and movements involving the persecution (and so on) of other
women as well as men, may at some level be prioritising other types of
identity over maternalist versions of gender identity. The other sources of
identity – for example, membership of a racialised, ethnic, caste or class
grouping – are more likely to afford a measure of power than most gender
positionings. If women are 'mothers of the nation', then mothers of other
nations (and classes) may be legitimate sexual targets in time of conflict.

Thus women's participation in atrocities, like men's, may be due to a
variety of factors, including coercion; wishing to affiliate as group members;
lack of ability to resist; fear of the consequences of resistance, wholehearted
agreement; and wishing to gain social power.

One implication of this (very preliminary) analysis of women's complicity is that we should not assume that 'empowerment' is always a positive phenomenon, whatever its current positive connotations in development discourses. Women, like men, may grasp at power where they find it – and the results may not be 'progressive', maternalist or relational in any usual sense. Just as many social movements exist, with no particular or necessary historical direction, there is no analytical reason to view women's actions as operating in a direction which will strengthen links among women as a gender group.

Conclusions

The first sections of this chapter critiqued parts of the globalisation literature both for tokenist analyses of gender and women's movements, and for unduly optimistic assumptions concerning the obstacles faced. However, this is not to argue that these analyses are completely mistaken. Women's movements as well as more amorphous forms of resistance(s) are indeed spreading across national boundaries, although constraints of space mean that these developments cannot be outlined in any detail here.

As noted, there are many forms of resistance against personalised forms of gender (and other) oppression which do not take any organisational forms (in part, precisely because the oppression appears to be 'personal'). Micro-scale resistances may, at least at times, have cumulative effects; it is likely that many changes in family life as well as in workplaces and farms have come about in this way. (See, for example, Castells' [1997] discussion of low birth rates in contemporary Italy, or Turner et al. [1997] on the refusal of Kenyan peasant women to plant certain cash crops.) This may not amount to a 'mass insurrection' (Castells 1997) but nevertheless signals change in gender relations in directions which may enhance women's gender status/es.

In organisational terms, women's movements are also growing. In some regions (Latin America, India), women's organisations have some strength. In other regions, organisations are more oriented to developmentalist goals such as income generation (Haynes 1997). Some earlier splits, for instance those between black and white feminists, while by no means erased, have perhaps become less pronounced (see, e.g., Alexander and Mohanty 1997). Part of this shift involves the growing mobilisation of women and some men in the South as well as the North, against widespread violence at various levels.

Globalisation throws up many challenges for women's organisations, nationally oriented as most are; yet there indeed exists reason to discuss women's movements as part of globalising processes. However, this remains only part of the story. Most social movements, and many individual resistances, 'provoke' – or entail – backlashes. That against women's movements has been discussed in certain respects (Faludi 1992) but is not integral to literature on politics or development.

Assuming that women can simply resist or organise, and that they will then become 'empowered', seriously underestimates the fears of a number of men who may be reluctant to lose gender power (and often, associated class/political) power. However, women may also fear changes in gender positionings; changes in the social status quo often cause apprehension (who knows what the consequences may be?). Non-nuanced views of empowerment through organisation can underestimate the complexity of power relations (Parpart 1999) as well as levels of coercion and violence against women's actions and organisations (Jacobson, personal communication, 1997; Jacobs 1998).

It is difficult to reconcile the growth of women's movements with the re-emergence of ethno-nationalisms. That the world encompasses rape camps as well as emancipatory movements is not easy to envisage. One line of thought is that unsettling of gender roles and positionings constitutes one among a complex of factors in the rise of ethno-nationalisms.

And a world in which women themselves not only participate in everyday 'othering' but in mass persecutions becomes even more opaque. Specific situations always call for specific historicised analyses. However, I have argued that the idea of 'empowerment' should be detached from a discourse in which the term is allied necessarily with 'right and good'. People's strivings for power can lead in many directions, some of which entail group closure, individual advancement, and toleration of/participation in abuse and atrocity.

As Friedman (1990) notes, fragmentation and universalism are part of one process. This is as true for a gendered analysis of globalisation as it has been for analyses which are gender blind.

Notes

1. In Gray's work, 'community' is a taken-for-granted concept.

2. Anderson (1995) notes differences in (a) the experience of democracy; (b) the lack of universalising beliefs, e.g. as in medieval Christianity; and (c) the relative absence of ordered hierarchies.

3. However, an assumption that only one 'correct' answer could exist, would be universalist.

Bibliography

African Rights (1995) *Rwanda – Not so Innocent: When Women Become Killers*, London: African Rights.

Agarwal, B. (1994) *A Field of One's Own*, Cambridge: Cambridge University Press.

Albrow, M. (1996) *The Global Age*, Cambridge: Polity Press.

Alexander, J. and C. T. Mohanty (eds) (1997) *Feminist Genealogies, Colonial Legacies, Democratic Futures*, New York: Routledge.

Alvarez, S. E. (1990) *Engendering Democracy in Brazil: Women's Movements in Transition Politics*, Princeton, NJ: Princeton University Press.

Anderson, B. (1983) *Imagined Communities*, London: Verso.

Anderson, J. (1995) 'The Exaggerated Death of the Nation State', in J. Anderson et al. (eds), *A Global World?*, Oxford: Oxford University Press.

Anthias, F. and N. Yuval-Davis (1983) 'Contextualising Feminism – Gender, Ethnic and Class Divisions', *Feminist Review*, no. 14.

— (1992) *Racialised Boundaries*, London: Routledge.

Appadurai, A. (1999) 'Dead Certainty: Ethnic Violence in the Era of Globalisation', in B. Meyer and P. Geschiere (eds), *Globalisation and Identity*, Oxford: Blackwell.

Aslanbegui, N., S. Pressman and G. Summerfield (eds) (1994) *Women in the Age of Economic Transformation*, London: Routledge.

Basu, A. (ed) (1995) *The Challenge of Local Feminisms*, Boulder, CO: Westview Press.

Bauman, Z. (1989) *Modernity and the Holocaust*, Cambridge: Polity Press.

— (1995) *Postmodernity and its Discontents*, Cambridge: Polity Press.

— (1998) *Globalization: its Human Consequences*, Cambridge: Polity Press.

Brah, A. (1993) 'Reframing Europe: Engendering Racisms, Ethnicities and Nationalisms in Contemporary Western Europe', *Feminist Review*, no. 45

— (1996) *Cartographies of Diaspora: Contested Identities*, London: Routledge.

Castells, M. (1997) *The Power of Identity*, Oxford: Blackwell.

Chant, S. (1997) *Women-headed Households*, London: Macmillan.

Chant, S. and S. Radcliffe (1992) 'Migration and Development: The Importance of Gender', in S. Chant (ed.), *Gender and Migration in Developing Countries*, London: Belhaven.

Chossudovsky, M. (1999) 'Human Security and Economic Genocide in Rwanda', in C. Thomas and P. Wilkin (eds), *Globalization and Human Security: The African Experience*, Boulder, CO: Lynne Rienner.

Cox, M. (1992) 'Global Perestroika', in R. Miliband and L. Panitch (eds), *Socialist Register*, London: Merlin.

Eisenstein, Z. (1996) *Hatreds: Racialized and Sexualized Conflicts in the 21st Century*, London: Routledge.

Elson, D. (1995) 'Male Bias in Macro-economics: The Case of Structural Adjustment', in D. Elson (ed.), *Male Bias in the Development Process*, Manchester: Manchester University Press.

Enloe, C. (1990) *Bananas, Beaches and Bases: Making Feminist Sense of International Politics*, London: Pandora.

Faludi, S. (1992) *Backlash: The Undeclared War Against American Women*, London: Chatto and Windus.

Featherstone, M. and S. Lash (1995) 'Globalization, Modernity and the Spatialization of Social Theory', in M. Featherstone, S. Lash and R. Robertson (eds), *Global Modernities*, London: Sage.

Fierlbeck, K. (1997) 'Getting Representation Right for Women in Development', in A.-M. Goetz (ed.), *Getting Institutions Right for Women in Development*, London: Zed Books.

Friedman, J. (1990) 'Being in the World: Globalization and Localization', in M. Featherstone (ed.), *Global Culture*, London: Sage.

Gellner, E. (1983) *Nations and Nationalism*, Oxford: Blackwell.

Gray, J. (1998) *False Dawn: The Delusions of Global Capitalism*, London: Granta.

Hall, S. (1992) 'The Question of Cultural Identity', in S. Hall et al. (eds), *Modernity and its Futures*, Cambridge: Polity Press.

Harvey, D. (1989) *The Condition of Postmodernity*, Oxford: Blackwell.

Haynes, J. (1997) *Democracy and Civil Society in the Third World*, Cambridge: Polity Press.

Held, D. (1995) *Democracy and the Global Order*, Cambridge: Polity Press.

— (1998) 'Globalization', *Marxism Today*, November–December.

Held, D. and T. McGrew (1998) 'The End of the Old Order? Globalization and the Prospects for World Order', *Review of International Studies*, vol. 24, pp. 219–43.

Hirst, P. and G. Thompson (1996) *Globalization in Question*, Cambridge: Polity Press.

Hobsbawm, E. and T. O. Ranger (eds) (1984) *The Invention of Tradition*, Cambridge: Cambridge University Press.

Jackson, C. (1997) 'Actor Orientation and Gender Relations in a Participatory Project Interface', in A.-M. Goetz (ed.), *Getting Institutions Right for Women in Development*, London: Zed Books.

Jacobs, S. (1997a) 'A Share of the Earth? Globalization, Land and Women's Movements in Southern Africa', paper presented to Society of Economic Anthropologists conference, Ajijic, Lake Chapala, Mexico.

— (1997b) 'Land to the Tiller? Gender Relations and Types of Land Reform', *Society in Transition*, vol 1, pp. 1–4.

— (1998) 'The Gendered Politics of Land Reform: Three Case Studies', in V. Randall and G. Waylen (eds), *Gender, Politics and the State*, London: Routledge.

— (1998) 'Rethinking "Bargaining with Patriarchy"', in C. Jackson and R. Pearson (eds), *Feminist Visions of Development*, London: Routledge.

Jayawardena, K. (1986) *Feminism and Nationalism in the Third World*, London: Zed Books.

Kahn, J. (1995) *Culture, Multiculture, Postculture*, London: Sage.

Kandiyoti, D. (1988) 'Bargaining with Patriarchy', *Gender and Society*, vol. 2, no. 3, pp. 274–90.

— (1988) 'Rethinking "Bargaining with Patriarchy"', in C. Jackson and R. Pearson (eds), *Feminist Visions of Development*, London: Routledge.

Kiely, R. (1998) 'Introduction: Globalisation, (Post-) Modernity and the Third World', in R. Kiely and P. Marfleet (eds), *Globalisation and the Third World*, London: Routledge.

Kofman, E. and G. Youngs (eds) (1996) *Globalization: Theory and Practice*, London: Pinter.

Kumar, R. (1995) 'From Chipko to Sati: the Contemporary Women's Movement in India', in A. Basu (ed.), *The Challenge of Local Feminisms*, Boulder, CO: Westview Press.

Long, N. and A. Long (eds) (1992) *Battlefields of Knowledge*, London: Routlege.

McClintock, A. (1993) 'Family Feuds: Gender, Nationalism and the Family' *Feminist Review*, no. 44.

McMichael, P. (1996) *Development and Social Change: A Global Perspective*, Pine Forge Press.

Mann, M. (1997) 'Has Globalization Ended the Rise and Rise of the Nation-state?', *Review of International Political Economy*, vol. 4, no. 3.

Meyer, B. and P. Geschiere (1999) 'Globalization and Identity: Dialectics of Flow and Closure', in Meyer and Geschiere (eds), *Globalization and Identity*, Oxford: Blackwell.

Miles, R. (1987) 'Recent Marxist Theories of Nationalism and the Issue of Racism', *British Journal of Sociology*, vol. 38, no. 1.

Mirza, H. S. (ed.) (1997) *Black British Feminism: A Reader*, London: Routledge.

Mittelman, J. (1996) *Globalization: Critical Reflections*, Boulder, CO: Lynne Rienner.

Molyneux, M. (1985) 'Mobilization without Emancipation: Women's Interests, the State and Revolution in Nicaragua', *Feminist Studies*, no. 11.

— (1994) 'Women's Rights and the International Context: Some Reflections on the Post-Communist States', *Millenium*, no. 232, pp. 287–313.

— (1998) 'Analysing Women's Movements', *Development and Change*, vol. 29, pp. 219–45.

Murthy, R. (1998) 'Learning about Gender Relations from Participation in Female Infanticide', in I. Gujit and M. K. Shah (eds), *The Myth of Community*, London: Intermediate Technology.

Nairn, T. (1977) *The Break-up of Britain*, London: Verso.

Parpart, J. (1999) 'Rethinking Participation, Empowerment and Development from a Gender Perspective', in J. Freedman (ed.), *Transforming Development*, Toronto: University of Toronto Press.

Peterson, V. S. and A. Runyan (1999) *Global Gender Issues*, Boulder, CO: Westview Press.

Rai, S. (1996) 'Women and the State in the Third World', in H. Afshar (ed.), *Women and Politics in the Third World*, London: Routledge.

Randall, V. (1998) 'Gender and Power: Women Engage the State', in V. Randall and G. Waylen (eds), *Gender, Politics and the State*, London: Routledge.

Robertson, R. (1992) *Globalization: Social Theory and Global Culture*, London: Sage.

Rowbotham, S. (1986) 'Feminism and Democracy', in D. Held and C. Pollitt (eds), *New Forms of Democracy*, London: Sage.

— (1992) *Women in Movement*, London: Routledge.

Saraswati, S. (1998) 'When the Earth is Female and the Nation is Mother: Gender, the Armed Forces and Nationalism in Indonesia', *Feminist Review*, no. 58, pp. 1–21.

Sarkar, T and U. Butalia (1995) *Women and Right-Wing Movements: Indian Experiences*, London: Zed Books.

Scholte, J. (1999) 'Security and Community in a Globalizing World', in C. Thomas and P. Wilkin (eds), *Globalization and Human Security: The African Experience*, Boulder, CO: Lynne Rienner.

Shaw, M. (1994) *Global Society and International Relations*, Cambridge: Polity Press.

Smith, A. (1979) *Nationalism in the Twentieth Century*, London: Martin Robertson.

— (1991) *National Identity*, London: Penguin Books.

Stivens, M. (1998) 'Theorising Gender, Power and Modernity' in M. Stivens et al. (eds), *Gender and Power in Affluent Asia*, London: Routledge.

Straub, E. (1992) 'Transforming the Bystanders', in H. Fein (ed.), *Genocide Watch*, Princeton, NJ: Yale University Press.

Tetreault, M. A. (ed.) (1994) *Women and Revolution in Africa, Asia and the New World*, Columbia: University of South Carolina Press.

Turner, T., W. Kaara and L. Brownhill (1997) 'Social Reconstruction in Rural Africa', *Canadian Journal of Development Studies*, no. xviii, p. 2.

Waters, M. (1995) *Globalisation*, London: Routledge.

Waylen, G. (1998a) 'Gender, Feminism and the State: An Overview', in V. Randall and G. Waylen (eds), *Gender, Politics and the State*, London: Routledge.

— (1998b) 'Gender Rights and the Institutional Arena', paper presented to *Gender, Democracy and the State in Latin America*, Institute of Latin American Studies, University of London, October.

Wilkin, P. (1999) 'Human Security and Class in a Global Economy', in C. Thomas and P. Wilkin (eds), *Globalization and Human Security: The African Experience*, Boulder, CO: Lynne Rienner.

World Development (1999) Special issue on 'Gender and Globalization', vol. 27, March.

Yuval-Davis, N. (1980) 'The Bearers of the Collective: Women and Religious Legislation in Israel', *Feminist Review*, no. 4

— (1997) *Gender and Nation*, London: Sage.

Index

engaged in violence, 14; in armed forces, 7 (in US, 12); in front-line combat, 5; in right-wing movements, 169; in security forces, 5, 8, 157; inflicting of death by, 164; joining Nazi Party, 12; leadership of, 71; marginalisation of, 110; nurturing role of, 81; participation in politics, 76; power of, 79–80; role of (in food production, 78; in global economy, 30; in peace-building, 71; in reproducing community, 166); support for violence, 46–7; waged employment of, 129, 130, 219; war against, 45–65

Women in Black, Belgrade, 53

Women Overcoming Violence conference, 52

Women Together for Peace, 181

Women's Defence Councils, 149

women's groups, establishment of, 73–4

Women's Hotline (China), 134, 135

Women's Journalists' Association (China), 133

Women's Legal Aid Centre (Brazil), 154

Women's Mayors' Association (China), 132, 133

women's movements: analysis of, 217; backlash against, 233; consultation with, 148; demands addressed to state governments, 223; growth of, 217; in Brazil, 148; in India, 168; in USA, 51; preference for use of term, 219

women's organisations, 132, 134; as extension of state, 125; in China, 132, 135; in Northern Ireland, 184; in Somalia, 70, 78; in USSR, 140; informal nature of, 222; national orientation of, 232

women's refuges, 153, 154, 159, 165

women's studies, 135; creation of units, 134

Women's World Day of Prayer, inter-faith service, 187

Workers' Party (Partido dos Trabalhadores) (PT) (Brazil), 154, 155, 156

World Bank, 34, 36, 224

World Economic Forum, 28, 42

World Trade Organisation (WTO), 35

Xiaoshan City Women's Writers' Small Group, 133

Yugoslavia, former, 10, 16, 47, 53, 55, 172; war in, 17

Yuval-Davis, Nira, 10, 88, 91

Zaire, 93

Zajovic, Staja, 53, 55

Zero Tolerance (in UK), 11

Zhenzhou University, women's studies at, 134